radical

*A Queer and Polyamory-Informed
Guide to Love Beyond the
Myth of Monogamy*

relating

MEL CASSIDY

ILLUSTRATIONS BY JOAN TRINH PHAM
FOREWORD BY KAI CHENG THOM

North Atlantic Books
Huichin, unceded Ohlone land
Berkeley, California

Published by   Cover art © nongnuch vikrutha via Getty Images
North Atlantic Books   Cover design by Amanda Weiss
Huichin, unceded Ohlone land   Book design by Happenstance Type-O-Rama
2526 Martin Luther King Jr Way
Berkeley, CA 94704 USA
www.northatlanticbooks.com

Printed in Canada

Radical Relating: A Queer and Polyamory-Informed Guide to Love Beyond the Myth of Monogamy is sponsored and published by North Atlantic Books, an educational nonprofit that collaborates with partners to develop cross-cultural perspectives; nurture holistic views of art, science, the humanities, and healing; and seed personal and global transformation by publishing work on the relationship of body, spirit, and nature.

North Atlantic Books's publications are distributed to the US trade and internationally by Penguin Random House Publisher Services. For further information, visit our website at www.northatlanticbooks.com.

The authorized representative in the EU for product safety and compliance is Eucomply OÜ, Pärnu mnt 139b-14, 11317 Tallinn, Estonia, hello@eucompliancepartner.com, +33757690241.

Library of Congress Cataloging-in-Publication Data

Names: Cassidy, Mel, 1982– author.
Title: Radical relating : queer, polyamorous, and somatic wisdom for living
    and loving in a post-monogamy world / Mel Cassidy ; illustrations by
    Joan Trinh Pham ; foreword by Kai Cheng Thom.
Description: Berkeley, California : North Atlantic Books, [2025] | Includes
    bibliographical references and index. | Summary: "Queer, Polyamorous,
    and Somatic Wisdom for Living and Loving in a Post-Monogamy World"—
    Provided by publisher.
Identifiers: LCCN 2024062128 (print) | LCCN 2024062129 (ebook) | ISBN
    9798889842453 (paperback) | ISBN 9798889842460 (epub)
Subjects: LCSH: Non-monogamous relationships. | Sex.
Classification: LCC HQ980 .C37 2025 (print) | LCC HQ980 (ebook) | DDC
    306.84/23—dc23/eng/20250222
LC record available at https://lccn.loc.gov/2024062128
LC ebook record available at https://lccn.loc.gov/2024062129

1 2 3 4 5 6 7 8 9 FRIESENS 30 29 28 27 26 25

*For Kokoni, Angeliki, Theodosia, Marianthi,
and all their brave foremothers and sisters
whose names I will never know.*

*In everlasting gratitude to GM, BM, and BN,
through whose grace and guidance all things
become joyfully possible.*

*And, to you, the reader: May we together
grow our relational ecologies towards a
kinder, more connected world.*

CONTENTS

FOREWORD

I was first introduced to polyamory as an eighteen-year-old, semi-feral, closeted baby trans girl, having recently fled my parents' home in Vancouver for the wilds of Montreal's anarchist queer scene. A proverbial Asian transgender Alice plummeting down the rabbit hole, I found myself suddenly immersed in wonders and wildness that were far beyond imagining in my previous life:

Non-monogamy! Genderqueerness! Free sexuality! Leatherdyke parties! Body positivity! Slut Pride! Three waves of feminism! Fisting workshops on college campuses! Sex work! Kink! It was a rush, to say the least. Had I died and gone to queer sexual heaven? Was this the Promised Land I'd fought tooth and nail to survive high school for? Or was this, like Alice's Wonderland, an alluring yet somewhat more sinister place?

The truth, as it so often does, lies somewhere in the grey space between extremes. The utopian project of Montreal's anarcho-queer community in the late 2000s and early 2010s was born out of a collective longing for erotic liberation, and, it must be said, heavily centered on the romantic sensibilities of mostly white, college-educated queer Gen Xers and millennials. The language of feminism and consent, as well as free sexuality, decolonial love, and transformative justice, lived alongside one another in our gorgeous fever dream, but we had yet to work out the tensions between them.

There was, perhaps, a youthfully naïve assumption among us that if we simply shared and talked about the vision of a world where everyone was both free *and* safe to love outside the norms of monogamy and the nuclear family, we could somehow bring that reality into being through force of will. As it turns out, however, actually doing liberated love and sexuality in real life—and finding the elusive balance of practices that allow for both safety and freedom at the same time—is somewhat more complex. It is this particular complexity into which Mel Cassidy's lovingly written and wonderfully practical *Radical Relating* fearlessly intervenes.

It's an unfortunate truism that revolutionary visions tend to carry with them the shadow of the cultural norms that they seek to transform, and the revolutionary potential of polyamory is no exception—whether in the experimental anarcho-queer bubble in which I spent my twenties or in the now more broadly mainstream versions of polyamory, or ethical non-monogamy (ENM), that have become popularized in the past decade.

As a young trans girl of colour, I found myself defaulting to polyamory often because that's what everyone I admired said was best—that is, because the cool kids were doing it. What I discovered was that polyamory could be a lot of fun, yes, but it could also be deeply confusing without the tools or skills to help me through it. Lovers who were older, wealthier, and more socially privileged could use polyamory jargon to belittle my emotional needs or to justify flat-out bad behavior. And even when things were going well, I didn't always know how to manage the intensity of my own emotions—in other words, polyamory was just as fraught as monogamy!

In this book, Mel Cassidy supports their readers through making sense of the reality that simply saying that a sexual or relational practice like polyamory (or monogamy, for that matter) is liberatory or ethical does not make it so. "Sexual freedom" is exciting when sexual repression is the norm—but in a patriarchal, misogynist context, "sexual freedom" can be quickly subverted into freedom for men to sexually harass or exploit women and trans people and then shame them for being "prudish" if they push back.

Similarly, polycules or relationship anarchy may sound like great alternatives to the restrictions of traditional marriage and the nuclear family, but in a society still entrapped in colonialism and capitalism, these concepts can quite easily be used to reinforce oppressive class and race dynamics. How revolutionary is relationship anarchy if it's just a rebrand for "white straight men doing whatever they want without caring about how they affect others"? How liberatory is a polycule if its structure centers the needs of legally married, middle-class couples who want to "experiment" romantically with young, racialized people who have shaky access to money and housing?

Radical Relating offers much-needed wisdom about how to navigate the experience of polyamory with deep care and awareness of the complexity of human emotions and relationships. Carefully researched, thoughtfully constructed, and full of heart, this book stands out in the growing body of literature on polyamory by seamlessly integrating the psychology of attachment with cutting-edge theories on trauma, social power dynamics, and a commitment to a way of being in relationships that centers justice, liberty, and pleasure for all. This is exactly the book my youthful, semi-feral self needed a decade and a half ago—a map to the wildness and the wonder that non-monogamy has to offer.

There is deep healing and transformative potential in Mel's writing and vision—this book takes long strides towards answering the questions of how to do polyamory well, what to do when it's not going well, and how polyamory really can become a bridge to collective freedom. There's a whole world between these pages. Read on and discover it.

Kai Cheng Thom, author of
I Hope We Choose Love and
Falling Back in Love with Being Human

ACKNOWLEDGMENTS

This book would not have been possible if not for the incredible courage, love, and support of so many in my relational ecology.

Thank you to all my teachers, guides, mentors, and ancestors in paths of yoga, Sufism, bodywork, somatics, movement, queerness, and liberatory practices. I am not sure by what grace I have had the good fortune to practice and study in so many rich traditions, lineages, and communities, but I know that my life and my work would not be what it is without all those who have come before me, and who in their own ways have taught me new ways of dancing in the world. And my deepest gratitude to GC, whose love, wisdom, and guidance has always led me to know the truth of my heart.

Huge gratitude to all the humans and animals in my extended anarcule who have provided emotional, spiritual, and practical support to this work and this writing process: to Alexandria, Ali, Bram, Calliope, Camille, Charles, Freja, Goose, Helena, Kaye, Kim, Kris, Marcia, Mars, Mercedes, Mia, Michelle, Miguel, Mira, Momo, Naia, Shivani, Van, and Xianny.

To all the additional people who have read and provided feedback on my writing and ideas through the years: Erin, Ivo, Jenny, Jess, John, Julie, Niels, Oliver, Sandy, and Sky.

Deep bows of appreciation to the members of the Solo Polyamory Facebook Group, the Vancouver Polyamory 101, Nanaimo Polyamory 101, and Open Comox Valley Groups, for always meeting my ideas with curiosity and openness, and exploring open relating together.

Huge thank-yous to Meg-John Barker for their mentorship, feedback, and guidance through the writing process, and to Lily Bruzas, who provided such valuable reflections during the editing process. Thank you as well to Barrak Alzaid and Irina Janakievska for both their lifelong friendship and professional writing support and encouragement.

Infinite gratitude to Ross Jenkins, Amie Alexis Allan, Marie Thouin, Xana Williams, and Charles Sullivan, who provided valuable feedback during the writing process of this book, and to the rest of my cohort of fellow Friday-morning writers who shared in the ups and downs of the writing process: Jess DeVries, Britta Love, Laura Mae Northrup, Shaun Miller, and Marcia Baczynski.

Thank you also to Eva Dusome, Eva Blake, Dave Macdonald and Sophia Graham, who offered such considerate feedback as the manuscript was nearing completion.

This book would not have been complete without the beautiful artwork of Joan Trinh Pham, whose art breathes delight and sensuousness into this work.

Thank you for bringing such brilliance and joy to the collaborative process with your art.

Thank you to Tim, Gillian, and everyone at North Atlantic Books, for getting curious, placing your trust in me, honouring my work, and recognizing the vision and scope of this book.

I am grateful for all the students and clients who have shared their stories with me through the years and trusted me to guide them. I am humbled by the willingness of those who have allowed me to share about our work together in the case studies provided in this text.

My everlasting thank-yous to Flow State Float House, for manifesting exactly when I needed you, and providing me with a somatic cocoon.

Thank you to the Pentlatch River, by whose shores so much of this book was written: for your whispers of encouragement, and your cool waters that continue to refresh my spirit when the journey has felt weary. Trusting in your flow has brought transformation beyond imagining into my life. My gratitude to all the caretakers of these lands that you flow through, both current and past, most especially to the K'ómoks, Pentlatch, Homalco, Wei Wei Kai, Wei Wei Kum, and Tla'amin peoples.

Thank you to the musicians whose music has nourished me through the writing journey, in particular Vidura Barrios, Amani Friend and Treavor Moontribe of Desert Dwellers, Random Rab, and Krishna Das. And also to all the neighbours who join me in keeping our local songbirds well fed and joyful.

Thank you to every person who has trusted me to support them in their journey: I have learned from you in every coaching session, every workshop, and every course. I remain in awe to have the privilege to do this work.

Finally, to all those, named and unnamed, who have been part of my relational journey, thank you for all the important lessons, and all the opportunities for growth.

INTRODUCTION

If you've picked up this book, chances are you're someone who is in some way curious about the alternatives to traditional monogamy. Perhaps you've been exploring alternatives to monogamy for some time, and you're looking for something different from the same repeating discussions about jealousy, scheduling, and relational hierarchy. Or maybe you're deeply into monogamy but you want to divest from the nuclear family and gendered, patriarchal assumptions in relationships. Or perhaps you've just felt frustrated and hurt by both monogamy and non-monogamy and are wondering if there's *any* way to have relationships that don't end in drama.

This book is for polyamorists who want to practice their non-monogamy with more feminism, more queerness, and more community-building. It's for monogamists who don't want to do relationships on autopilot. It's for everyone who dearly believes a better way to love and live exists. It's for change-makers who aspire to rewild the ways we love.

The underlying assumption in monogamous literature is that a romantic partner must be a sexual partner and that a successful romantic relationship is the only noble and worthwhile goal of relating. Your soulmate must be your *sole* mate. Mainstream relationship advice is often written with the assumption that the reader is probably white, Western, neurotypical, relatively untraumatized, and able-bodied. Non-normative experiences (and challenges) in relationships are often invisible. Meanwhile, in non-monogamy literature, many materials that newcomers rely on are based on the author's journey of what worked for them, and they can fall short when it comes to the rich diversity that non-monogamy can include.

In my own relationships, I yearned for a guidebook that could speak to the undercurrent of how the hangover from monogamy was so deeply internalized that it continued to play out in non-monogamous dynamics. I wanted something that would name the ways that other systems of oppression, like racism and misogyny, intersected with monogamy and continued to show up even in non-monogamy. I longed for something that went beyond the logistics of dating multiple partners, and that spoke to the experience of the mind, body, heart, and spirit as they navigate complex relational structures that go against the grain of what's been accepted as status quo. My quest for resources and practices that could support a more holistic, embodied, and trauma-sensitive approach to relationships has become my life's work, and is presented to you in this book.

And yes, this book contains what worked for me, but I hope that it offers a liberating structure for your own relationships that empowers you to craft a path that's authentic for you—even though our backgrounds, experiences, and the kinds of relationships we seek might be very different.

A Radical Journey

The word *radical* comes from the word *root*. I've always sought to understand the root of things. For much of my life I felt like a perpetual outsider, swimming in a soup of cultural influences and intergenerational traumas, straddling ways in which I've been privileged and ways in which I've experienced marginalization. I've been married and divorced. I've been pregnant twice and miscarried twice, and I'm a survivor of assault. I've unpacked internalized homophobia and transphobia to be able to embrace myself as a genderqueer bisexual woman.

I'm a second-generation "third culture kid," with a mix of Irish, English, Greek, and Roma ancestry, and come from a matrilineal line of women who have survived genocide and Nazi eugenics. I hold dual British and Canadian citizenship, but neither nationality feels true to who I am. I'm diasporic and nomadic: born in the UK, raised in Kuwait, and a long-term visitor on K'ómoks Territories in so-called British Columbia. I'm a feminist and an anarchist, and I'm also deeply spiritual, with a lifetime of study in a lineaged tradition of Shaivism.

I've challenged my own internalized mono-normativity—the idea that monogamy is the only possible pathway to healthy relationships—and today I live my life as a solo polyamorous person. To me, that means that I'm my own primary partner. I also believe that when we separate our personal experiences from the social fabric we exist within, we obscure a bigger picture of ongoing systemic oppression that we're all working to survive, and I wholeheartedly subscribe to the ideas of relationship anarchy. My not-so-secret polyamorous agenda is that I want all of us to have an easier time growing and sustaining loving, kind, and compassionate relationships, where we all feel free to be our most authentic self.

But I'm not here to teach you how to be polyamorous. This work is for anyone and everyone who is questioning monogamy and seeking their own path in relationships. I invite you to delve into the root of your desires, explore the narratives you've inherited about relationships, and embark on a transformative journey that will deepen your connection with yourself, your loved ones, and the world around you.

I invite you to join me in a relational revolution: a reimagining of the ways we relate with one another, growing from the roots of why and how we relate and imagining new possibilities for what relationships can look and feel like beyond the status quo of traditional, compulsory monogamy.

All relationship forms are welcome here—monogamous, polyamorous, sexual, platonic, and everything in between. We can all shake off restrictive models of patriarchal expectations, gender roles, and the nuclear family, and step into a new paradigm: where secure attachment is experienced through networks of relationships, sex is not the primary measure of relational success or fulfilment, self-sacrifice is no longer seen as a love language, and diverse relational ecosystems supplant the narrow path of escalating relationships.

This isn't a journey to undertake lightly: letting go of prescriptive monogamy is easier said than done. Along the way, we can be confronted by both inner and outer complexity, a complexity that can sometimes brew storms of chaos. Many who attempt to leave the traditions of monogamy behind struggle to adjust and feel pulled back by mono-normativity.

SOMATIC PAUSE
Orienting to This Work

I invite you to take a moment to pause and enjoy stillness in whatever way feels good and is accessible to you. In this moment of stillness, you might notice your breath, hear a pleasing sound, feel the textures of your clothing, or observe a cherished memento in your space.

Notice: Do you feel a sense of anticipation, excitement, or perhaps agitation? Does your mind feel at ease, or is it filled with questions? Notice what's happening to your body as you pause: Is there tension in your muscles, or are they relaxed?

Now pay attention to your senses and notice if anything brings you a feeling of pleasure, ease, happiness, or softness. You may notice a pleasant smell or a way of moving your body that feels good to you right now. What is this feeling of pleasure like? Is it warm? Does it bring ease to your body or your mind?

As you feel this sense of ease return, notice any thoughts, feelings, sensations, or questions that come up for you. You may find returning to this Somatic Pause activity useful as you read this book.

Polyamory Isn't (Necessarily) Revolutionary

I've been practising polyamory—consensual non-monogamy, done with honesty, transparency, and compassion—for well over a decade, and I can tell you: Polyamory is not revolutionary. At least, not inherently. Polyamory can be part of a liberatory practice, but it is not a guarantee of that, nor is it necessary to live a post-monogamous life. The real revolution isn't in having multiple partners—honestly, that part is optional. It's in challenging monogamy itself.

The threads holding monogamy in place as the framework for how we create relationships in our colonial-corporate culture are fragile and worn; pulling at that single thread of monogamy is enough to unravel the whole tapestry of the status quo in Western society.

When we pull at that thread, we challenge notions of scarcity and dominance. We question the idea of "ownership" over people, resources, and capital. We unwind gender roles and the unspoken expectations of behaviours in any relationship, romantic or not. And we dismantle the walls of siloed relationship styles that say you are not allowed to prioritize your friends over your partners and that you cannot, must not, resource-share with your loved ones beyond a single spouse.

Monogamy isn't the only thread we can pull at; any thread of the status quo is enough to begin your process of unravelling. Once the threads are unravelled, you can start to weave a new tapestry, one inspired by your own deepest, most authentic, and aligned vision of what you desire your relationships to be.

You Have Permission to Be Messy with This Work

This work is created for people like you who are questioning the linear pathways for relationships offered by monogamy, who find themselves dissatisfied with the status quo around exclusivity of affection in relationships, the social misfits and cultural rebels who want to find a different way of relating but don't know how they're going to navigate these uncharted territories. Consider this a guidebook as you discover your own path in relationships. It will help you understand the lay of the land in a new way, and develop a deeper understanding of yourself and your loved ones, as you grow joyful, embodied, and authentic relationships for everyone involved.

There's no "perfect" way to do things, so get ready to invite your inner perfectionist to be a little gentler with you. This work is not a substitute for therapy, but things may come up for you as you read that you might want to talk to a therapist, counsellor, coach, or friend about. Also, this book isn't going to address systemic traumas directly. However, you might find it easier to do so when your relationships cease to be a source of stress and, instead, become part of a resilient landscape that empowers you against systems of oppression.

How to Use This Book

This book is laid out in four sections:

- **Why:** The first section offers an overview of the challenges of prescriptive monogamy and consensual non-monogamy and why this work matters.

- **What:** The second section introduces the framework for Radical Relating, including detailed overviews of each aspect.

- **How:** The third section offers an overview of core skills that support Radical Relating.

- **Where:** The fourth and final section of this book invites you to envision the possibilities of where Radical Relating can take you.

In the book, you'll also find three kinds of activities: Reflective Journaling prompts, Somatic Pauses, and ingredients for your Relational Toolkit. I encourage you to keep a journal or make notes in whatever way works for you as you progress through this book.

Reflective Journaling: These are questions and prompts for you to contemplate and journal. Some of these can also be used as prompts for book clubs, discussion groups, and conversations with loved ones. They offer you an opportunity to record what you are thinking and doing.

Somatic Pause: These are practices you can do privately that invite you to tune in to the sensations and feelings in your body, sometimes alongside gentle movement. We'll explore more about what somatics are in chapter 5. They support your nervous system as you read and offer moments to connect with yourself and notice what you are feeling.

Relational Toolkit: These are ongoing practices you may want to return to again and again and integrate into your daily life, both with partners and alone. They offer you an opportunity to put into practice everything that we are exploring in this book.

In addition, you'll also find several stories that illustrate aspects of this radical journey. A few are personal shares, but most come through people I have known: coaching clients and students from my Monogamy Detox course as well as friends in my extended community. All individuals have consented to share their stories and have had a chance to review the context in which their story is being shared.

You may come across terms that are new to you; in the glossary you'll find definitions. Some of these words come from the polyamorous lexicon, others from somatic practices, and a few are contemporary terms.

You will also find three beautifully hand-drawn illustrations by Joan Trinh Pham that enhance some of the core ideas presented in this book. Joan and I have known each other since the earliest days of my non-monogamous adventures, and she has a gift for synthesising complex ideas into visual form. I am honoured that she has created such beautiful art illustrations for this book.

Please hold yourself with compassion as you read. There may be parts that feel challenging—or that you disagree with entirely. And that's okay. If you find your mind feeling overwhelmed, put the book down. If you feel like reading chapters out of sequence, that's also okay! You may want to read the book through and do each activity as you come to it, or read the whole book through before going back to do the activities. There's no right way or wrong way to approach this. I've written this book with versatility in mind, and I hope that you'll come back to it again and again.

So, let's start Radical Relating.

Why

In this section we look at why this work of Radical Relating matters:

- the history behind **monogamy** and **non-monogamy** and how both have been influenced by **patriarchy, colonialism,** and **white-supremacy culture**
- why monogamy isn't working
- what a **post-monogamous** paradigm might include
- what the obstacles are to getting there

You'll be invited to consider how you've internalized **mono-normativity** and to think about how your ancestors practised relationships.

We'll also examine why taking a **trauma-informed** approach to moving beyond monogamy is so important, why the practices of somatics are particularly helpful on this journey, and the four principles or pillars that can support us as we explore this.

1

UNRAVELLING MONOGAMY

Love is a Verb, not a permanent state of enthusiasm.

—ESTHER PEREL[1]

I got married when I was twenty-two because I thought that was what you were supposed to do when you were twenty-two and in love. I didn't realize my expectations about love would end up being toxic to our relationship, and I had no idea how to express my needs and desires. The stories I told myself held us both back, and for many years, I felt like I was flying on autopilot.

After two miscarriages, a botched attempt at an open marriage, and an affair, we realized neither of us was happy existing in a relationship that didn't meet either of our needs. Instead of fighting to exist in a state of compromise, we amicably went our separate ways.

Excitedly, I jumped right into a non-monogamous life, aspiring to be polyamorous, which I understood to be a form of honest non-monogamy that happens with the full knowledge and consent of everyone involved. Early in my dating experiences, I met someone I felt was my "soulmate." The connection was intense, and we felt like we'd known each other for lifetimes! But we had very different lifestyles, and despite the great sexual chemistry, that relationship didn't last long.

Nursing a broken heart, I felt lost and uncertain about how to engage in relationships for a while. I realized that what was holding me back was the mythology I'd been fed since childhood—not just the "one day my prince will come" narratives—but all the expectations and stories about what a partner would do for me and how social norms defined a successful relationship. I started to examine my experiences and how often I'd put aside my needs and desires while trying to become who I imagined my partner wanted or needed me to be. I began to see that the people I was dating were doing the same with me too.

Several years later, when I began my practice as a relationship coach, I found that almost all my clients—both monogamous and non-monogamous—were working with some form of leftover mono-normative stories, filled with unspoken and unconscious expectations, holding them back from happy and ful-filled relationships.

Why Do We Do Monogamy?

Monogamy is typically defined as:

- lifelong or long-term
- mutually exclusive
- sexual and/or social
- a dyadic pair bond, meaning between two people only

In humans, monogamy often leads to marriage, and relationships usually adhere to a pattern of inevitable escalation, also known as the relationship escalator. We'll take a deeper look at this in chapter 3.

Like many traditions, lifelong monogamy makes sense at particular times, in particular places, for particular people. Monogamy seems to be emotionally stream-lined, logistically simpler, and offers a possibility for financial stability as well as sexual health and safety. Many of us have grown up not realizing that there are any accept-able alternatives to monogamy. A commitment to lifelong fidelity with one partner is, for many, something that inspires them to move through inevitable times of con-flict and to seek the possibilities of repair. However, almost everyone at some point experiences the end of a monogamous relationship, be it through break-up, divorce, opening up, or death. When that happens, our safety and stability are disrupted.

But, humans haven't always practised monogamy. In her book *Eve,* Cat Bohan-non references how early human societies were likely communal and matrilineal, while in *Sex at Dawn,* Christopher Ryan and Cacilda Jethá trace the origins of monogamy to the dawn of agriculture and the emergence of property ownership and inheritance rites.[2] How things have changed! Today, monogamy has become the predominant form of socially expected and accepted romantic partnership, and even though the expectations of monogamous relationships can vary signifi-cantly from culture to culture, and even from region to region, monogamy has become enshrined as a global relational ideal. Even within countries and cultures where polygamous marriages have been historically practised, there has been a gradual trend to conform to Western standards of monogamy.

Monogamy can be effective for creating resilience and experiencing safety and stability, but this is not a safety we can guarantee will last. We're told that having one devoted partner means a more stable environment in which to raise a family, that it will grant us more financial security, and that a single sexual partner is healthier and safer. We might be promised that we'll have someone to look after us in old age and who will have our back when times are tough.

In some parts of the world, monogamy perks might also be gender-specific: where women face obstacles to employment and having independent finances, they may socially need a man to provide financially, and in some cultures, a man may be expected to have a wife who will take care of his home and children to take care of his legacy.

All these benefits are possibilities, never guaranteed, and aren't determined by a relationship's monogamous nature but by the values and efforts of the people involved. Any monogamous partnership can experience bereavement, loss of income, cheating that impacts sexual health, and many other things that disrupt the monogamous ideal.

Patriarchal Monogamy

Patriarchy is one of the longest-running and most widespread social systems in human history, detrimental to all different genders, albeit in various ways. It has a long history of being domineering and is deeply woven into the histories and fabric of most of the world today. As the late Black feminist scholar bell hooks wrote:

> Patriarchy is a political-social system that insists that males are inherently dominating, superior to everything and everyone deemed weak, especially females, and endowed with the right to dominate and rule over the weak and to maintain that dominance through various forms of psychological terrorism and violence.[3]

The predominant model of monogamy today is rooted in patriarchal traditions based on cis-heteronormative pairings, where men historically held power or ownership over women. While modern Western culture may reject the notion of a woman being her husband's property, internalized dynamics of ownership can still show up in romantic partnerships across all genders—this is patriarchy at work. Even in same-sex relationships, one partner may be expected to take on traditional roles, like homemaker or breadwinner.

Patriarchal monogamy isn't the only system impacting our experiences of relationships.

Monogamy and Colonialism

Monogamy has historically been used as a means for controlling colonized and enslaved populations. In a 2017 talk at the University of British Columbia, Indigenous scholar and sexuality expert Dr. Kim Tallbear expanded on how pre-colonial relationships were not defined along monogamous lines:

> Part of "saving Indians from their savagery" meant pursuing the righteous monogamous couple-centric nuclear family, co-produced with private property, including the partitioning of the tribal land basin into individually owned allotments held under men's names.[4]

Tallbear goes on to quote Cree-Métis feminist Kim Anderson:

> One of the biggest targets of colonialism was the Indigenous family in which women had occupied positions of authority and controlled property. The colonial state targeted women's power. It tied land rights to heterosexual, one-on-one lifelong marriages, thus tying women's economic well-being to men who controlled the property.[5]

When Canada passed anti-bigamy laws in 1890 it made non-monogamous First Nations families illegal and punishable by imprisonment. This happened only a few years after the Indian Act of 1876, which saw the federal government exert control over most aspects of Indigenous life, including land management, housing, education, marriage, and even what professions people could train in. It is still the foundation of colonial governance over First Nations in Canada today. Similarly, the Indian Penal Code of 1860 imposed a ban on Christian polygamous marriages in British-controlled India. These are only two examples. Compulsory monogamy has been, and still is, a tool of colonization: a means of disrupting the communal bonds of peoples who oppose colonization.

As we question monogamy and explore new paradigms of relating, we also need to reckon with the traditions, legacy, and impacts that monogamy (and its imposition) has had on Indigenous and traditional community-nourishing practices. And we must remember that the effects of this imposition are not just found in history but are continuous and ongoing, and impact all our lives to this day.

The Nuclear Family

The concept of a nuclear family emerged in the United States in the 1950s. This introduced the idea of family as not just one man and one woman in a monogamous marriage, but that you also had to have two or three children, a home, one or two cars, and a white picket fence. It was part of a propaganda campaign to return women to the home after many had entered the workforce during World War II, and also to combat the rise of socialism by encouraging siloed family units that would purchase the new goods being churned out by the former war factories repurposed toward consumption-based American industry.

While it started in the United States, the prevalence of the nuclear family as the centre-point in Hollywood sitcoms and cartoons exported this idea to the world. On the other side of the planet in the 1980s and 1990s, I grew up watching the dysfunctional goings-on of fictional families that in no way resembled my own, but like many, I was fascinated with them. The nuclear family, glamorized as an ideal way to raise children and experience family, is now an aspiration for many.

But the nuclear family is not necessarily as healthy as it's made out to be, and in pursuing it, we lose an important connection to something more. In a March 2020 article for *The Atlantic*, "The Nuclear Family Was a Mistake," journalist David Brooks writes,

> We've made life freer for individuals and more unstable for families. We've made life better for adults but worse for children. We've moved from big, interconnected, and extended families, which helped protect the most vulnerable people in society from the shocks of life, to smaller, detached nuclear families (a married couple and their children), which give the most privileged people in society room to maximize their talents and expand their options. The shift from bigger and interconnected extended families to smaller and detached nuclear families ultimately led to a familial system that liberates the rich and ravages the working-class and the poor.[6]

The nuclear family is indeed intended to keep us consuming rather than sharing, competing rather than collaborating, and at the core of it all is the idea that life-long monogamy is the secret to happiness in life.

White Supremacy Culture and Monogamy

Embedded within the colonizer-imposed patriarchal monogamous practices and the narratives of the nuclear family are qualities of *white supremacy culture*. Jewish-American activist Tema Okun coined the concept of white supremacy culture to describe culturally embedded practices that white colonizing powers use to create hierarchy based on racialized values, and which disconnect and divide white people from Black, Indigenous, and people of colour, BIPOC from one another, and white people from one another too.[7]

White supremacy culture isn't just about race or skin color, and you don't have to be white to perpetuate it: It is structurally embedded and personally internalized ongoing oppression that creates an artificial hierarchy of human worth, and it collaborates with patriarchy, ableism, and other forms of oppression. The ideology shows up in cultural beliefs, values, social norms, and the systems that govern our politics, economics, and relations. There are many specific qualities that Okun has identified, but in summary, it supposes that there is an ideal way to be human: to be white, able-bodied, cis-gendered, heterosexual, thin, and rich, and hold power over resources. Any deviation from this implies being less human: If you are a person of colour, disabled, queer, fat, poor, and share your resources, then white supremacy culture considers you inferior.

White supremacy culture prizes monogamy and the nuclear family. These concepts help to create hierarchies: for example, those who are married versus those who aren't, or those who have children versus those who don't. Three specific ways that the values of white supremacy culture show up strongly in monogamous relationships are:

- One right way: Monogamy is the only way to have healthy relationships and raise a family; anyone doing differently is inferior.
- Fear of "temptation" leading to failing at monogamy, which would make one inferior, and which in turn restricts emotional intimacy.
- Individualism: Each monogamous pair, or in modern times, nuclear family unit, exists separately from others and must be self-sustaining. Seeking help or support from outside is a personal failure and means you are less worthy within systems of white supremacy.

Addressing the ways that we've internalized white supremacy culture means challenging the idea of the nuclear family, questioning the Western biases of attachment theory (discussed below), and broadening the ways we explore and express intimacy, especially platonic non-sexual intimacy.

And yes, this is all easier said than done: The values and rules of white supremacy permeate so much of our world today. Unpacking these internalized narratives can be a lifelong journey for everyone, no matter the colour of your skin, your ethnic and racial background, or what your lived experiences of marginalization have been.

Monogamy and Attachment

In the 1950s, researchers Mary Ainsworth and John Bowlby observed how infants responded to separation and reunion with their parents. They proposed that our desire to form attachments with romantic partners mirrors or compensates for our early attachment experiences.

Since the 1950s, we've learned that attachment styles aren't fixed and can change based on our partners' behaviours and responsiveness. We might gravitate towards secure attachment with someone we feel completely comfortable and safe with, experience anxious attachment when we fear abandonment, or avoidant attachment when we seek to protect ourselves from the pain of loss. Or we might experience disorganized attachment, where we oscillate between states of safety and deep mistrust of the safety we feel.

While childhood attachment may influence adult relationships, we're not bound to repeat those patterns. Indeed, through self-awareness and healthy relating practices, many people can develop secure attachments in adulthood, even if they had no baseline for this as infants.

Remember: most of the research that led to the creation of attachment theory was done on families existing in a Western paradigm of relating, where the nuclear family model was the default. This is fundamentally founded in colonial relationship structures, where infants are raised primarily by one or two parents, with minimal daily interaction with the extended family or village. We change schools, we move around, and our social surroundings are prone to shift. Only our adult caregivers remain consistent, and they may not necessarily be able to provide the space we need to develop a sense of embodied, or somatic, safety.

This starkly contrasts the interconnectedness of community, village, and tribal connection that is the basis for attachment in most cultures worldwide. People who live most of their lives in a single place may have an experience of attachment with the land, and we can hear this in how Indigenous and displaced people around the world talk about their homes, traditions, communities, even their spiritual cosmology. Survivors of the Palestinian Nakba of the late 1940s kept the keys to the homes stolen from them as a symbol of their relationship to their ancestral lands, passing these keys to their children and grandchildren in the hopes of return. At the first World Romani Congress in 1971, the Romani peoples, displaced from Northern India and nomadic for many generations, created a flag to symbolize diasporic unity: with a strip of green to represent the land and a strip of blue to represent the sky, this flag reflects being in relationship to the landscape. A red wheel or dharmachakra in the centre represents their origins in India and symbolizes the journey in caravans across Asia Minor, the Levant, and Europe.[8]

The idea that attachment is only attainable through an exclusive romantic partnership is part of mono-normativity: the internalized stories we have about relationships, based on monogamy. Think of the 1950s North American nuclear family: financial security on a single income thanks to the father, and everything in the home harmonious thanks to the housewife mother. Even in the 1950s, this was primarily attainable for people who were white, heterosexual, and able-bodied. For everyone else—people of colour and queer and disabled folks—it was often only achievable through extreme sacrifice and effort. To succeed in creating one's own nuclear family was, in many ways, a means to earn social privilege.

SOMATIC PAUSE
Confronting Internalized Mono-Normativity

Take a few breaths and move your body gently in any way that feels good for you.

Notice how your body, mind, heart, and perhaps even spirit respond to this exploration of white supremacy culture, patriarchy, the nuclear family, and mono-normativity. Notice what emotions, sensations, or other feelings arise for you.

For many, thinking about this can bring up grief. You might notice this grief as anger, or perhaps deep sadness. You might sense an energy rushing through you, like heat. You may feel numb and cold. It is okay to take a moment to notice these sensations and acknowledge them as part of your experience.

It's possible that what you're feeling right now is a small reflection of how you've felt when trying to engage with the expectations of monogamy and mono-normativity.

Before you continue, take a few more breaths, give your body a gentle shake, or let out a sigh.

Monogamy Isn't Working

According to data provided by resource website Divorce.com, in the United States 60 percent of spouses married between ages twenty to twenty-five will divorce, and second marriages have a 60 percent divorce rate.[9]

So why isn't it working? There are many possible answers to this question, but I always come back to it never truly working to begin with. As a system, compulsory patriarchal monogamy is reliant on control and conformity to a set script and parameters of behaviour. It's imposed and restrictive. As more people are inspired to break into nonconformity in other aspects of their lives—such as gender expression, sexuality, the ways that we work, and so forth—and reclaim agency—especially from colonial and patriarchal hierarchical capitalist-colonial systems that exploit workers—we have been collectively pulling at enough threads that the monogamous mindset is unravelling.

Once you see the weaving behind monogamous mythology and how it has not supported you in being an embodied, joyful, and authentic being in your relationships, it's natural to want to seek an alternative. As we confront how monogamy hasn't fulfilled its promises to us and strive to be liberated from the oppressive systems that are interwoven with compulsory monogamy, it's natural to ask, What are the alternatives?

2

EXPLORING NON-MONOGAMY

Around the world, we can find examples of Indigenous cultures that have practised non-monogamy for millennia. The Blackfoot and Cree are among the First
Nations peoples who have practised plural relationships for generations. They have
no word to distinguish between monogamy and non-monogamy.[1] In Tibet, fraternal polyandry, where brothers might share a single wife, supports population
management and equitable sharing of limited resources.[2] Polygyny, the practice of
having multiple wives, was widely practised in the Abrahamic religions—Judaism,
Christianity, and Islam. Christian churches moved towards monogamy around the
seventh century, while the first record of turning away from plural marriages in
Judaism comes from the tenth century.[3] In some branches of Islam, polygamy is still
practised, although as Islamic scholar Leila Ahmed points out, in the matriarchal
cultures of pre-Islamic Arabia and the Levant, both polygyny and polyandry were
equally acceptable matrimonial options.[4] These are just a few examples of how
non-monogamy is a long-standing practice in non-Western traditions worldwide.

REFLECTIVE JOURNALING
Non-Monogamy and Your Ancestors

What do you know about how your ancestors might have practised non-
monogamy? You might not have to look far. Perhaps in your family there are
examples of affairs or polygamous or bigamous relationships. Sometimes affairs
were known of and even supported by a spouse.

You might also consider the broader cultural approaches to non-
monogamy. There are examples of non-monogamy in all countries, throughout
history, and in all cultures, both honest and dishonest.

As you examine how your ancestors practised non-monogamy, you may
also notice how they might have been shamed, punished, or coerced into more
monogamous ways of relating.

How do you feel about the traditions of non-monogamy that your ancestors practised?

Through the influence of feminism and feminist values over the last two hundred years, non-monogamy has been reimagined. *Feminism* is a term that is often misunderstood: Some assume that it is solely about giving women the vote or granting women equal power to men. But at its core, feminism seeks to dismantle hierarchies by fostering anti-oppressive, non-hierarchical paradigms. Feminism today challenges systems that automatically privilege any group.

The first wave of feminism in the 1800s was the age of suffrage and campaigning for women to have the vote, go to school, and take their place alongside men in the workplace. Relationships in the Western world began to be reimagined. If women were not property and could have agency, what would then become of relationships? Early experiments in non-monogamous community building, like the Oneida community, emerged. In 1914, Emma Goldman wrote the essay "Marriage and Love," questioning romantic assumptions and challenging the social basis for marriage.[5]

The second wave of feminism in the West was an age of women's empowerment. Revolutions in birth control in the 1950s made the free love movement possible. Feminist writers like Octavia Butler and Ursula Le Guin deconstructed patriarchy, while Robert Heinlein explored the idea of multiple marriages through science fiction stories. The group marriage–based Kerista Commune, who would go on to coin *compersion* to describe "sympathetic joy," was formed.

The 1980s and the advent of the AIDS crisis saw a shift in both feminism and non-monogamy and the heralding of a third wave. While intersectional feminism (a term coined by Kimberlé Crenshaw in 1989) highlighted the disparities between white women and women of colour in the Western world, queer communities were fighting for gay rights and pushing back against the stigmas that HIV carried. This was also the era in which the term *ethical non-monogamy* first emerged, and in 1997 both Deborah Anapol's *Polyamory: The New Love Without Limits* and Dossie Easton and Janet Hardy's *The Ethical Slut* were published. These books painted new possibilities for non-monogamy. It didn't have to be group marriages and communes; you could be autonomous and have ethically non-monogamous relationships with multiple consenting adults.

In the early 2000s, the scope of feminism had grown to include dismantling all systems of oppression. Many Western countries have now legalized same-sex marriage, there is broader sex education in schools and more legislation to support trans rights, and much more. In 2006 Andie Nordgren published the Relationship Anarchy Manifesto in Europe,[6] and in 2012 the Supreme Court of British Columbia recognized that consensual non-monogamy was not a violation of Canadian anti-bigamy laws. Responding to a need for consensual non-monogamy–affirming therapy, numerous individuals have been inspired to pursue their counselling, psychotherapy, and psychology degrees with the non-monogamous client in mind. Social media and stronger interest from publishers means there's more support than ever for newcomers to non-monogamy.

According to the Organization for Polyamory and Ethical Non-Monogamy, approximately 5 percent of the population of the United States currently practise some form of non-monogamy, and up to 6 percent of people would prefer non-monogamy over monogamy.[7] Surveys in the UK suggest that 7 percent of the population have been involved in consensually non-monogamous relationships at some point in their lives, while a survey in Spain indicated that almost half the population agreed it was fine to have more than one loving relationship at a time.[8]

Modern Non-Monogamy

While there's one clear pathway to follow in monogamy, people today might do non-monogamy in many ways.

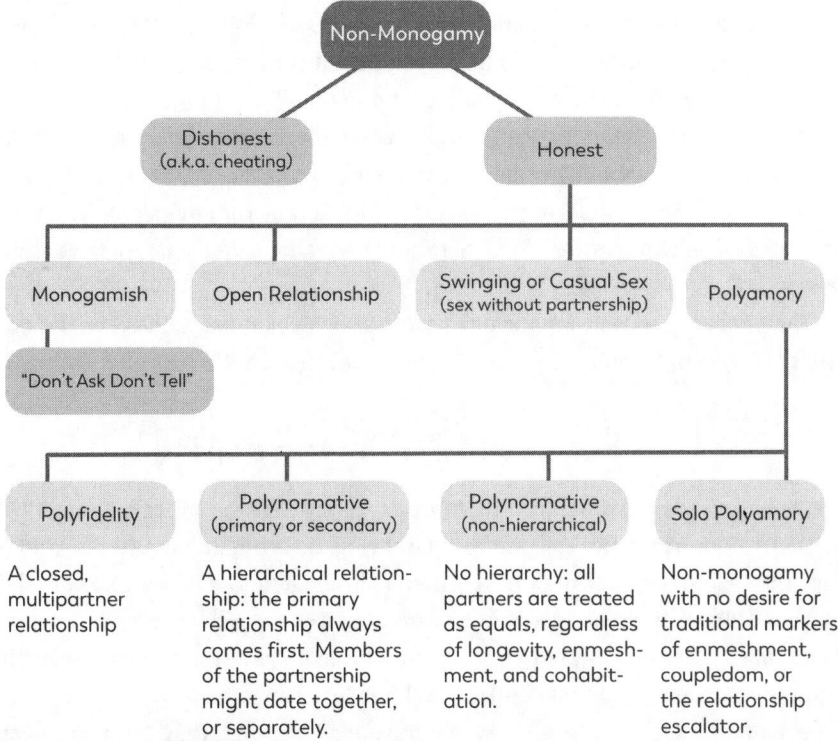

Figure 2.1. The scope of non-monogamy

Non-monogamy as an umbrella term encompasses infinite ways to explore relationships, and within those ways there can be infinite diversities in infinite combinations. We might be dishonest about it (also known as cheating), or we can be honest. People might be monogamish and experience functional monogamy but have a consensual and agreed openness to enjoy sexual relationships with others only under particular circumstances, such as hookups while travelling.

In open relationships the scope of how they relate with others outside a primary partnership is limited to relationships that don't include emotional enmeshment. They might be swingers, either as part of a couple or as a single individual, enjoying casual sex without dating or developing partnerships with the people they have sex with. This might happen within organized settings, such as sex parties or "lifestyle events," or it may be more informal.

Some seek polyamory and the possibility of multiple loving relationships, but even within that, some may look for polyfidelity (exclusivity within group relationships), or they might unicorn hunt (seeking a third partner together with a spouse), or explore hierarchy through having a primary partner and dating others as secondaries.

And then there's Solo Polyamory: non-monogamy but without the desire for the relationship escalator or any kind of traditional enmeshment, such as sharing finances, cohabiting, having a wedding, and so on.

Within all these different ways, people might engage in various approaches to sex (they might be asexual, greysexual, or practice aspects of BDSM), have different capacities for emotional intimacy, and hold different attitudes about how they integrate or don't integrate their partners into their family life, work, or friendship networks.

The approach to non-monogamy that has seen the most focus over the last twenty years is polyamory.

What Exactly Is Polyamory?

The word *polyamory* was coined by Morning Glory Zell-Ravenheart in her 1990 article "A Bouquet of Lovers" to describe the open, loving, committed relationships she shared with her multiple partners. She wanted to differentiate her relationship style from the better-known forms of non-monogamy in North America at the time: religious polygamy (one man with many wives), swinging (usually heteronormative and couple-centric), and free love (open sexuality with no relational commitments). She believed in cultivating "ongoing, long-term, complex relationships. . . rooted in deep mutual friendships."[9]

Many refinements to the definition of polyamory have been offered since then. Loving More, a nonprofit organization dedicated to education and support of polyamory as a valid choice in loving relationships and family lifestyle, defines it as "emotionally connected relationships openly involving three or more people."[10] Wikipedia offers that it is "the practice of, or desire for, romantic relationships with more than one partner at the same time, with the informed consent of all partners involved."[11] The Canadian Polyamory Advocacy Association says that it is "the practice, desire, or acceptance of having more than one intimate relationship at a time with the knowledge and consent of everyone involved."[12]

There are subtle differences between each of these definitions, and you may encounter many more variations on these themes. Some of these definitions can raise more questions than they answer. If polyamory is a form of ethical non-monogamy, by whose ethics are actions to be measured? If polyamory is done with the full knowledge and consent of all involved, what exactly is "full knowledge"? Who needs to have it? Are we defining consent as giving permission, or is consent a collaborative agreement process?

One of the other questions that often arises about polyamory is whether or not it is an orientation. It's certainly not a sexual orientation, such as bisexual or straight, since it's not about the gender of who one is attracted to. But might poly-amory be part of a kind of relational orientation, existing on a spectrum that moves from exclusivity and monogamy on one end to promiscuity and multigamy on the other? If we're defining polyamory as being honest and consensual, maybe it would be more accurate to say that non-monogamy is the orientation, and polyamory is one way, among many possibilities, of practising non-monogamy. This might be akin to the difference between saying you're religious and defining your religion. Personally, I consider non-monogamy to be my relational orientation, because I have always crushed on multiple people at a time, and solo polyamory is how I practise it currently. However, I recognize that could one day change.

For my peace of mind, I define polyamory as: a form of honest non-monogamy and practice, or openness to, engaging in multiple loving relationships with honesty and consent.

Ethics and Consent in Non-Monogamy

In the 2020s, ethical non-monogamy (ENM) has become a common shorthand in online dating profiles. Clinicians and researchers tend to avoid ENM, favouring consensual non-monogamy (CNM) instead, in recognition of the cultural sub-jectivity of ethics and how, in a colonial and patriarchal society, ethics are often strongly influenced by things like internalized white supremacy, covert misogyny, and more.

Having lived in and been raised around a medley of cultures, traditions, and ethical codes, I have difficulty accepting that there is a universal ethic. I personally gravitate towards the idea of dharma, a Sanskrit word used in Hinduism and Buddhism to represent living in a way that invites kindness, compassion, and consideration.

In recent years, some writers and advocates have been dropping any kind of qualifier before non-monogamy, pointing out that we don't differentiate between ethical-unethical or consensual-nonconsensual monogamy in our everyday language. Some have also explored alternative phrases to describe the scope of non-monogamy, including terms like *multiamory, multigamy,*[13] *bonogamy,*[14] and *polyphilia.*

If you're exploring a world beyond monogamy and feel confused by all these questions and the many ways you see people defining their non-monogamy, I assure you that you are not alone.

I like to talk about non-monogamous dynamics in a way that aims to normalize them. However, I don't want to dismiss the value of conscious and intentional monogamy: I know this works for many people, and I don't think that being monogamous excludes the possibility of benefiting from this work. Many have dipped their toes into honest non-monogamy, had profound experiences, learned a lot, and then returned to monogamy with more confidence, clarity, and relational maturity than before. And, for the record, I don't think that non-monogamy is necessarily the solution when monogamy is hard. If you find it hard to sustain one loving relationship, sustaining multiple loving relationships may be even more challenging.

People explore non-monogamy for many reasons, including attraction to more than one gender or more than one person, or because they have diverse relational desires that a single partner could not meet. Some may be drawn to it as a means to actively challenge social notions of ownership and jealousy, or as an extension of wanting to live according to feminist and queer principles of agency and autonomy. Some may look beyond monogamy because it has either never made sense to them or never worked for them or anyone in their life. Some are drawn to non-monogamy as part of decolonizing their ways of relating and reclaiming something closer to their ancestral practices of love and kinship.

My Polyamorous Awakening

My journey into non-monogamy began in childhood when I'd play make-believe and tell stories about a fantasy princess I imagined myself to be who had not one, not two, but three husbands! My mother was shocked by this story and explained to me that one could only have one husband at a time, so I reluctantly rewrote my princess tale.

In high school I crushed on many people, reluctant to date any of them, preferring to make out at parties, because I thought that if I did date one, I would have to stop crushing on the others, and I didn't know how to do that. I remember reading a teen magazine article about a woman who lived with her two boyfriends and thinking how that sounded really cool. It was also in high school that I had my first experience of non-monogamy: sneaking off to make out with my ex-boyfriend behind the school auditorium even after he started dating someone from another school. I asked if he wanted to stop what we'd been doing, and he said no. I asked him if he wanted to tell her about us, and he said no. Seventeen-year-old me was already leaning into open relationships and aspiring towards values of transparency and consent, even though she wasn't quite there yet.

But it was a decade before I began to explore non-monogamy in earnest. In that time I tried to be a "responsible grown-up": a university degree (check!), getting engaged (check!), getting married and moving to my husband's hometown in Canada (check!), trying to have children and experiencing two confirmed miscarriages. And then having an affair and subsequently separating from and divorcing my husband.

By the time my honest non-monogamy journey began in earnest I was twenty-nine years old, separated, and living in a small community on a peninsula in British Columbia on Shíshálh territories. The next decade would see me move to the hub of polyamory that is East Vancouver, dive head-first into being a bisexual and solo polyamorous hot mess, and experience a smorgasbord of everything within the non-monogamous umbrella: married partners with hierarchy, married partners where I was invited to be part of the family, married partners where I never met their spouse, short-term recreational relationships, long-term recreational relationships, orgies, festival hookups, metamours (the partners of my partners) who became friends and metamours who I was never able to get along with. I had amicable break-ups and not-so-amicable break-ups.

For over a decade, I've been solo polyamorous—to me this means that I'm my own primary partner. But this doesn't mean I don't have meaningful, loving relationships. My relationship landscape has included deeply significant emotional relationships, including long-term ones. I have one long-distance erotic-kink friendship that's been going on and off for a quarter of a century, and several loverships that defy definition but hold a tender space in my life. Within my polyamorous journey I've also dipped into swinging and sex parties, dabbled with the idea of nesting and moving into a hierarchical relationship with one partner, and navigated several incidents of intimate abuse.

There have been many times in my journey when things have been messy, and I'd like to think I've learned from every mess. For all the ups and downs, stepping into a post-monogamous way of living and loving has been the best self-development workshop for me. If I went back in time and told seventeen-year-old me what was in store, I don't think my teen self would have believed it possible. Heck, I think even my twenty-nine-year-old self would have been highly suspicious! But over the past decade and a bit, I've found every core belief has been held up and challenged—some have changed, some have not, and the journey has been, at times, terrifying, intoxicating, dizzying, overwhelming, nourishing, and ultimately, liberating.

If you are interested in a kind of relating that includes multiple loving relationships, you may find that polyamory is not just about exploring individual intimacies but also about challenging how we have internalized the dominant culture. Whether it's your ultimate destination or not, exploring non-monogamy can help to undo the knots of patriarchy, colonialism, and imperialism you carry, and to weave a new narrative that is authentic and connects you to many hearts, providing you with a broader network of loving and compassionate support.

White Supremacy Culture in Non-Monogamy

As we explored in chapter 1, white supremacy culture is a toxic and violent system that permeates our modern world and says human worthiness is determined by the extent to which we are white, thin, able-bodied, and rich and hold control over resources. It intersects with patriarchy and colonialism to attempt control over our sexuality, our intimacies, and our relationships.

Even when we are working on moving away from mono-normative and cis-heteronormative ways of being and relating, internalized white supremacy culture can show up in our non-monogamy. Three common behaviours that you might experience in non-monogamous relationships that come from internalized white supremacy culture are:

- Avoidance of conflict: Agreeability is equated to safety.

- Resource and power hoarding, including love, money, time: This can show up as hierarchy, or its cousin, sneakyarchy.

- Expectations of conformity or ostracizing nonconformity: a rhetoric that there is "one true way to poly."

AVOIDANCE OF CONFLICT

In white supremacy culture, those who hold power may feel entitled to comfort, and conflict, being something that disrupts comfort, isn't tolerated unless it is done politely and non-disruptively. As a result of equating agreeability and niceness to comfort, and comfort to safety, anyone who does bring up conflict or differences or even draws attention to harm or abuse can be accused of being harmful or disruptive.

It may seem paradoxical that within non-monogamous spaces there is a culture of avoiding conflict, since the more people you relate with, the harder it is to avoid conflict and difference. However, since white supremacy culture has taught us to avoid conflict, we may lack the skills to navigate conflict in healthy ways and wish to avoid it because our unfamiliarity makes it feel overwhelming and scary.

RESOURCE AND POWER HOARDING

In patriarchal forms of non-monogamy, this looks like accumulating many partners of the same gender who do not have other relationships, or only with their primary partner's sanction, for example, polygamy. In feminist polyamorous spaces, resource and power hoarding can manifest in overt relational hierarchy, such as primary partners being prioritized over secondaries, or sneakyarchy: covert hierarchy where, despite no primary-secondary labelling, there is still some kind of pecking order that places less worthy partners as lower priorities. Sometimes this power hoarding shows up in social spaces as unwillingness to share positional power in organizing community, gatekeeping of knowledge, or making unilateral decisions on behalf of others without consulting them.

EXPECTATIONS OF CONFORMITY

The idea that there is one true way to be polyamorous, or a single ethical code that governs all non-monogamy, is deeply embedded with the internalized ideas of perfectionism that we get from white supremacy culture. Sometimes people hold onto the idea of a gold standard because they feel under pressure to justify their non-monogamy within a culture that prioritizes monogamy and glamorizes the nuclear family. This even shows up from time to time in the literature and social media created by advocates for non-monogamy. But this has consequences: Those who don't adhere to the expected way of doing non-monogamy may be bullied and socially ostracized by other non-monogamists, and if they've already been othered by monogamists, they may feel very isolated.

As we'll explore in the following few chapters, stepping into the new territory of non-monogamy when all you've had role-modelled is monogamy can feel daunting. There's so much more to think about and track, leaving some who try to explore it without support feeling exhausted, tapped out, and craving the comparative simplicity of monogamy. Many of the structures you'll find me sharing in this book are ones I either learned and adapted or created from scratch in my moments of feeling exhausted in polyamorous relationships. They supported me in reframing how I was relating in a way that wasn't tied up within terminology or bound by hierarchical or egalitarian structures. Over the years, I have found that they have helped many others explore non-monogamy too.

SOMATIC PAUSE
Reflecting on Non-Monogamous Relationships

Take a moment to move and stretch your body in a way that feels comfortable for you. Notice what you're experiencing in your body right now after reading more about polyamory and other types of non-monogamy. What is it like to think about how oppression shows up in non-monogamy? Have you experienced any of these yourself?

Notice if any part of you feels tension, and invite your breath to move into those parts. Notice if any part of you feels open or perhaps hopeful. You can invite your breath to move through these parts of yourself.

Take a moment to remember the people in your life who have cared for you and supported you. You might imagine them around you, or you might think of a memory that includes them. Notice how your body responds to remembering them. Is there a change in your breathing? Do your mind and body relax?

However your body is responding, take a moment to notice this consciously, and then shake your body out for a few seconds before continuing.

3

POST-MONOGAMY

In the last chapter we looked at the parallels between the waves of feminism and non-monogamy. I'd argue that we're seeing the beginnings of a *post-monogamous* wave of feminism. It may be only the first swell, yet to grow into a cresting wave, but in this wave many through-lines are converging: human rights, socialism, feminism, intersectionality, queer politics, and non-monogamy.

We are primed for this post-monogamous paradigm. In the face of economic recession, the ecological crisis driven by climate change, the COVID-19 pandemic, wars, genocides, and more, the monogamous nuclear family fails to meet our survival needs. As we seek more security through relationships, many are turning toward wider communities that provide connection, healing, and a sense of belonging, helping to restore lost traditional extended kinship networks. In essence, if the nuclear family was designed to isolate us, we're now rebelling and looking for ways to feel more connected, in order to survive and thrive together.

More people are considering relational ecosystems as an alternative to the relationship escalator. New economic realities mean that more people are deconstructing their nuclear family, creating anarcules: anarchic networks of relations not bound by imposed order or other assumptions but formed through mutuality, alignment of values and interests, and collaborative agreement. An anarcule could include romantic partners, lovers, chosen family, platonic partnerships, nesting mates, friends, children, elders, nonhuman companions, and more. We'll look more closely at anarcules in chapters 11 and 20.

What Exactly Is Post-Monogamy?

A post-monogamous paradigm would be one where monogamy is no longer considered the default for intimate relationships.

Instead of pursuing relationships in search of safety within systems that divide us, we'd seek out relationships as a means of collectively surviving and thriving. Rather than isolated dyadic partnerships being prioritized above other relationships, we'd experience connections as interdependent, relational eco-systems, balancing individual agency and the collective care of community-resourced attachment experiences. Instead of family dynamics where elders and children alike feel isolated while the working adults strive to provide for them, we'd have intergenerational experiences where all ages have multiple loving connections with people who support them. And we'd relate in ways that were kinder, more compassionate, more considerate, and honouring the humanity in everyone. If we started to make these shifts within our personal, intimate lives, maybe we'd be better resourced to move into a new paradigm that makes the current nuclear family–centric, resource-hoarding paradigm obsolete and once again be able to form kinship networks and nurture chosen family freely.

But we face obstacles to getting there. Internalized mono-normativity, alongside white supremacy culture, patriarchy, colonialism, and the narratives of the nuclear family, won't disappear overnight, nor will they evaporate just through reading this book. However, understanding exactly what these obstacles are and learning how we can begin moving through them is a smart place to start.

Obstacles to Post-Monogamy

Divesting from white supremacy culture is challenging when racism, ableism, and misogyny are all embedded in the systems that govern our social, economic, and relational freedoms or lack thereof. We can sometimes feel trapped, feeling like we have no choice but to submit to its narratives if we want to survive and thrive.

Even if you don't have the capacity or ability to effect change on a structural level, you *can* effect change on a personal level, starting with your intimate relationships and how you connect with others:

- learning how to show up for relational conflict with kindness, compassion, and trauma-informed skills to support yourself and others;
- embracing collaborative processes in relationships;
- growing respect for the tapestry of experiences a rich and diverse relational ecology offers.

The starting point for all of this is to learn how to care for yourself—the self that white supremacy culture may have told you is unworthy, or that it may have told you is more worthy than others. Caring for ourselves begins with noticing what's happening inside our nervous systems and how that affects our desires, choices, and responses to change.

The Monogamy Hangover

At the root of internalized mono-normativity is the monogamy hangover. This describes the leftover mythology of monogamy, which says that as long as we adhere to the rules of lifelong exclusive partnership, we'll be rewarded with economic stability, social safety, emotional security, and more.

If we've leaned heavily into this mythology with the hope that one day we'll be safe, secure, and stable in an exclusive partnership, anything challenging that dream will feel threatening. Anger, sadness, depression, rage: all of these are emotions we may be familiar with in the wake of any break-up or relationship-changing event. The hangover of monogamy, especially as it happens in non-monogamous relationships, can show up in bargaining, denial, doubt, and panic, all aspects of grief. We can be so conditioned to rely on monogamy to orient ourselves in our relationships, and our life in general, that even years into exploring open relationships, lingering mono-normative notions and assumptions can crop up in how we approach our non-monogamous relationships.

We can examine the monogamy hangover through four core areas: why we seek relationships, what we want from them, where we hope they will go, and how we engage in them.

Why We Seek Relationships

We are relational creatures that thrive through connection. The reasons we seek monogamous relationships are summarized in the following four sections.

THE RELATIONSHIP ESCALATOR

The relationship escalator, a term coined by Amy Gahran, refers to the default trajectory of relationships encouraged by modern Western cultures. It's a familiar fairy tale: Two people meet, like each other a lot, meet each other's parents, decide to move in, maybe get married, have kids, and then retire. Success on the relationship escalator is equated to success as a grown-up, and the goal is to die without ever leaving it.

In her book *Stepping Off the Escalator,* Gahran describes five key components of escalator relationships:

- Sexual and romantic exclusivity between two, and only two, partners.

- Merging life infrastructure and identity: sharing a home and other resources, such as finances. Also identifying strongly as a couple or family, perhaps to the extent that the individual identities of partners start to be eclipsed.

- Hierarchy. Some relationships are considered more important than others, and thus "win" by default in many situations. On the escalator, since you're allowed only one sexual-romantic partner, that relationship is considered more important than almost every other relationship, such as friendships, with the possible exception of parenting.

- Sexual connection, at least at the beginning of the relationship. Sex often fades or disappears, especially in long-term monogamy.

- Continuity and consistency: Escalator relationships aren't supposed to pause or step back to a less-merged state.[1]

Being on the relationship escalator is celebrated, and we are encouraged to "settle down." When we do, we may feel more loved and validated by family members, elders, and friends. For both serial monogamists and those in consensual non-monogamous relationships, multiple relationship escalators are possible, either simultaneously or overlapping: if one falters, there's a backup to ensure they will never fall completely off.

Stepping off, or worse, falling off the escalator is socially discouraged and shamed. People who have gone through divorce or adultery may be judged or socially ostracized, and newly single people may feel pressured to get back to dating so that they can get back on the escalator quickly.

BELIEF IN "THE ONE"

Go to any bookstore's section on relationships and you'll find books about finding and keeping your "soulmate." However, when we believe that another person is our one-and-only soulmate, what happens when we meet someone else? Indeed, the hold of this mythology is so tremendous that cults and self-improvement empires have been built upon the promise of finding and keeping one's "twin flame."

When going through break-ups or opening up a relationship, an internalized belief in "the one" can trigger insecurity about oneself and how you've related to the relationship. Thoughts of, *If I'm not their "one," someone else might be,* and, *Their connection with their other partner is so strong, they must be soulmates,* are not uncommon.

PERSONAL VALUE TIED TO RELATIONSHIP

In my early thirties, I briefly worked at a dating agency catering to busy professionals seeking monogamous soulmates. Most clients, in their mid-forties to early fifties and dating for the first time since divorcing their high school or college sweethearts, often gave feedback that while they liked their match, they couldn't introduce them to friends. Upon deeper probing, I realized this wasn't just about social compatibility but rather social standing. Many of these clients sought partners who could elevate their status, fearing rejection from their social circles if their partners didn't meet unspoken standards. As some grew tired of the dating cycle, they expressed fears of social exclusion for being unpartnered, feeling they were seen by their friends as less worthy without a partner.

In societies where women are not afforded true equality and equity, a partner's social, economic, and professional status may matter greatly. The hangover kicks in when we measure our self-worth based on the type of partners or suitors we attract or find compatibility with, especially when focusing on superficial qualities such as appearance rather than emotional availability, relational attunement, and other compatibility aspects. Furthermore, if we have internalized that we only have worth based on the worthiness of our partners, then our sense of self-worth may struggle when we are unpartnered or find ourselves unexpectedly single.

SAFETY IN PARTNERSHIP

Relying on partnership for safety is precarious, yet it is still a primary reason many seek monogamous relationships. Social systems often prioritize married couples for foster parenting, adoption, or hospital visitation rights. In some parts of the world, single individuals continue to face disenfranchisement, whether through financial restrictions or political exclusions.

When a partnership doesn't provide the sense of security we seek and we lack the resources or support to find it elsewhere, we may attempt to "lock things down." This could involve pushing the relationship along the traditional relationship escalator, such as having children or making significant joint investments, creating obligations within the relationship, or even resorting to strategies like love bombing, where we flood a partner with affection, praise, or gifts in an attempt to secure a commitment via obligation and transactionality.

REFLECTIVE JOURNALING
Why Have You Sought Out Relationships?

Why have you sought out meaningful relationships?

Have there been social, economic, and cultural influences that have affected the way that you approach or view relationships?

Are there fairy tale stories, family anecdotes, or other narratives that have shaped what you view as the reasons for intimate relationships?

What We Seek: Expectations of Relationships

Monogamy offers hope of security, and sometimes the unsatisfying familiar feels more comfortable than the risk of venturing into unknowns. When I ask folks why they don't leave a relationship that seems to be holding them back from what they need, they respond that they feel more security within the relationship than outside of it. Two of the most common expectations of relationships are permanency and telepathy.

PERMANENCY

The expectation of permanence creates anxiety around change, with even small shifts feeling like signs that the relationship is ending. Temporary changes in a relationship dynamic can feel catastrophic when you believe whatever is true now must remain forever.

Expecting permanence can also lead to complacency. Couples may avoid seeking therapy or coaching out of fear that doing so might create change, and change is seen as bad. Yet whether navigating life solo, with one partner, or with many, relationships' inherent complexity and flux are unavoidable. Relying on a false sense of permanence can hinder the development of somatic resilience and conflict intimacy (we'll explore these in more detail throughout this book), paradoxically making it harder to adapt to inevitable changes.

TELEPATHY

Have you ever felt that your partner should magically know what you want without you ever asking or hinting? We can be afraid to ask for what we want or communicate boundaries. When the stakes are high, it can feel safer to avoid direct communication and rely on passive behaviours—what my colleague Marcia Baczynski calls desire smuggling, where we hint, suggest, or subtly manipulate our desires into conversations. This can show up in both monogamy and non-monogamy and is common when couples face new experiences like opening up a monogamous relationship. Unspoken assumptions about roles and responsibilities as well as projecting our desires onto our partner, such as both partners assuming they'd be the focus of a potential threesome, can create tension that ultimately sabotages happiness.

Even when we do attempt direct communication, words don't always have the same meaning for everyone. For instance, in English, the word *orange* can refer to both a fruit and a colour; similarly, many words and concepts can hold different interpretations within relationships. This makes even clear communication susceptible to misinterpretation. Over time, misunderstandings can multiply, especially in long-term relationships where meanings may shift or assumptions go unchecked. Phrases like "taking the relationship to the next level" can create confusion—does it mean something sexual, moving in together, meeting families, or just deepening emotional intimacy?

REFLECTIVE JOURNALING
What Expectations Have You Held of Your Relationships?

Are there behaviours or actions that you've hoped for in a partner?

Have you experienced frustration at a partner being unable to meet an expectation in the relationship?

In what ways have you tried to smuggle your desires into a relationship, perhaps by hinting heavily or projecting your desires onto your partner?

Where We Want It to Go

Many of us tend to hold to the idea that relationships will be lifelong and include aspects of inescapable entanglement: till death do us part. These are some of the more frequently held ideas of how we are supposed to engage once we are in a relationship, and these primarily centre on merging and maintaining forever, whatever the cost.

MERGING

Merging extends from the "one true soulmate" myth, where the relationship becomes more important than the individuals in it, leading to the sacrifice of individuality for the sake of togetherness. Over time, couples may start to dress alike, adopt similar speech patterns, or be seen by others as a single, inseparable unit.

Simply becoming a little more like our partners is relatively benign. The expectation that partners should do everything together can, however, lead to uncomfortable compromises and inaccurate assumptions: *If my partner wants this, I should want it too,* or assuming, *If I want something, of course my partner will support it,* or even, *If my partner doesn't want this, then I shouldn't either.* This can result in relationships becoming insular, friendships and family being neglected, and people focusing solely on each other. This is true in non-monogamy as well as in monogamy, and navigating the feelings of enmeshment and merging with multiple partners simultaneously is a common challenge in non-monogamy. Merging dynamics can also play into coercion, abuse, or chronically avoiding conflict.

MAINTAINING FOREVER, NO MATTER THE COST

The expectation that an emotionally connected relationship must involve taking the relationship escalator—and in polyamory, the assumption that all partners are on the relationship escalator—can prevent us from admitting when a relationship has run its course or needs to change. It might lead us to feel that the need to make a change somehow reflects our not putting in enough effort.

The cost of maintaining a relationship the way it is forever can be huge. If the individuals in the relationship are not open to the dynamics, expectations, and general sandbox of the relationship changing over time, feelings of resentment will inevitably emerge. Staying in a situation that we are enduring, rather than one we are enthusiastic about, can impact our physical and mental health. Elevated stress levels from living in relational resentment can affect our immune system, cardiovascular system, and ability to recuperate from injuries.

REFLECTIVE JOURNALING
Where Have You Wanted Your Relationships to Go?

Have you experienced feeling frustrated or perhaps uninterested in a relationship that didn't seem to be progressing in a particular direction?

How have you handled a mismatch in desired direction in relationships? Has this ever precipitated the end of a relationship?

How We Measure Success in Relationship

To be successful in a relationship is seen as a reflection of our capacity to be successful in life itself. These are three of the most common markers of our success in monogamous relationships, often taken as proof that we're succeeding at that relationship escalator:

- perfectionism
- sex equals success
- self-sacrifice

PERFECTIONISM

Perfectionism, as we experience it today, is deeply rooted in white supremacy and often tied to ideas of purity. The subtext of perfectionism is usually ableist, stigmatises mental health challenges, and shames bodies that don't meet white-supremacy standards of thinness and athleticism. This legacy of perfectionism has harmed our ancestors and continues to reinforce oppressive systems, keeping us in cycles of self-criticism and societal judgment.

Aspiring to be perfect can sabotage our happiness and sense of fulfilment. We also risk holding others to unrealistic standards, straining our relationships by imposing our ideals of perfection onto them. This expectation stifles true intimacy, as the pressure to be the perfect person for our partner pulls us away from authenticity. Trust erodes when we lose that authenticity, and disconnection grows in our relationships.

SEX EQUALS SUCCESS

One of the most common causes of panic in relationships is a decrease in sexual activity. I've often heard people worry that they should be having more sex with their partners or fear that they are no longer sexually attractive. Some even end relationships because they no longer feel turned on by their partner. These anxieties stem from the belief that a healthy relationship must include a lot of sex, and that changes in sexual dynamics signal a problem. In non-monogamous dynamics I've seen individuals focus on relationships with more exciting sexual chemistry, sometimes neglecting the need to address sexual dissatisfaction in their existing partnerships.

While a change in sexual chemistry can sometimes be an indicator of underlying issues, it's entirely natural for desire and libido to shift over time. Expecting a relationship to remain sexual, or treating sex as obligatory within a romantic relationship, can lead to resentment and bitterness that becomes an obstacle to intimacy.

SELF-SACRIFICE AS A LOVE LANGUAGE

Have you ever found yourself putting others' needs before your own, to the detriment of your mental, emotional, and physical health, and thinking it demonstrates how deeply you love them? We've been taught that sacrificing ourselves in relationships is noble and a symbol of love. This can lead us to expect similar sacrifices from others, sometimes keeping score in a tit-for-tat approach to love. We might sacrifice any number of things: our time, our dreams, our bodies, our resources, and more. We learn to tolerate and endure things that are uncomfortable and even harmful to us, once again bringing on relational stress that can impact our health.

Even if you reject the idea of being your partner's property, holding onto self-sacrificing behaviours can signal that some part of you still feels beholden to them. This feeds into codependency and other unhealthy patterns, where enduring what drains us is seen as virtuous. Many of these narratives stem from limiting beliefs and societal expectations we've internalized, like heteronormative gender roles, religious norms, social pressures, and the lingering effects of purity culture and inadequate sex education. When we buy into this mindset, we risk crossing into the dangerous territory of harm and abuse. Although the harm is often to ourselves, constantly trying to rescue a partner can also harm them and damage the relationship.

REFLECTIVE JOURNALING
How Have You Evaluated Your Relationships?

When you've found yourself weighing the options of continuing or ending a relationship, what factors have you considered? Is there one that is more important than others? Are there dealbreakers for you?

What do you consider being a good partner to look or feel like?

If the monogamy hangover arises from the grief of letting go of the mythology of patriarchal monogamy, then working through our monogamy hangover is a process that requires us to discover a new paradigm for relating—one that is thoroughly liberated from the limiting, transactional frameworks that patriarchal monogamy, colonialism, and the nuclear family have imposed. As we gather the unravelled threads of the monogamous tapestry, we can weave something new, fresh, and unique for ourselves.

REFLECTIVE JOURNALING
Recognizing Your Monogamy Hangover

Take some time to think about how you've internalized mono-normativity. You might reflect on the previous prompts in this chapter.

What stories, narratives, and life experiences have influenced your beliefs about relationships?

As a child, what did you see role-modelled for you about relationships, and what did others tell you to expect of partnership?

Why do you seek out relationships with others, and what expectations have you held of your partners in those relationships?

How do you know when a relationship needs to change, or to end?

Embracing Post-Monogamy

A post-monogamous wave of feminism offers us exciting possibilities: a queering of relationships beyond the sexual intimacies that patriarchy has positioned as paramount, a cultivating of intergenerational connections that better support the raising of children, a movement away from individualism, consumerism, and chronic codependency in an unsustainable corporate capitalist hellscape, and into a collectivist, compassionate, mycelial, and communal social ecology.

Societal change on a global scale takes time—years, decades, or even centuries. I'm acutely aware that, as I write of equity and community care, people in some countries face imprisonment or execution for supporting women's bodily autonomy. Even in Canada, the hard-won rights for women, trans people, and people of colour are constantly at risk, and we have yet to achieve justice, healing, and recognition for First Nations, Inuit, and Métis peoples.

And yet, while societal change may move at what seems like a snail's pace, with the pendulum swinging back and forth every few years between conservative patriarchy and progressive feminist values, we can still, every one of us, deconstruct and dismantle the ways that systems of dominance impact our most intimate spaces.

I invite you to cultivate hope: If we, non-monogamous or not, can succeed in making progress towards post-monogamous, feminist, radical relationships by cultivating our relational ecosystems and growing our anarcules of loving connections, then perhaps we, as humanity, stand a real chance of thriving into the future.

SOMATIC PAUSE
Going Beyond Monogamy

Take a moment to pause and breathe.

Think about how you experience connection and relationships in your life right now and what obstacles you've faced. Notice if tension arises when you think about these obstacles, and give your body a moment to shake, stretch, or move in a way that feels good to you.

Now, think about someone you have a non-romantic connection with that you have enjoyed, even if you don't know that person very well. Notice what sensations or emotions arise when you think about this person. Do you feel ease, a sense of openness, perhaps an experience of expansion? How much space do you feel you can take up when you're around this person? How much space do you feel they can take up around you?

Imagine what could be possible if more relationships felt like this.

What could be possible in your relationships if the limitations of mono-normativity didn't hold you back? How might sensations of ease and openness expand into all your relationships?

I invite you to place a hand on the part of yourself that feels most open and warm, and take a few breaths before continuing.

4

BECOMING TRAUMA-INFORMED

In this chapter, we explore what trauma is, how and why it shows up in our relationships, and how understanding and working with it supports us to confidently grow post-monogamous relationships. Trauma-informed relating isn't just about understanding trauma: It's an active process where we seek to resolve the past, honour the experiences of the present, and hopefully reduce the risk of future overwhelm or harm.

We're going to look at a few different definitions and perspectives on trauma, but I want to be clear that it isn't just something that happens as a consequence of isolated, intensely painful experiences. Trauma can arise from being overwhelmed beyond our ability to cope, from events moving so fast we don't have time to process them, and also from confusion and feeling lost in our relationships. Challenging mono-normativity can sometimes leave us feeling lost, confused, overwhelmed, or like things are moving too fast. When we're scared or overwhelmed, we're more likely to fall back on the familiar patterns of mono-normativity. Becoming trauma-informed can help us recognize when stress or overwhelm might lead us to revert to old habits, empowering us to make more intentional and liberating choices in our relationships.

Understanding and working with the ways that trauma shows up in our relationships requires self-reflection, humility, and perseverance. It is also not just an intellectual pursuit: Learning about trauma and then growing a relationship with it takes time. In many ways, trauma-informed relating is an art.

REFLECTIVE JOURNALING
What Is Your Relationship to Trauma?

What do you understand trauma to be? Do you think of it as something that happens to other people, or do you have a sense of what your trauma might be?

Have you ever talked to anyone about the painful experiences you've had? What does it feel like to receive support or not receive support?

Is there anyone in your life who has experienced a lot of hardships in life who you see thriving today?

What Is Trauma?

Trauma can be understood as a consequence of adverse or disruptive experiences that happen without the support to cope with, process, and integrate them: our nervous system goes into a state of alert to protect us from harm, but when it never finds resolution—in other words, we never find a way to come back to safety—those self-protective responses can continue to manifest in various situations, even in the absence of harm. Think of how you might flinch at the sound of a car hitting the brakes. If you've ever been in a motor vehicle accident, your body might tense up and brace for an impact as if you are in the car itself, even if you are safely indoors and not in any danger.

While we might commonly associate trauma with extraordinarily horrific events like genocide, war, personal injuries, or interpersonal violence, trauma encompasses so much more than that. Some of us have experienced hurt and harm early in life, such as the pre-verbal trauma when infants are separated from caregivers, whether forcibly by the state or due to caregivers needing to return to work. Childhood experiences like bullying, social ostracization, inappropriate adult interactions, violations of our agency by family members or other adults, and encountering societal and systemic issues like ableism, racism, and homophobia can also leave us with an imprint of trauma. As adults, abusive relationships, poverty, health crises, environmental disasters, social unrest, migration, and witnessing harm to others can all contribute to overwhelming our nervous systems.

There is also intergenerational trauma, passed down through family lines, including genetic changes and also behavioural coping mechanisms that are passed down like family traditions. Geneticists have found DNA alterations can occur as a consequence of adverse experiences. As an example, the children of holocaust survivors have been shown to have more challenges in adapting to stress. In minority communities that have experienced oppression, it is noted that there is an increased occurrence of chronic health conditions, such as heart disease, cancer, dementia, and more.

Trauma is not a contest: there are many different examples of experiences that can create disruption and leave someone with trauma. Two people could go through the same experience and have drastically different trauma, depending on their prior experiences and the way they're supported afterwards. Someone can experience something incredibly horrific, but with access to resources—such as community, friendship, skilled healers and therapists, and time—they can live so that the pain from their past does not cast shadows over their present.

REFLECTIVE JOURNALING
Intergenerational Trauma

What kinds of intergenerational trauma might there be in your family?

- What stresses and challenges did your parents or grandparents face, and how much do you know about how they handled it?

- Are there specific stories of traumatic events that your family of origin or your culture hold to be of particular significance? Examples include wars, migrations, and historical events. How are these events commemorated today?

How did your family of origin adapt to cope with disruptive and traumatic events?

Are there habits or behaviours or perhaps beliefs that they passed down to you?

Have you ever seen these show up within your relationships?

Trauma as Disruption

Right now, some part of your marvellous brain is aware of the space you occupy, registering the temperature, the lighting, the presence of people, and the elements surrounding you. Your brain processes sensory information from sound, smell, sight, taste, and touch, assessing potential changes or shifts that may necessitate a response.

Much of this process occurs automatically. While our responses are not always perfect—for example, putting on a sweater because we feel cold at home, while ignoring the draft from an open window—we can generally navigate our environments effectively and safely. Occasionally, when we have very painful experiences, we learn to interpret certain events, words, circumstances, behaviours, or people as indicators of risk, and we may have self-protective responses to those indicators that make sense to us, but to others seem disproportionate. There are also times when we lack the context to understand what we are experiencing, and thus cannot know whether we are actually safe or not. In Somatic Experiencing (discussed in depth in chapter 5), this is known as disrupted orienting.

Think of a time you visited somewhere new. You might have purchased a guidebook or downloaded some articles about where you were going. You might have studied a map and figured out where you'd be staying, where the attractions were, and maybe you looked up some restaurants you'd like to dine at. Perhaps you talked to friends who had been there before and asked for their recommendations. This is part of how you orient your nervous system to engage with being in a new place. If you arrive at your vacation destination and find that the maps are inaccurate, that an attraction you had hoped to see is closed for the season, or that the restaurants can't cater to your dietary needs, you might find yourself feeling agitated and anxious as your nervous system experiences the disruption of expectations being dashed and facing unexpected changes instead.

Similarly, when we embark on open relationships, we seek guidebooks and articles that tell us what to expect. We also reach out to people who have done this before us and ask for their advice. However, the landscape of open relating is so vast and filled with possibilities that it is impossible to be prepared for it all. Our ability to orient towards safety is disrupted when we don't have enough context to understand our new experiences.

There will always be a few folks who enjoy the thrill of wandering without a guidebook, but even the boldest of adventurers can find themselves caught unprepared for what they encounter. In the same way, venturing into non-monogamy without a contextual framework for our experiences can be overwhelming. As a result, our nervous systems may respond in the same ways that we respond to disrupting and traumatic experiences: panic, anxiety, and controlling behaviours can all show up as we attempt to establish some semblance of direction in this vast and open landscape.

My Experience of Disrupted Orienting

My early polyamory journey was a storm of overwhelming and complex events: alienation from my homophobic mother after coming out as queer, navigating new boundaries while recovering from a harmful relationship, relocating to a new city and struggling to find community, and grappling with financial uncertainty despite holding three jobs.

I was carving out my path as a solo polyamorist in a community dominated by couples seeking a third. I was confused that every person I went on a date with seemed to have a different definition of polyamory. Amid all this, I could not recognize just how overwhelmed I truly was.

I found myself people-pleasing with partners and holding back from asserting boundaries out of fear of alienation, only to grow frustrated and exhausted when I felt I had no space for myself. My emotions oscillated between exuberance and overconfidence (attempting to "fake it till you make it") and private moments of despair and sorrow.

So much in my life was changing and I didn't know which way was up. I often felt like I was treading water. To try to make sense of it, I began writing a blog to reflect on my experiences and articulate what I was learning about relationships. I created a personal road map by deciding to be in a primary relationship with myself, and as soon as I had that clarity, navigating things felt a little less stressful.

Even so, I would still face challenges in my relational world, where my nervous system would feel disrupted again and my self-protection responses would take over. It took several years to understand my deep-seated drive toward self-protection amid both disorienting and overwhelming experiences.

Trauma as Relational Rupture

From the moment we are born, the presence of loving relationships registers in our nervous system: if we are fortunate to have many kind, loving, nurturing adults around us, we may grow up feeling supported and safe, whereas if our adult caregivers are unkind, emotionally unavailable, or unable to meet our needs adequately, we may feel the urge to protect ourselves from possible loss, harm, or abandonment, and relationships might not feel like they are an adequate source of support.

When any relationship ends, whether through break-up or bereavement, our lives experience rupture. Without additional supportive relationships like friends, community, or other partners, we may feel isolated, lament the relationship, or dwell on the past to the point that it becomes hard to engage with new connections. Or we may become fixated on planning for the future to the point of struggling to engage with the present. We do this because to sit with the pain of loss is hard, especially if we do not feel supported or understood, or don't feel like we're permitted to grieve the loss of a relationship.

Another definition of trauma is the "loss of relationship." This can be a loss of relationship with others or ourselves. It can also be seen as a loss of relationship to the present. One of the ways I notice trauma coming up with my clients is that they have a hard time staying present to our conversation. They might jump around a timeline as they describe events, or keep returning to something from the distant past. In some partnerships, one or both partners might loop back to a moment in their relationship where there was pain or hurt, and struggle to see the loving connection available in the present. I think of this aspect of trauma as time-travelling, and our nervous systems often need time and support to relearn that the present moment can hold safety, pleasure, and joy. Indeed, new research supports this: In a 2023 study, a team from Yale University conducted scans on the brains of twenty-eight people with PTSD, and based on the neural activity in the brain, found that traumatic memories aren't just remembered; they are relived.[1]

Trauma can also be a loss of relationship with self: Our self-protection mechanisms can urge us to run from ourselves, to fight ourselves, to go numb to ourselves, and to capitulate to others and override our own needs for the sake of maintaining an external relationship. This loss of relationship to self is usually momentary. As it passes, sometimes with ease, sometimes with a bit of work, we can regain our sense of relationship with ourselves. Other times, the disruption might feel continuous, or the stressful event exhausts us. In such moments, we may find ourselves feeling reminded of past traumas or may feel so internally dysregulated that we feel swallowed by the gravitational pull of trauma.

I see a loss of relationship to self when clients struggle to talk about themselves. I might ask clients how they are doing, and they tell me instead about their partners. Or I ask them to describe their feelings, and they describe what they've been doing in their day. Even though they may not be able to answer the question I have asked them, what they do share tells me a lot: A person who is struggling to connect to themselves may not feel safe enough to be with themselves, and there may be trauma at work.

Trauma doesn't happen in isolation. If one person in a relationship feels activated, under capacity, or challenged by a situation, chances are their partners may experience the change in their behaviours as causing disruption to their own nervous systems. Navigating trauma within relationships can get tricky. We all bring our wounds from childhood and past romantic relationships, potentially interpreting our present experiences through the lens of past pain.

SOMATIC PAUSE
Gratitude Practice

Take a moment to think about the people in your life who have supported and loved you, especially through particularly challenging times.

How did they support you?

What encouraging things did they say or do to demonstrate their support and care for you?

Are there ways in which they are still part of your landscape today?

Trauma as Grief

I invite you to consider grief as a nervous system response to the loss of something or someone who participated, even if it was in a seemingly small way, in your network of attachment—the core people, places, and relationships around you that help you feel safe, secure, and stable.

Even if you haven't named it as grief, you may know that feeling: the emotional pin-bowling and pretzelling as you wrestle with loss, the sensation of tightness in your chest when you are reminded of something painful from the past, the dizzying dreams that loop memories and moments over and over, and the emotional numbness that comes with realizing that what was will never be again.

In any kind of relationship, there is grief with break-ups, discovering a partner has broken an agreement or other acts of infidelity, the loss of a beloved animal, the loss of a child, disappointment upon discovering an incompatibility. In the arc of a romantic relationship, grief comes alongside differentiation. Having been besotted with new relationship energy, which helps us see how we are compatible with our partner and can build a fantasy of the relationship to aspire to, differentiation is the phase where we slowly come to reclaim our self-identity and begin to experience how we are different, and seek out the grounded reality of the relationship potential. Sometimes that process is gentle; sometimes it is sudden. But with the shattering of a fantasy, there is also the grief of its loss. We take a closer look at this in chapters 9 and 18.

Exploring post-monogamy involves a fundamental grief. It is mourning the promises of mono-normativity and the dreams we had pinned on those promises. In open relationships, we might be confronted with differentiation sooner than in monogamous ones, simply because we have more opportunities to have our fantasies of someone challenged by other relationships. We might also experience:

- the grief of saying goodbye to the monogamous fantasy when opening a relationship up
- the vicarious grief of supporting a partner through a break-up
- the grief of losing a metamour when your partner breaks up with them
- the grief of realizing that a hoped-for polyamorous configuration just may not be possible
- the grief of rupture within a communal living situation
- the compounded grief of losing multiple partners when a polycule breaks up

And there may be many more. During grief, the nervous system recalibrates and reorients to the world. This takes an incredible amount of energy, and the resulting stress can manifest as physiological symptoms: fatigue, increased appetite, loss of appetite, irritability, confusion, memory challenges, comprehension difficulty, blurred vision, weight gain, weight loss, sudden bursts of euphoria, insomnia, even nightmares.

Grief spirals through stages: denial, anger, bargaining, depression, and acceptance, sometimes separate and sometimes all together, each like a unique note in a complex melody. Grief in our relationships can lead us to avoid pain and discomfort. We might distract ourselves in other relationships, or seek out endless reassurances from our partners while ignoring relational issues. In complex relational dynamics grief as anger might extend towards ex-partners, their new relationships, or metamours. We might try to bargain by making deals with ourselves, hoping circumstances will improve if we just make certain changes. We might choose to stay with relational discomfort, hoping that everything will eventually get easier.

Grief can also show up as depression: feelings of loneliness, diminished self-worth, and doubts about our own desirability, especially when we are dealing with shifting relational dynamics.

REFLECTIVE JOURNALING
Acknowledging Grief

Think about a time you knew a relationship was changing. What were the signs that the relationship was changing? For example, conflict arising, a de-escalation of connection, or seeing less of one another? How did you respond to the signs of change? Were there things you said or did that reflected a desire for the relationship not to change—or that tried to accelerate the changes?

Is it different if you are the person initiating change in a relationship versus when the other person wanted things to change?

How would you respond if your current relationships—romantic, platonic, familial, or otherwise—were to change?

The very nature of post-monogamous relationships, whether opening up an existing relationship or beginning new relationships without an assumption of monogamy, holds risk, uncertainty, and unknowns. The complex dynamics of open relating can shake up our internal status quo, causing old wounds, hurts, and painful memories to surface—experiences that we must try to make sense of within the context of new ways of relating, even while still trying to figure out what those new ways are.

Perhaps it's not entirely surprising that well-meaning therapists and individuals with limited understanding of non-monogamy and alternative relationships sometimes dismiss them as harmful. However, open relationships can be a catalyst for the shaking of our inner worlds and are not necessarily the root cause of the disquiet we experience. That root cause lies in the systemic, intergenerational, and personal traumas and pain that we may hold in our psyche, and how we have adapted to and integrated, or not, around them.

Even in healthy and well-resourced relationships, the ways we have adapted to survive hurt, harm, and a lack of safety in the past can profoundly impact our ability to be present to our loved ones. We may shut down in the face of conflict or, conversely, feel compelled to stoke conflict. These safety-seeking responses can inadvertently sabotage intimacy, subsequently hindering our ability to relate. This impact isn't just felt individually; it can ripple through the dynamics of all our relationships, including friendships, metamourships, and our wider polycules and anarcules.

Self-Protective Responses in Relationships

Self-protection responses, sometimes called trauma responses, are instinctive reactions stemming from primal, physiological changes that occur when our nervous system perceives a threat to our safety. These responses serve us well when we are unsafe, facing attack, or otherwise threatened. When the nervous system enters a state of alertness, it readies us to either fight or flee (the flight response), accompanied by an increased sense of energy and a heightened heart rate. If the nervous system has been frequently engaged in fight or flight or encounters numerous overwhelming threats, it may shift into a state known as freeze. Another common self-protection response is fawn, a survival strategy involving attempts to please the threatening person.

Self-protective responses are normal and natural. They arise because we feel unsafe; their purpose is to return us to safety. Most of the time, they are temporary, and as soon as our nervous system experiences safety, we drop the behaviours associated with self-protection. However, sometimes we can get stuck—especially if we don't find safety, can't trust the safety that we do find, or feel continuous threats.

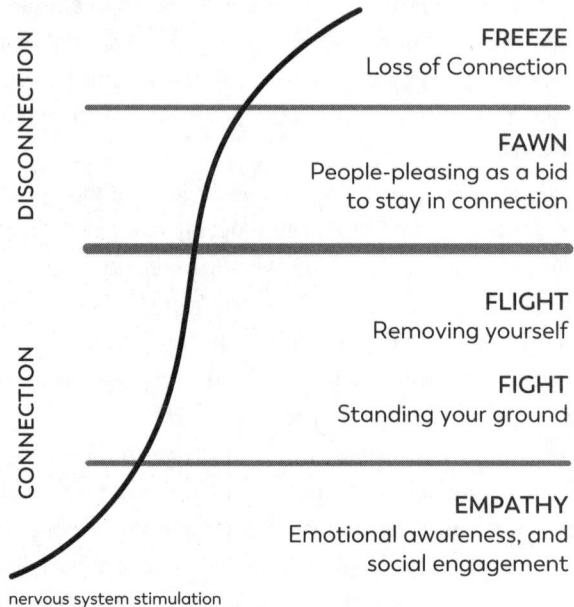

Figure 4.1. Self-protection and nervous system stimulation

We come back to these four self-protective responses a few times in this book, but here's a brief look at what these self-protection responses can feel like in our bodies, and how they might show up in relationships:

Flight response: a primal urge to run away. Humans have muscles involved in movement that tense up, ready to flee from danger. You might notice this through your lower back, hips, and legs. In flight, our brain may feel anxious, our breath shallower, and our heart racing. In our relationships, the flight response might result in avoidance of conflict or withholding information from a loved one that we fear might lead to conflict. We might want to push or rush through any dis-comfort we feel to maintain connection with our partners, and slowing down can feel scary because in slowing down we feel more—more of the good things, and more of the uncomfortable things. This can also show up as distracting yourself by staying busy, perhaps by dating more people or by taking on more than you have the capacity to do.

Fight response: a primal urge to defend ourselves from a threat. We may feel our centre of gravity move lower in our body, a psychosomatic response to ensure we can assert ourselves. The phrases *digging your heels in* or *standing your ground* evoke what it might feel like to move into a fight response. In our relationships, a fight response might look like stubbornness, rigidity, inflexibility about scheduling, or an inability to find compromise. Sometimes it can show up as a lack of compassion and empathy or verbal responses that berate, shut down, or minimize loved ones.

Freeze response: a strategy for managing overwhelm. When we have lingered for a long time in either fight or flight, or highly disruptive events happen, we shut down. In this state, moving our bodies may feel difficult and perhaps impossible. Processing words may feel hard. Attuning to emotions can feel challenging. In relationships, this can show up as forgetting conversations moments after they have happened, or heavily projecting onto or daydreaming about a partner. Some people try to silo their relationships and keep connections compartmentalized, which can work as a short-term strategy. However, if practised over an extended time, it can play into disconnected experiences for the hinge partner and even impact the clarity of communication between all parties.

Fawn response: a strategy for safety that puts our needs and boundaries aside for the sake of others. It can be a bid to avoid an escalation of nervous system stimulation that would take us into freeze, and an attempt to stay connected. It can be much harder to notice because it's natural to find ourselves agreeing to the desires of our loved ones. However, capitulating to partners or potentially telling partners only what we think they are comfortable knowing, rather than information they might find upsetting, can indicate a fawn response at play. Another way I have seen this show up is when a partner offers empty reassurances despite a situation carrying risk and potential discomfort.

REFLECTIVE JOURNALING
Recognizing Self-Protection Responses

Which of these four self-protective responses do you gravitate towards when you feel nervous or uneasy in a relationship: flight, fight, freeze, and fawn?

How do you notice this showing up in how you behave with your partners?

Are there any self-protective responses you notice your loved ones do more frequently?

Remember: it is normal and natural to feel these responses arise within us when our relational equilibrium is disrupted and we don't feel safe. They become a challenge in our relationships when they continue to occur—either disproportionately to the perceived threat, or when a challenge is continuous and there is no opportunity for the nervous system to find reprieve from activation other than a freeze or shut down, even after the threat itself has passed.

This last scenario, where we stay activated in the absence of threat, is an incomplete self-protection response. It can feel like being stuck in a loop. We ride a proverbial hamster wheel of emotions, sometimes oscillating from one mode to the next, from flight to fawn to fight to freeze, though not necessarily in that order, and keep cycling until something supports our nervous system to know that we are safe enough to re-engage with the present moment.

Think of a time you struggled to sleep because an argument wasn't resolved, or you held back from asserting a boundary with a loved one. While our nervous systems usually have good resilience to navigate this stress in the short term, if the issue is never addressed and our nervous system never moves back into an experience of safety, these responses can become stuck. The behaviours associated with self-protective responses can come to dominate our relationships, and the stress within our nervous system can even manifest in physical tension, pain, or other psychosomatic symptoms. This can lead us to feel like we are perpetually on the verge of a breakdown, or like we cannot escape relational stress and conflict.

Ezmi's Story
Resolving Incomplete Self-Protection Responses

Ezmi came to me during a challenging time in one of their relationships. They and one of their partners had found themselves locked in conflict, and Ezmi was struggling to understand the hurt this partner was feeling, and also having a hard time identifying and asserting their boundaries.

When we started working together, Ezmi shared with me that they had been experiencing a lot of lower back and hip pain. They were also navigating some family challenges at home. As our session unfolded, we discovered that self-protective responses of flight and freeze were coming up strongly in their life. In many different situations, Ezmi's boundaries weren't being honoured, and they felt they had to bite their tongue and hold back from asserting themselves. As a consequence of this stress and the ways it made them feel stuck, they found it uncomfortable to stay present in many activities and interactions, contributing to conflict with their partner.

In our first session, I invited Ezmi to move their feet as if they were walking and then let that movement come up to their legs and hips. As they did so, they continued to describe the frustrations they had been having about asserting boundaries and how that made them feel. We spent some time exploring the flight response through movement and imagining what it might be like for them to walk away from the things that had been creating stress. By the end of the session, Ezmi's hip pain had dissipated, and they felt more resourced to engage with their partner again.

Over more somatic coaching sessions, Ezmi was able to trace their self-protective responses to specific moments in youth when core needs for loving and safe connection had gone unmet, and they had not had the kind of support they needed. As our somatic work continued over several months, Ezmi began to experience a shift in how they were relating with their partners, family members, ex-partners, and new people they were starting to date. Ezmi described the sensation as being like many components of a computer having been dusted off, moved around, and finally coming online.

Increasingly, they noticed their nervous system distress before the self-protection responses kicked in and were able to pause the activation and return to experiences of safety and greater openness to connection.

Windows of Capacity

Many of us spend our lives addressing one alarm after another, and might not immediately be able to tune in to the sensations of feeling safe enough. This feeling of being safe enough is called being within our window of capacity. For some, this might feel like ease, tranquillity, happiness, or joy. For others, they notice it when they can tune in to sensations of pleasure or become aware of pleasant sensory experiences. You might feel steady in your body as if comforted from within. Some find that familiar surroundings, music, or even television shows help them to access more capacity; for others, it is easier to sense when we are with specific people with whom we feel understood and cared for. When we have a wider window of capacity, we can be more responsive to the world around us, more engaged and connected with others. Capacity can be a helpful way to think about the energy you have to engage in stimulating activities without overwhelming your nervous system. We explore this idea a little more in chapter 6, and go into depth on capacity in chapter 15.

Trauma-Informed, Not Just Trauma Aware

Trauma-informed relating is about more than acknowledging trauma: It's developing a relationship with it, which can be a lifelong journey. To embrace the trauma our loved ones may carry with them asks that we deepen our own capacity for empathy, compassion, and understanding of the ways trauma and self-protective responses show up. Without the context, resources, and some basic understanding of how nervous system stress plays out in relationships, we may feel overwhelmed or scared by a partner's self-protection responses, and we may feel the urge to dismiss them, minimize their pain, or even gaslight them because we are uncomfortable or unsure how to engage.

The ways we respond to the trauma and distress of others can also activate our own nervous systems into self-protection. Think of how you respond when you hear of atrocities happening in war: For many, comprehending them will be overwhelming; some may be able to understand some part of it, but not all. Even those who have themselves survived atrocities may find it challenging to connect to their empathy when they hear of atrocities happening to others if the pain they carry still feels raw. It can sometimes feel easier to hold space for the trauma of people we relate to in some way, whether that's because of gender, racial dynamics, socio-economic class, or background. And when we love someone who carries trauma that we might not have personal reference points for, engaging with their trauma can feel overwhelming.

As we explored in the previous chapters, mono-normativity and the nuclear family have often resulted in a lot less relationship to village and extended family as well as a diminished experience of platonic friendships. All of these relationships are significant when we are working on moving out of self-protection and defence, and on a journey to resolve our grief and pain.

The journey of healing from trauma doesn't happen in isolation: our relationships with ourselves, our partners, our friends, our families, and our communities are an essential component of resourcing our experiences of safety and support. Trauma-informed relationships are compassionate, patient, spacious, noncoercive, and loving. A trauma-sensitive relationship is mutually respectful and honours the most important dynamic in any relationship: each individual's somatic experience of safety.

Trauma-informed relationships are like physiotherapy for our psyche: We grow our capacity for nervous-system resilience, address the scars from the past, and remedy the patterns of behaviour that no longer support us. They are spacious and compassionate. They aren't rushed. They ask us to hone awareness of our personal and collective needs and cultivate resilience rather than greater endurance. As we navigate the presence of trauma in our bodies and our relationships, we can not only potentially heal from the disruption and pain of our past, but we can grow in ways of relating that allow us to show up as authentic, embodied, and fully present to all that is.

5

WHY SOMATICS?

I've already used the word *somatics* in the last few chapters, and in my coaching practice, it forms the foundation for trauma-informed work. Let's examine what somatics is, where it comes from, why so many people working with trauma love it so much, and how somatic practices might support us in our journey away from mono-normativity.

Somatics Have Animistic Roots

Somatics is a broad umbrella term that also refers to specific modern practices drawn from and inspired by several specific Indigenous traditions but incorporating contemporary wisdom and studies. In traditional settings, practices to support the nervous system were woven into the fabric of everyday life, with no need to see them as a separate set of practices: Dance, music, meditation, the use of art, and pleasure practices can all be considered somatic. This includes the traditions of Yoga from South Asia; Yoruba and hoodoo practices from Africa; Huna and other Indigenous spiritual practices from around the Pacific Rim; Sufi mysticism, considered a branch of Islam, but which may pre-date it; and the shamanic practices of northern Asia and throughout the Americas. All these practices support growing more capacity to be present, whether our experiences are pleasant or challenging, nourishing or gruelling.

The modern field of somatics has been critiqued for cultural appropriation, and this critique is valid and important. You might notice that many of the people I name as key figures in the somatics movement of the twentieth century have been male, white, and Western. While non-Western practices undoubtedly inspired them, the origins of these practices are rarely acknowledged in their teaching materials. Yet in some of these traditions, such as Yoga, to divorce the practices from their origins and lineage is seen as taking away the medicine from the practice, and what was once beneficial can become poison.

This doesn't mean that somatics cannot benefit you, and I don't think it means you can't practise somatics. What I would encourage you to do is to explore what kinds of traditional practices in your own ancestry align with somatics: for example, traditional forms of music and dance, ancestral animism and spirituality (not to be confused with organized religion), and celebrations that mark life milestones or the changing of seasons. More practitioners and teachers are exploring pathways of re-indigenizing and reclaiming somatics. Just a few examples of people growing a new movement that reintegrates somatic practices with traditions in which they originate are Nkem Ndefo, creator of the Resilience Toolkit; Resmaa Menakem, founder of the Cultural Somatics Institute; and two-spirit indigequeer psychotherapist Roger Kuhn.

My own understanding of modern somatics is supported by a lifetime of practice in Yoga and Tantra traditions, as well as some studies of Sufism. I can tell you that I've experienced meaningful shifts in my relationship to my own self and my trauma through both my time spent in Yoga ashrams and also in working with somatics. I don't think one is better; instead, I think of it as different medicine for different conditions. In deference to these lineages and my position as a student of them, and not a teacher of them, I'm not directly referencing their somatic practices. I encourage you to seek out the somatic practices that nourish and support you, and to be curious about your own ancestral traditions that can complement this work.

Modern Somatics

The ancestors who developed traditional forms of somatics experienced different challenges and stressors than we experience today. They didn't have to address the intergenerational trauma of being deep in patriarchal monogamy, white supremacy culture, or the separation from community brought by the nuclear family. Today, many cultures face obstacles to accessing their own Indigenous wisdom: Some languages have been lost, the wisdom keepers of traditions persecuted, and the traditional ways of life in which these practices were embedded have been heavily disrupted.

The modern concept of somatics started in psychology circles in the mid-1800s, borrowing the word *soma* from both Greek and Sanskrit. In Greek, *soma* refers to the body and has been adopted in biology to refer to the body's cells. In Sanskrit, *soma* appears in the Vedic texts describing a divine elixir that grants immortality, and in the Bhagavad Gita as a substance that absolves all suffering. Nineteenth-century somaticists believed that the soul could not experience illness, and therefore all ailments, including mental ones, resided in the body.

In the mid- to late twentieth century, movement theorist Thomas Hanna used the term to describe an emerging field of bodywork and movement practice that supported mind-body integration. Hanna was inspired by yogic disciplines and contemporary movement and bodywork teachers like Moshé Feldenkrais, Ida Rolf, and Rudolf von Laban. Hanna sought the means to support humanity through what he described as a time of radical change. Writing in his 1970 book *Bodies of Revolt,* he states:

> As we close out the last third of the twentieth century, we are witnessing the closing out of an immensely long period in human culture and, simultaneously, we are experiencing an abrupt and sharply accelerated mutation into a radically different human culture. . . . In brief, in a technological environment that is radically new, a radically accelerated environmental adaptation is taking place. . . . And, for good or for ill—depending on one's cultural and somatic stance—this identification of evolution and revolution will henceforth be the future situation of a technological human society.[1]

In other words, he experienced the rapid changes brought about by technology as heralding not just change but change that was happening so fast that it might take a lot of work to keep up. What might Hanna have thought of the AI revolution or how the rapid pace of innovation impacts our brains, physicality, mental health, and capacity for interpersonal relationships?

Hanna's work would not have been what it was without the influence of Eleanor Criswell, his partner. Criswell studied Yoga under the guidance of several spiritual and scholarly experts. Criswell writes in *How Yoga Works:*

> Somatic yoga has to do with the evolution of the person—mind, body, and spirit. It leans heavily on sensing your life's work or destiny. The various practices facilitate being able to hear more and more messages from your inner wisdom or guidance.[2]

Together, Criswell and Hanna founded the Novato Institute in 1975 and began researching, using biofeedback, the impact of different practices on the nervous system. They arrived at a modality for movement that integrated functional movement practices, with some forms borrowed from Hatha Yoga, alongside mindfulness and self-reflective engagement. This has come to be known as Hanna Somatics, and its key features include:

- Pandiculation, wherein you move parts of the body all the way from contraction to expansion and back. Think of rolling a shoulder forward, and then rolling it back, and then forward again.

- Slowing down to better notice sensation and support reconnection of mind and body.

- Awareness of the body in startle and self-protective responses from the perspective of physical trauma, for example, in car accidents and sports injuries.

Hanna and Criswell's work sits at an intersection of physical practice and philosophy that was part of a larger movement in the late 1960s and 1970s exploring how mental and emotional experiences impacted the body and psyche. Building on the work of Austrian psychoanalyst Wilhelm Reich, who explored what he called "holding patterns" in the body, bodyworkers like Jack W. Painter and therapists like Dr. Rafael Estrada Villa sought to integrate bodywork, massage, and touch work as a means for both physical and emotional release of long-held traumas.[3] In 1969, California scientist and researcher Peter A. Levine began working with the body's self-protective and defensive impulses to help people suffering from the stress of trauma find relief. Levine would go on to hone this practice and develop what we now know as Somatic Experiencing. In the introduction to his groundbreaking work, *Waking the Tiger,* Levine writes,

> For thousands of years, oriental and shamanic healers have recognized not only that the mind affects the body, as in psychosomatic medicine, but how every organ system of the body equally has a psychic representation in the fabric of the mind. Recent revolutionary developments in neuroscience and psycho-neuro-immunology have established solid evidence of the intricate two-way communication between mind and body. . . . Beyond the mechanistic, reductionist view of life, there exists a sensing, feeling, knowing, living organism. This living body, a condition we share with all sentient beings, informs us of our innate capacity to heal from the effects of trauma.[4]

Key features of Somatic Experiencing include:

- pendulation, wherein the nervous system is guided from states of feeling open and grounded to states of activation and arousal, often referred to as fight, flight, freeze, and then back into a state of openness.

- titration to slow stimulation and allow for greater awareness of sensations to support increased mind-body connection.

- awareness of the nervous system and how the startle, self-protective, and defensive responses can affect the body, mind, heart, and spirit.

You might notice how similar this is to Hanna Somatics. Both Somatic Experiencing and Hanna Somatics offer a non–culturally specific way to explore how overwhelm and self-protective responses impact the body, mind, heart, and spirit; they both use practices that move between states of safety and openness to states of tension and self-protection and back into safety and openness. They encourage moving gently. Nothing is rushed; everything is slowed down and done with mindful awareness. Any discomfort or agitation is addressed so the individual returns to awareness of the present. In any experience of somatics, you should only ever go to the edge of where you feel okay to go.

This may feel counter-intuitive: Western culture expects us to push ourselves to overcome discomfort. We might feel an impulse to rush when an experience is distressing, as if this might bring us relief sooner. Early in my somatic movement practice, I learned that rushing to finish or trying to speed up to get in more movement repetitions takes away from self-awareness and increases the risk of injury. In teaching Hanna Somatics to the enthusiastic students at my local seniors centre, I often need to remind the students to slow down, and slow down even further.

Likewise, it can be dysregulating to rush into the depths of a traumatic memory without first practising the skills needed to resource and support the nervous system. When a client is hungry to dig deep into an experience, it's my responsibility as a practitioner to help them slow down and stay connected to the things that support their nervous system. When they rush, it becomes much more challenging to stay present and aware of the sensations they are experiencing, be they pleasant and nourishing or difficult and painful.

Moving slowly, we grow aware of the possibilities of openness, groundedness, and freedom within ourselves. We can also begin to make sense of experiences where too much was happening for us to be able to process in the moment. Incomplete self-protective responses in our psyche and our body can find resolution— and in so doing, we can be more aware of our present rather than feeling stuck in the past or yearning for the future.

Many modern mind-body practices might fall under a broader umbrella of somatic practices that support physical and mental well-being, for example, ecstatic dance, Pilates, Gestalt therapy, Reichian therapy, Rolfing, Deep Flow Bodywork, and many more. Other activities and practices such as sensory deprivation floating, conscious and intentional plant medicine use, spiritual rituals, meditation, and even consensual sexual practices can potentially support or enhance somatics for some, although they might not inherently include elements of pendulation, titration, or moving gently and slowly.

Somatics offers opportunities for us to experience embodied change, the kind of change that goes beyond mental gymnastics and affects us at deep fundamental levels, shifting how we respond to the world around us, and giving us greater capacity to be present to our relationships. Regularly engaging in somatic practices can support:

- enhanced awareness of one's boundaries and capacity
- integrating after periods of dissociation or dissociative responses
- recovery from physical trauma or injury
- recovery from emotional trauma or injury
- improving nervous system regulation
- improving body awareness and mobility
- improving mental health and mental outlook
- enhanced ability to differentiate between relationship experiences and move through intense emotional experiences

Somatic Parts

Somatic practices offer pathways for us to become more integrated as individuals, as relational beings, and as living organisms existing in a shared global ecology. While some practitioners might approach somatics from a purely mind and body perspective, I explore it through the dimensions of mind, body, heart, and also spirit. You'll notice these concepts come up repeatedly in this book, so let's look at what they refer to:

Mind: The mind is more than just our brain; it extends through the entire neural network of the body. Our nervous system receives input from the world around us, and the mind interprets that information and responds, always seeking to attain safety: a state in which we experience ease within our bodies. Our minds can instantly feel safe when we connect and resonate with others. Knowing that we share values and visions with others brings a sense of familiarity, and from that familiarity we find the seeds of growing community: a network of support that maintains safety.

Body: Our bodies are infinitely responsive to our surroundings and experiences, and yet, in Western culture, we're often taught from an early age to disengage from the language of our bodies. We might move our bodies in restricted and rigid ways, sometimes even in clothing that limits our range of movement. We live and work in high-stress environments, which can further lead us to disconnect

HEART

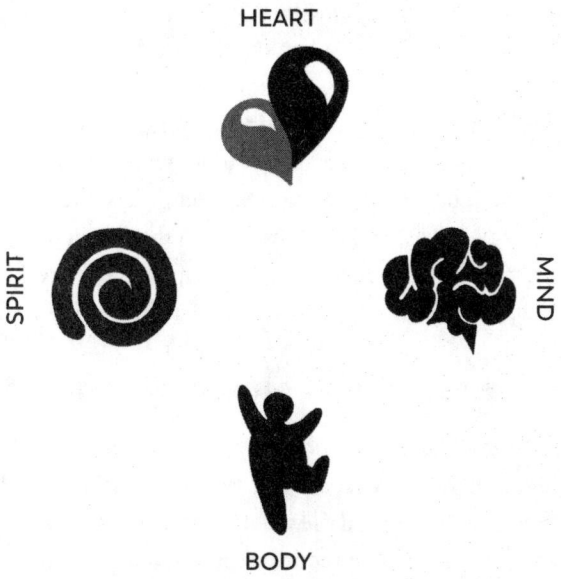

SPIRIT

MIND

BODY

Figure 5.1. Somatic parts (icons by Joan Trinh Pham)

from the sensations of our bodies. Our bodies have incredible resilience and adaptability. When a body has experienced an injury, we can often adapt as we heal. A body in safety is comfortable, warm, and at ease. Its boundaries are honoured and it honours the boundaries of others. I sometimes talk about being embodied. This refers to a capacity to feel and hold an experience within our bodies.

Heart: Our heart is all about feeling seen, heard, and understood. We might seek to be embraced for the full spectrum of who we are, including all the complexities of our hearts. Acknowledging the parts of ourselves that feel unsafe, and gently reassuring them as a grandparent might do with a young child, we can create spaces for ourselves to experience a safer relationship with our own emotional journey through life. The heart holds our emotions: joy, sorrow, anger, surprise, grief, and so much more. To connect with our hearts is to explore a kaleidoscope of emotional experiences.

Spirit: If you've grown up within a dogmatic religious context, the word *spirit* might have particular connotations for you. What I mean by Spirit in this context is the ineffable essence of who we are. Maybe that's a soul, or perhaps the electrical current that moves through our neurons and brain, firing off the signals that keep our body functioning and engaging in the world. Our spirit is both our creative source and the dwelling place of erotic joy. Cultivating spiritual safety is about creating space and permission in ourselves and for others to be messy, make mistakes, and let go of perfectionism. When our spirit is liberated from the shackles of shame, new possibilities open for self-expression and connection with others. Spirit is nourished through gratitude, cultivating forgiveness, lightening the burdens of blame we may hold, and honouring our joyful being. Spirit is beyond that which we can see, touch, taste, smell, or hear, but it is something we can sense through loving energy. Spirit can be the fire within that inspires us, drives us, and sustains us. Spirit might also be the felt sense of our values and ethics that defines how we show up in the world.

Somatics, Non-Monogamy, and You

Remember that the goal of white supremacy culture is disconnection: from ourselves, from others, and from nature. Somatics can help us to come back into connection with ourselves, others, and the whole world around us.

Applying somatics within the practice of post-monogamous relationships has tremendous potential. Just as Thomas Hanna envisioned the somatic movement as a resource for coping with the rapid changes in society and politics in the 1960s, and Peter Levine's work has helped thousands around the world deal with the aftermath of overwhelming events, so too somatics can help us navigate the novel and sometimes overwhelming experience of moving into a post-monogamous paradigm. Somatic practices can support us as we orient to new paradigms, help us work with our fears and hesitations around change, support healthier relationships with ourselves and others, and help us heal from the impacts of oppressive systems that have enforced and imposed monogamy.

When the excitement and titillation of open relating and non-monogamy can feel so enticing and pull us into rapid changes and quick decision-making, somatic practices offer us moments of pause in which we can metaphorically, and sometimes literally, catch our breath and take stock of transformation occurring both within us and in our relational field. Somatic principles like slowing down can support us in our alternative relationship practices to better orient and gauge what's happening amid so many relational dynamics.

Not only this, but as we explore further in the coming chapters, when the excitement of disrupting the status quo of patriarchal monogamy turns into overwhelm, somatics can help us return to connection with all our parts, develop new neural pathways to support engaging with relationships differently, and grow greater capacity for engaging in radically new ways.

SOMATIC PAUSE
Your Relationship to Trauma

All of us have a relationship with trauma, and most of us have probably experienced some kind of trauma, even if we've never talked to anyone about some of the painful and challenging experiences we've had.

Sometimes even talking about trauma in general terms can stir up any unresolved pain, so be gentle with yourself as you read the next chapter, where we discuss and explore trauma in more detail.

As you continue to read, notice if your mind feels distracted, if your body feels agitated, if you begin to feel emotional (sad, angry, and so on), or if you start to feel like it's hard to stay focussed.

If you do feel that way at any point, I invite you to pause, move around, and take a little break before continuing. You might explore peddling your feet as you sit, mimicking the movement of walking, or stretching your arms up and out to your sides if this is comfortable and accessible for you. You can also explore releasing any stress or tension by letting out an audible sigh.

6

THE PILLARS OF
TRAUMA-INFORMED RELATING

The essence of trauma is a disconnect from the self. Therefore, the essence of healing is not just uncovering one's past, but reconnecting with oneself in the present.

—GABOR MATE[1]

Everyone has had experiences of feeling scared, uncertain, or overwhelmed in a relationship. Maybe you felt butterflies in your stomach when going on a first date, or noticed apprehension about broaching a tender subject with a loved one. Or perhaps you've felt fearful of your partner's response to something you've done.

These moments are normal, and very human. We don't want to hurt the people we love or let anyone down; we want to stay in loving connections. However, we live in ways that are inherently overwhelming for our nervous systems. Late-stage capitalism, climate change, the stimulation of media consumption, and ongoing systemic oppressions contribute to stress that means sometimes even the little moments of extra pressure feel overwhelming if we haven't cultivated the skills of resilience.

Working with the ways our self-protective responses have coalesced around trauma can be a lifelong journey. Ignoring how we feel and trying to push aside our responses to pain, loss, and overwhelm—trying to "fake it till we make it" or bypassing our feelings to "keep calm and carry on" only hinders this journey, causing the grief of trauma to fester and then seep out in the form of disruption and struggle in our relationships.

Sometimes ongoing overwhelm in a relationship creates a cascade of successive reactions, which might look a little like this: One person feels overwhelmed, their partner tries to support them and then feels overwhelmed themselves, leading them to dismiss their partner's experience (fight), emotionally or mentally check out from the relationship (flight), become unresponsive to their partner's needs (freeze), or fall into self-sacrificing and put aside their own needs (fawn). These in turn trigger protective or defensive responses in the first partner, who was already overwhelmed. Before they know it, both partners can feel pulled into a vicious and exhausting cycle that perpetuates stress and overwhelm.

For many of us, once this cascade starts, we feel like we have to hold on for dear life and ride this roller coaster until it's done. Any attempt to squash the cascade can feel futile, and the idea that there might be another way to navigate it might sound far-fetched when we're grasping tightly.

A relationship can quickly become a vortex of pain, confusion, and complex activation when we don't understand what's happening, why it's happening, or what we can do to step out of the cycle. In these kinds of vortexes, we might feel like we are in free-fall: lacking support, untethered, and with no idea when we will find solid ground to stand on.

While all of our self-protective impulses have at one point served us in the short term, in the long term we become so accustomed to them that we live our lives in protective and defensive modes that can lead to rupture within our relationships. These self-protective behaviours can mean that we pull away from emotional presence. When we deny, avoid, or ignore the internal reality a loved one is experiencing in this way, we deny their truth and judge who they are being. This drives a wedge between us, and we also hurt our own hearts.

The Pillars of Trauma-Informed Relating

To help us understand what makes up a trauma-informed relationship, I use four key principles or pillars: orientation, resilience, resolution, and engagement. These function together cohesively, rather than linearly, and while some aspects can be practised in solitude, the goal is to enhance our capacity for being in loving, kind, and compassionate relationships, including returning to connection and relationship after any loss or relational disruption.

Let's take a closer look at each of these pillars.

Orientation

Orientation is about safety. By observing and cognitively making sense of our experiences, the nervous system has more context to understand our relationship with the world around us and the beings in it, and gradually begins to access greater capacity for these relationships. Confusion, uncertainty, and ambiguity are allayed through

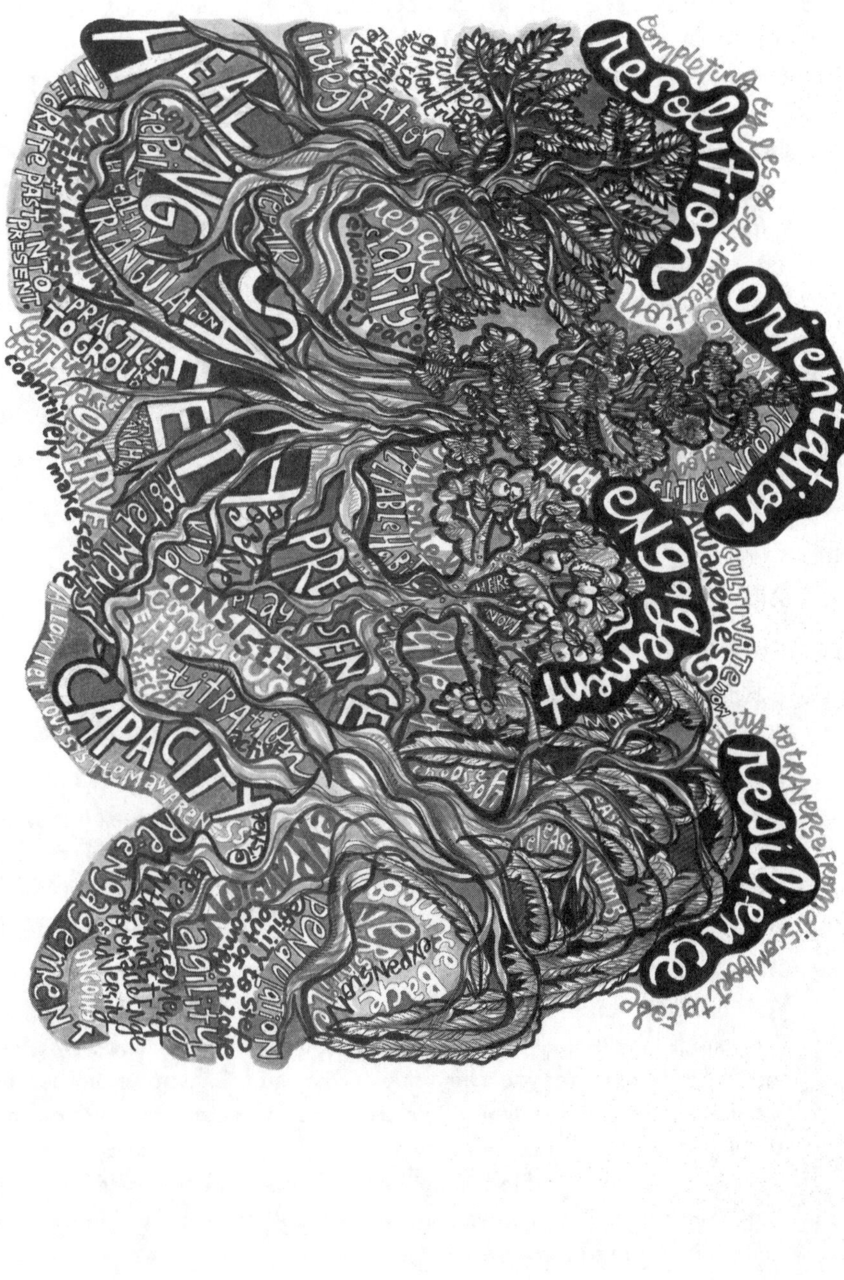

Figure 6.1. The pillars of trauma-informed relating imagined as a forest (illustration by Joan Trinh Pham)

the process of orienting. Orientation practices that ground our nervous system can act as anchoring or resourcing, enabling us to take small risks and venture into the unknown without fear of being carried away by the unfamiliar.

In monogamy, we often orient ourselves to the relationship escalator and other assumptions of lifelong fidelitous pair bonding. Without these in non-monogamy, we might feel disoriented. If you've ever spent any time in any kind of polyamory or non-monogamy discussion group, you may have noticed how often people ask questions like, "How does this work?" and "Is my experience normal?" All these questions can indicate a struggle to orient and looking to others more familiar with the landscape to help. As part of this process of orienting, polyamorists have developed a reputation for being a nerdy bunch (guilty as charged!): writing blogs, creating diagrams, coining new terms, scribing books, and broadcasting about their experiences on social media. As they do so, they're offering maps, landmarks, and guidance that can help those who are new to orient better and understand what polyamory is all about.

This book offers a framework to support you in orienting within the relational ecology of a post-monogamous world, and thus contribute to how you resource the experience of safety.

RELATIONAL TOOLKIT
Orienting Practices

Explore these orientation activities, and notice which ones allow you to experience greater ease, calm, focus, and capacity in your nervous system.

GROUND YOUR FEET
If it's available to you, stretch your toes out and move your feet. If movement isn't available to you, you can imagine yourself doing this. You might remember digging your toes into warm sand or walking on soft grass. Try practising this several times daily, taking your shoes off if possible. If it is safe to do so, you can explore what it's like to be barefoot outdoors.

ATTENTION OUT
Turn to look to your right and then your left. Look up and then look down. Turn to look behind you, under your chair, above your head. Consciously notice what is around you: Do you see items of a particular colour? Can you touch anything? What shapes do you notice? Our eyes and hands can receive information about the space we are in and inform our nervous system that we are not in danger. Consciously noting our surroundings supports our minds in knowing we are in a familiar and safe space.

NOURISHING YOUR SENSES
Collect some textures, smells, colours, images, tastes, and sounds that give you pleasure. Fuzzy blankets, essential oils, photographs of loved ones, a favourite piece of music: what these are for you will be unique for you. When you feel the tension of your nervous system becoming activated, reach for these items. By supporting your senses to experience pleasurable things, your nervous system will be soothed.

MAP IT OUT
Draw a map of your neighbourhood with the landmarks around you. If you were giving someone directions to your home, how would you guide them to your home without using street names? Invite your friends to join you with this, and see what landmarks they notice.

Resilience

Resilience is an ability to re-engage with the present, even when challenging experiences are ongoing. It describes our ability to step outside of our comfort zones, experience discomfort, be it physical, emotional, mental, or otherwise, and then return to a state of ease and comfort. Resilience isn't the same as "toughing out the hard stuff"; rather, it's about honing our ability to resource ourselves amid challenging experiences and come back to connection, even when those experiences have a lingering impact.

Think of how you might respond to someone saying something unkind to you. You might shut down and grow numb to protect yourself from feeling the impact of those words. This is a great self-protective response in the short term. But if you often experience these unkind words said to you, you might find you stay shut down, even to the point where you tune out of the signals your body is giving you about hunger, pain, and fatigue. This is an example of endurance. We look at this more in chapter 15 when we explore boundaries and capacity.

On the other hand, with a greater capacity and practice of resilience, you might hear the unkind words, feel yourself armour up in self-protection, and then be able to release or complete this response, perhaps through self-dialogue, movement, or the support of others, and then be able to engage again with others and with yourself, releasing any numbness and coming back into a fuller experience of sensation. You'll find some practices to help you with this in chapter 18.

Think of it as your ability to bounce back. Sometimes we have a lot of capacity for resilience. You might find it easier to tackle a difficult task if you are rested and nourished rather than trying to do it when you are exhausted and hungry, for example. Resilience isn't just something we experience as individuals; our relationships can also be resilient. A resilient relationship can weather the storm of disruption—whether that's conflict, rupture, or the introduction of a new being into the relational landscape, be it a partner, a child, or an animal, for example. Resilient relationships are versatile in how they orient and have a lot of practice in the repair process.

In somatic experiencing, resilience is experienced as pendulation: a natural release in the nervous system that allows our self-protective and defensive responses to complete, enabling us to become more present in the here and now. We move out of stimulation and can access more connection. Sometimes we must consciously practice this process to make it easier. Think of the relief you feel at the end of a stressful workday. Walking away allows your body to complete a flight response. Even cleaning your home can feel cathartic, as it sometimes provides a completion of a fight response.

Over time we can develop resilience skills, like recognizing our body's signals to rest, and knowing what supports a nourishing rest. We may even feel supported enough to step out of our comfort zones, taking a risk to explore new experiences. Cultivating resilience can also feel vulnerable. It often requires releasing the armour we use to get through experiences that haven't felt safe. This vulnerability can be overwhelming, especially in the face of ongoing threats like discrimination, oppression, or abusive relationships. Alone, we might feel compelled to increase our defences. But when supported by friends, family, and community, we may be more resourced and find resilience that is kinder and gentler on our psyches.

Growing your capacity for resilience doesn't mean you won't experience difficult or hard things in your relationships. What it does mean is that when those difficult and hard things happen, you'll feel more resourced and supported to engage with them in loving ways. Even if your capacity for resilience feels small at first, know that it can grow with practice and over time.

RELATIONAL TOOLKIT
Resourcing Resilience

What makes you feel disconnected or alone in your relationships? What behaviours, activities, or events activate your feelings of aloneness, or seem to lead to disconnection between you and your loved ones? This could be specific words, phrases, or even tone of voice. It could also be habitual behaviours like checking the phone while in a conversation or withdrawing from physical contact.

How do you notice that you're feeling disconnected from others? Do you withdraw, or do you reach out with more urgency? How do your loved ones react when they feel disconnected, and are your responses similar or different?

What activities or interactions help you feel connected with loved ones? What are your ways of expressing love? Do you like to be of service, share physical touch, give and receive words of affirmation, make things for your loved ones, share creative ideas? Can you plan to share in these activities more?

What sensory tools remind you of your connection to loved ones? Objects, colours, smells, flavours, textures, sounds—all of these can be powerful reminders of our positive experiences with someone and rekindle our experience of connection. Do you have a favourite shared playlist? Is there a smell that reminds you of them? What are your partners' favourite colours, and are they anywhere in your space? Can you co-create something to remind you of your connection?

Resolution

Resolution is about healing: untangling the experience so we can make sense of it, and then resolving our incomplete self-protection responses. In so doing, we welcome the part of ourselves dwelling in the past to join us in the present. Resolution of the things we've experienced in relationships often comes *through* relationships, and by cultivating healthy relationships that support us, whatever our self-protective responses may be.

Sometimes we begin the healing journey by returning first to relationships with others. Other times, we start by coming back to the relationship with ourselves. Being in a relationship doesn't just mean we show up to spend time with someone. It means being present with whoever we relate with—person, nature, pet, self—and aware of what is occurring in the relational space from moment to moment, whether that's feeling the touch of a partner next to you in bed, listening empathetically to a dear friend, or staying engaged with a child in distress.

One of the ways I've found it helpful to think about the impacts of trauma is as a kind of time travel. When we experience something traumatic—too much happening too fast and without an opportunity to process it fully—everything gets tangled up in a twisted, confusing mess. Even when we try to move on with our lives, a part of our brain may feel stuck in that moment because it is still trying to make sense of it. This is why we may have flashbacks or feel like a past tragedy is about to repeat itself. A part of us continues to live in the past, stuck on a moment that it cannot process and trying desperately to figure out how to protect itself from something it might not even fully understand.

In my own journey of trauma healing, I've found it helpful to redefine what "healing" means for me. I no longer see it as "everything will be easy and like it was before the pain." Instead, I've come to experience healing as a state where I'm able to internally shift my relationship to the painful experiences I've had, so that they don't hold me back, limit me, or negatively impact my ability to relate with others. I've found that getting to this takes more than talk therapy, although that is absolutely a helpful part of it. What has supported me the most is consciously creating positive and empowering experiences with others that help override the imprint of negative ones, alongside completing the cycles of self-protection that trauma had me stuck in. I share a personal story about this in chapter 13.

RELATIONAL TOOLKIT
Resolving Self-Protection Part 1

When you feel yourself struggling with being pulled back by past experiences that your brain is still trying to untangle and process, try out some of these activities to help you experience some resolution to your self-protection response. These aren't intended to be a solution to trauma but instead are simple things that you can do solo to support your nervous system to move towards resolving a threat response. You can physically practise these movements, or you can imagine or visualize yourself doing them. We'll explore more practices in chapter 18.

Freeze—dorsal vagal stimulation: Explore gentle movements through your joints or moving in ways that curl and uncurl your body, such as curling up in a ball and then stretching out like a starfish. Some people find it helpful to feel warmth on their back or on their belly.

Flight—sympathetic stimulation: Explore mobilizing the lower part of your body. This could mean walking, but it could also include any other lower-body movement, like cycling, jumping, or even just peddling your feet back and forth. Some people find it's helpful to go for a short excursion or move from one room to another.

Fight—sympathetic stimulation: Explore mobilizing your upper body, such as gently turning your head to look around you or rolling your shoulders back and forth. Some find engaging their hands in physical activity helpful, such as gardening, kneading bread, lifting weights, or carrying things.

Engagement

Saying that we're trauma-informed or thinking about being trauma-informed isn't enough: We have to actively live it to the best of our abilities. Being trauma-informed in our relationships is an ongoing practice that takes consistency, conscious effort, and active engagement.

Engagement isn't just about doing something; it's about creating reliable, consistent habits. Conscious engagement supports us to be more present in the here and now rather than feeling stuck in the past or lost in hopeful fantasies of the future. While there are limits to what we might be able to do to prevent the stress and disruptions of climate change, war, economic collapse, and so on, we can still do so much to support nurturing compassionate spaces within our relationships.

Some examples of conscious engagement practices that we can do in our relationships include: regular check-ins (see the example in chapter 19), crafting relationship agreements (covered in chapter 17), learning more about how self-protective responses interact with our own, and doing physical activities together, from practical things like tidying the house or running errands, to more pleasurable things like dance or exchanging massage or other touch.

RELATIONAL TOOLKIT
Engagement Practices

These are some simple practices you can do with a loved one to mutually support your nervous systems and grow a greater capacity for resilience. They are not meant to be seen as solutions to systemic or relational trauma, but they can help reduce the impacts of systemic and relational harm. Remember that you retain personal choice and agency whenever you engage with others. You have the option to be part of someone's journey of trauma healing and integration. You also have the option to say no to any invitation from others.

Doing any activity for fifteen to twenty minutes can help let the nervous system know you are resourced and safe.

Activities for your heart: Listen to or play music together, spend time with animals or beloved family members and friends.

Activities for your mind: Play a card game, video game, or board game; read a book out loud to each other; discuss a podcast or something you've learned recently.

Activities for your body: Go for a walk together, dance together, work on a physical task like cleaning the house, or offer each other a gentle massage.

Activities for your spirit: Share a ritual together, create a collaborative art piece, or cook a shared meal.

These four pillars—orientation, resilience, resolution, and engagement—can support you to move through your relationship experiences with greater capacity in your nervous system, making it easier to engage with moments that are overwhelming, to hold compassion for a loved one in distress, to share deep empathy with those that are in pain, and to navigate the moments when you are the one in distress or pain with more ease.

PART 1 SUMMARY

In this section of the book, we have taken a look at the history of monogamy and non-monogamy, including the influences of **colonialism, patriarchy,** and **white supremacy** on the ways we relate. Knowing that monogamy doesn't work for everyone and that the model of the nuclear family is outdated, we've identified the **monogamy hangover** that arises from internalized mono-normativity when trying to explore non-monogamy, looking at how this can be tied to a quest for somatic safety, and emphasizing the need for compassion and a trauma-aware approach to **post-monogamous** relationships.

We have also set the foundations for understanding **somatic** practices and trauma, including intergenerational trauma, trauma as a consequence of early life experiences, and trauma as nervous system disruption. We've examined the common self-protective responses that arise when we feel unsafe or are in a state of distress: **fight, flight, freeze, and fawn.** We've explored how these can each manifest in our relationships, influencing our behaviours, communication, and ability to connect with our loved ones. We've introduced the idea of the **window of capacity** and the experience of feeling safe enough within our nervous systems as a foundation for authentic connection with others. We've also discussed why being trauma-aware isn't enough and why a **trauma-informed** approach to our relationships, emphasizing empathy, patience, and compassion, is essential.

You can return to the activities and reflections in this section whenever you want support in understanding your relationship to trauma, both your own and the trauma that your partners may hold, to help you begin the journey of becoming trauma-informed in your relationships.

What

In this section, we orient to a new map for relating that incorporates **queerness** and **anarchism** and that will help you break free from mono-normativity in a trauma-informed and somatically integrated way. It goes beyond the relationship escalator and the nuclear family and invites a **landscape of relating** that allows for a more radical approach to relationships.

Within this landscape, we'll explore four distinct **quadrants—emotional, social, practical,** and **erotic**—each representing a core aspect of relationships. Within each quadrant, we delve into four progressive **layers: awareness, safety, intimacy,** and **relationship.** These layers and quadrants will form a multidimensional map to guide us through a deeper understanding of ourselves and how we relate.

Within each chapter you'll be invited to reflect on your own relationship landscape, quadrants, and past experiences of relationships.

7

QUEERNESS AND ANARCHY

"Queer" not as being about who you're having sex with (that can be a dimension of it); but "queer" as being about the self that is at odds with everything around it and that has to invent and create and find a place to speak and to thrive and to live.

—bell hooks

Anarchism: The philosophy of a new social order based on liberty unrestricted by man-made law; the theory that all forms of government rest on violence, and are therefore wrong and harmful, as well as unnecessary. . . . Anarchism is the great liberator of man from the phantoms that have held him captive.

—EMMA GOLDMAN

To offer more context for what we're about to explore in this section, let's first look at what *queerness* and *anarchy* mean. These terms are often misunderstood, even sometimes by those who identify with them, yet they are crucial components of our Radical Relating journey.

Anarchism: From the Greek *an-archos,* meaning "to be without rule." Anarchism is a set of social and political values that seeks to disrupt systemic power structures. In anarchism, the individual is liberated from participating in hierarchies and cultures of dominance and control through nourishing networks of relations that aim for egalitarianism and anti-oppression.

Relationship anarchists critique, question, rewrite, and sometimes reject the prescribed rules for relating. The emphasis on anti-oppression as a social movement means that Relationship Anarchy (RA) communities aspire to reform social order with a focus on community care. Anarchy may often be misunderstood as chaos, but its roots lie in questioning the accepted rules of society, commerce, and who gets to be in charge. Anarchy is like that precocious child who insists on asking, "Why? But why? *But why?*" Relationship anarchists have, at various times, been called sex radicals or free lovers, and have been found within movements of feminism and abolitionism. They have a long and rich history of questioning the institution of marriage and gendered roles in relationships.

In *Relationship Anarchy,* Juan-Carlos Pérez-Cortés records that relationship anarchy as a modern-day philosophy and practice began to emerge in the summer of 2005 at an anarchist retreat in Sweden, where Andie Nordgren, Jon Jordas, and more than fifty others gathered to talk about anarchism and relationships. Nordgren, who would go on to write the relationship anarchy manifesto, emphasized "the need to shift to a feminist perspective that is not heterocentric, getting beyond the logic of the free love of the '70s."[1] Since then, the ideas of relationship anarchy have been explored, discussed, and practised worldwide—and not without misunderstandings and hiccups.

One common misconception is that relationship anarchy is a type of non-monogamy, or that it opposes monogamy, but this isn't necessarily the case. Pérez-Cortés shares,

> Each individual decides to what extent they can or want to challenge social normativity according to their interests, possibilities, and circumstances. Presenting Relationship Anarchy as the "good" version of open relationships, swinging, free love, polyamory, or consensual non-monogamies has the secondary effect of censorship or disapproval of those or other models that actually involve interesting disruptive processes that are very important.[2]

This means that it is possible to practise romantic or sexual monogamy as a relationship anarchist. The key is that social normativity is challenged. In the case of someone who is romantically monogamous, this might mean pushing back against the assumptions of gendered roles, the nuclear family, and other aspects of mono-normativity. Monogamous relationship anarchists might prioritize growing community relationships over romantic ones and might even decentre sexuality and romance altogether.

Pérez-Cortés emphasizes that relationship anarchy isn't an all-in-one solution, nor should it be taken as a philosophy or practice that celebrates individualism. He writes,

> Just as how the solution to low wages is not another side hustle, the answer to the problem of the normative couple as a bubble that isolates and prevents relationships from forming a network of support, care, and mutual understanding is not the "freedom" to multiply the bubbles.[3]

Relationship anarchy frames relationships from a nonconformist perspective deeply rooted in feminism and community care. For many, it also reflects the principles of queerness.

Queer: A multifaceted word with multiple definitions.

1. A sexual identity that doesn't correspond to heterosexual norms.

2. A gender identity that doesn't correspond to binary (man-woman) norms.

3. A general term referring to all people under the LGBTQIA2S+ umbrella.

4. A way of describing any way of being that challenges cultural norms and status quo.

In the nineteenth century, *queer* was used to disdainfully describe men who didn't conform to the prescribed expectations of masculinity and were therefore assumed to be gay. In the twentieth century it continued to be used as a term to other gay men, women, and non-binary individuals, and even within the mid-century gay scene the term was not always looked at favourably.

The reclaiming of *queer* since the 1980s has been for many a way of owning one's difference and inherent nature being beyond social norms. *Queer* today can refer to someone's sexual orientation—an umbrella term that can encompass gay, lesbian, bisexuality, pansexuality, and more—or to refer to someone's gender—trans, non-binary, intersex, genderqueer, or genderfluid. I used to feel mystified by the term and confused about whether people using it meant it about their orientation or their gender. A non-binary and pansexual friend explained to me that for them, it could refer to both. As I began to understand queerness in more depth, I realized that I identified with the broad range it encompassed and that my attraction to multiple genders, as well as my internal sense of gender—something fluid that moves between femme and androgyny—was quintessential to my own queerness.

Queerness has come to represent a questioning of normative ways of relating. No longer limited to just sexuality and gender, some consider non-monogamy, and even polyamory specifically, to be a kind of queerness. To be queer is to situate oneself on a spectrum of possibilities that doesn't accept limitations of binary gender, heterosexual attraction, and mono-normative ways of being. I think a good argument can be made that questioning the relationship escalator and challenging the norms of mono-normativity and patriarchal monogamy is in itself a queering of relationships—although I do caution that adopting the label of queer because of your relational orientation may not necessarily mean you gain access to LGBTQIA2S+ spaces without also holding a queer sexual orientation or gender experience.

If you've never thought about these ideas before now, and you find that something in you is stirring as you read this, know that it is not too late to step into your own queer experience.

Becoming Anarcho-Queer

Anarchists and queers have often aligned in a desire to live freely, love openly, and be liberated from systems of control. Queerness questions social rules about gender, sexuality, and relationships. Anarchy deconstructs the accepted or given order of things and re-creates an order that is personal and collaborative rather than universally imposed. Queerness and anarchy combine to birth new worlds where everyone's innate agency is respected, personal and communal networks of chosen family and mutual aid are grown, and safer spaces offer alternative ways of being and relating, allowing for deeper expressions of love. These worlds open us to community organizing along horizontal, collaborative, non-hierarchical principles, helping us to better resist oppression and abuse by corrupt state and colonial powers.

Anarcho-queers reimagine the entire system and structure of how we relate. The relationship escalator and the rest of the monogamy hangover can be left behind, and the rewilding of the relationship landscape can begin, taking us boldly towards that post-monogamous world.

There are political factions who want to control and take away sexual and relational liberties. They fear that sexual radicalness and an ongoing queering of relationships will threaten their power, and I think they are right about that. Once you pull at one thread of the status quo, the whole tapestry begins to unravel. And if the tapestry of dominance culture—including patriarchy, colonialism, and white supremacy culture—unravels, those who have hoarded power and resources will likely lose them.

What most queers want is just to live their lives without fearing for them: to love without interference from governing systems, and without pressure to conform to their expectations. The harder it becomes for us to do so within the systems and structures we exist within, the more we will want to rebel and create systemic and structural change.

8

THE RELATIONSHIP LANDSCAPE

Stepping away from the culturally ingrained and familiar ways of being with one another, ways we hope promise security and stability, can feel disorienting. We might find ourselves feeling afraid and sometimes lost as we face new and unfamiliar things. And anytime we experience confusion while trying new things, we're more likely to lean back on the old and familiar, even when it isn't something we want. This inevitably happens at some point to every person exploring alternative relationships.

Just as someone might stay in an unhealthy or unfulfilling relationship because they are uncertain how they will make life work on their own, we hold on to the scripts that are more familiar to us because we feel comfortable with them. We know how to navigate them, and even the discomfort they carry is something we're accustomed to dealing with. And, if we're scared of doing things in a new way, we'll default back to the familiar we have had practice with. This is why, for example, even when someone is actively seeking polyamory, a common response to jealousy is a request to close down the relationship's openness in some form. Some part of our psyche is still convinced that exclusivity equals fidelity, which equals safety.

Our personal sense of safety develops in infancy and childhood, influenced by everything from breastfeeding and skin-to-skin touch with our caregivers to illness in the family, generational trauma, and more. As children who feel unsafe, we might respond by crying, throwing a tantrum, pushing people away, hiding away, or seeking out the company of a trusted friend or adult. As adults, we might still follow these patterns, albeit in slightly different ways. As part of the growing up process, we learn that holding tightly to what we feel certainty about can help us feel safe. When your sense of safety feels threatened in relationships, it's a natural response to dig in your heels and hold on to what you already know. This can make things feel much less scary when you're breaking out and exploring territory with no guidebook. This is the essence of the monogamy hangover: We fall back on learned monogamous behaviours because we're more practised with them. Shaking off this hangover means stepping into uncertainty and relating in ways we may not feel competent or even sure of.

In this chapter, we'll explore alternatives to those familiar monogamous pathways of relating. As we explored in chapter 3, one of the foundational elements of the monogamy mythology is that of the relationship escalator. This metaphor represents the linear trajectory of the inevitable progression of relationships: from dating to moving in together to meeting each other's parents, possibly getting married, and then eventually retiring and one day dying. It is seen as one of our primary strategies for creating safety, security, and stability in our lives. The goal is to get onto the escalator and to stay there for life.

Even when you're challenging patriarchal and monogamous norms by exploring things like open relationships, polyamory, and other forms of consensual and honest non-monogamy, elements of the relationship escalator tend to show up, simply because we've come to rely on it as a signifier of safety, stability, and security in relationships. Having grown up immersed in cultural messages about the worthiness of a relationship derived from being on this escalator with a person, we gravitate towards it, like a moth to a flame—even when we don't necessarily want all the trappings of it. When you find yourself in relationships that don't involve the escalator, you might feel unsafe, destabilized, and insecure in otherwise very loving relationships. What we need is an alternative model to this escalator that encompasses the nuances and complexity of the diverse forms that post-monogamous relationships can take.

The Relationship Landscape

Instead of the relationship escalator, I invite you to consider a relationship landscape. Rather than a singular pathway, the relationship landscape is about cultivating what works with your relationship ecology. Just as a garden can contain various types of soil and nutrients, and some parts might be suitable for growing big trees while other parts are better for shade-loving plants, we ourselves have our own relationship landscapes with different terrains capable of supporting a thriving ecosystem of relationships—as long as those relationships are planted in the right kind of soil and have the right type of conditions.

You already have a landscape of relationships. Even if you haven't been aware of it until now, it's there, shifting and changing with the seasons of your life. The people around you as you grew up would have formed your earliest landscape of relating. Some of these people, such as siblings or parents, might still be part of your landscape today. Over time, as you have formed friendships, moved cities or perhaps countries, changed jobs, dated new people, and perhaps had children of your own, your landscape will have changed, just as the physical landscape around us can change through the seasons and the passing of years.

Like with any natural landscape, we can nurture a conscious and active relationship to our relationship landscape. We may find ourselves weeding out connections that drain us, transplanting relationships when they aren't thriving where they are, and planting seeds for new connections that we actively seek to nourish. Instead of being on the linear trajectory of the relationship escalator, we get to be the gardener of our landscape. And there is adventure to be found in exploring the ecology we find there.

Understanding Your Ecology: The Four Quadrants Model

Ecology is the study of how all living things are related to one another: how plants, animals, fungi, and all elements of nature interact within an ecosystem, a collection of relationships that form a community. The idea behind relationship ecology is that we are not entirely separate from the beings and elements we interact with. It isn't just people we relate to within our landscape; we are affected by the temperature each day and how much sunlight exposure we have, by the food we nourish ourselves with, by the animals in our lives, and by the people we engage with. All these aspects of our landscape are impacted by their own interactions with us.

Thinking of this as an ecosystem is also a way to gently push back against the individualism that is prevalent in mono-normative ways of thinking and embedded within ideas like the nuclear family: Rather than being isolated and feeling a need to be heroes in our journey, we can find strength and resilience through the inter-connectivity of all the relationships that co-exist and support one another, moving towards more communal ways of approaching relationships.

When we've been used to the singular pathway of intimate relating offered by the relationship escalator, relating with people within this diverse landscape can seem intimidating, so I like to break this down into four quadrants.

The Four Quadrants

Consider thinking about these quadrants as sections of your landscape. Some areas may feel abundant while others might feel sparse. Some quadrants may feel very closely related for you, perhaps with lots of overlap, while others may feel compartmentalized or walled off from the rest of your landscape. Whatever you are beginning your relationship landscaping journey with is okay. We explore more about how to understand each quadrant and nourish them in the following few chapters.

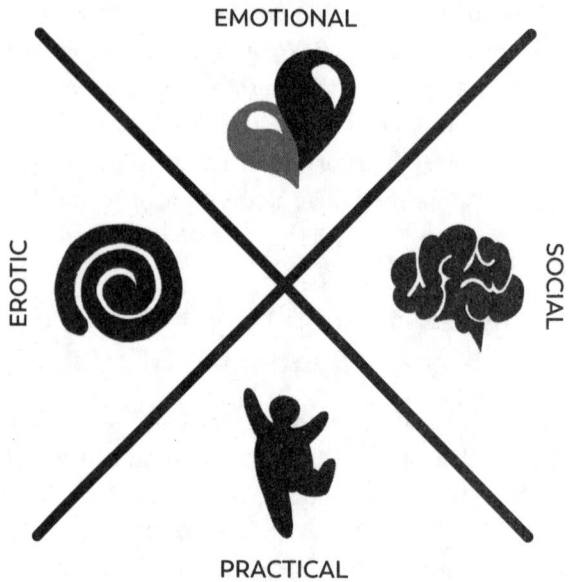

EMOTIONAL

EROTIC

SOCIAL

PRACTICAL

Figure 8.1. The four quadrants (icons by Joan Trinh Pham)

The Emotional Quadrant

The emotional quadrant is about how we relate in our hearts. The people we hold close in our emotional quadrant might be those we feel safe talking to about our feelings or those we experience profound emotional intimacy with.

This is where we feel our big feelings and find the people we feel safe enough to share our deepest emotions with. We might commiserate together through moments of grief and celebrate together the moments of joy. These relationships might be with family members, children, parents, or friends. We might develop emotional relationships with people we have had a specific shared experience with, such as being on a retreat.

The emotional quadrant can feel vulnerable to include others in, and it might take time for a relationship to flourish in this space. You may even have experienced welcoming someone into your emotional world but then found that the other person didn't reciprocate by including you in their own emotional life.

The Social Quadrant

The social quadrant is about forming relationships through sharing thoughts and ideas. The extent to which you feel safe speaking your mind in some spaces but not in others can reflect an inner sense of feeling understood and connected to others in your social quadrant.

The people we hold close socially tend to share similar values or beliefs. We may go on to develop deeper intimacy with some of these people—think of the bond you might have had with people who have the same place of worship as you, or who love the same fandom series as you. You probably feel very safe around these people. And yet you might feel safe to express your beliefs or talk about politics with only a small number of trusted friends with whom you share a particular flavour of social intimacy.

Humans often form social groups based on shared values. Anything related to how we think about things, like our education and our belief systems, could be included in the social quadrant. Consider your own friendship groups and communities. Are there specific values or ideas shared between you?

It's worth noting that intellectual attraction, sometimes called sapiosexuality, can exist in this quadrant. There's some controversy around this term, with criticism being that to be attracted to intellect becomes ableist against those who may have disabilities that affect their cognitive capacity, but I like to think of it as an attraction to someone's mind, however their mind expresses itself. This could include how people with similar neurodiversity are drawn to one another and form friendships and community. Since this relates to the mind, ideas, and expressing one's beliefs and values, I include all this as an expression of the social quadrant.

The Erotic Quadrant

The erotic quadrant is about our sensuality and our creativity. It's the pleasure-seeking part of our landscape. For some this might be sexual, but it doesn't have to be. Think of the delight you experience when eating a delicious sweet piece of fruit, or the joy at hearing a beautiful piece of music. The people we feel safe with in this quadrant give us space to be ourselves, and the people we develop intimacy with both encourage us to be ourselves and are curious to know who it is that we truly are.

The erotic quadrant represents our sexuality, but it isn't limited to sex. If your experience of eroticism has only ever been connected to sex, consider this an invitation to expand your definition of what eroticism can be. Those on the asexual spectrum may find their erotic quadrant is primarily about creative expression and filled with people and experiences that inspire them. Indeed, many find that this quadrant is the source of their creativity and self-expression. In erotic relationships, we celebrate the essence of who we are and honour the essence of who others are. There are many creative and expressive ways to celebrate each other, for example, collaborating on projects together, cooking a meal together, or curating a beautiful experience for others to enjoy. For some, the erotic quadrant might even be experienced as a place where spiritual connection occurs.

The Practical Quadrant

The practical quadrant is about our physical space and well-being. You might share a practical relationship with a partner, a child, a roommate, or a beloved pet. Our practical relationships also extend to who we co-parent with, work with, share financial commitments with, such as a business partner or a former romantic partner, or the quality of connection we have with our neighbours. Who we welcome into our physical space, be it our physical home or our personal bubble, matters. You might feel safe to welcome your friends and friends of friends for dinner or a movie night, but have only a select few who you feel comfortable having stay over for a whole week.

Disabled folks, including those with chronic illness, may have specific needs and boundaries in their practical quadrant. This could be due to accessibility (for example, needing a home to be scent-free), or it could be something that supports them in managing their condition, such as having their own bed, rather than sharing a bed with a partner. Since anyone can become disabled—and many of us do as we age—the needs we have in this quadrant, and the ways we engage with others here, can shift dramatically over time.

A Note on Spiritual Relationships

When I teach this model of the four quadrants, I am often asked about spiritual relationships. Where these exist for different folks may vary. I experience spirituality as being very closely related to the erotic. I didn't always think of it this way, and at different points thought it would go with the social, as in spiritual community, or with the emotional, as devotional practice is a form of spirituality. When I considered how I explored the erotic quadrant, and the way I explore my own personal spirituality, I found correlation. If spirituality is important to you, consider how it shows up differently in each quadrant.

REFLECTIVE JOURNALING
Thinking About the Four Quadrants

In your journal, draw a circle or square (it doesn't need to be precise) and divide it through the middle into four equal sections. Label these sections according to the quadrants: emotional, social, erotic, and practical.

Consider who is essential to you in your life—you can include people from your childhood who were important too—and write their names in any quadrant you think your relationship with them has been in.

Notice when you are unsure about putting someone in a single quadrant, and when one person is in multiple quadrants. Do you have many names in a single quadrant? Is one of the quadrants sparser than the others?

The Four Quadrants in Other Forms

This model went through a few different drafts before I came to the form it takes today. Along the journey of adapting and evolving it, I discovered some other places where structures very similar to the four quadrants show up. These are just a few examples, and each has enriched my understanding and appreciation of this concept. I encourage you to explore any other expressions of the four quadrants you encounter.

Indigenous Traditions

The medicine wheel is a concept common to many Indigenous spiritual traditions in North America. The wheel is often divided into four parts, representing different archetypal elements that offer reflections of wisdom to how we exist as beings in the world. In this model, the four aspects can be seen as movements in a cycle of human experience: growth, wholeness, protection, and nourishment. In *Soma-cultural Liberation,* two-spirit indigequeer therapist Roger Kuhn shares,

> The medicine wheel has been culturally appropriated by many Western prac-
> titioners who have benefited financially from the oppression of Indigenous
> knowledge systems. . . . Medicine wheels differ depending on the Indigenous
> culture that is using them. The medicine wheel is often represented in four
> colours (red, yellow, black, white), four directions (north, south, east, west),
> four seasons (winter, spring, summer, fall) and four experiences (body, mind,
> emotion, existential).[1]

I first encountered the medicine wheel while living on the Coast Salish territories of the Pacific Northwest of North America. These teachings have been preserved in many ways and in some cases, sadly, appropriated. If you wish to study these traditions, please seek out teachers and learning resources offered by those who are part of these traditions.

In Buddhism and Hinduism, the world is seen to consist primarily of four elements: earth (physical matter and practical things), water (fluid matter, both

Figure 8.2. The relationship landscape (illustration by Joan Trinh Pham)

external and internal, including the fluids associated with emotions), fire (anything that produces warmth), and air (the breath, also expansion). These are explored in many ways through the different branches of spiritual practices throughout South and Central Asia, including Vedanta, Ayurveda, Shaivism, and others. A fifth element, ether (spirit), is added in some iterations. These concepts have influenced modern Western culture and have also been appropriated.

If the concepts of quadrants, elements, or directions show up in any of the spiritual and Indigenous traditions you are part of or have studied, you may want to refresh your relationship to these and explore how your traditions can inform how you relate to this model of the relationship landscape. If you are interested in learning more about Vedanta, Shaivism, Buddhism, or other spiritual traditions of Asia, I recommend that you seek out teachers who are immersed in these traditions and who have studied with respected lineages. .

Somatics

As we explored in chapter 5, somatics are practices for integrating the self in the relationship between mind, body, heart, and spirit. When I studied Hanna Somatics, we were encouraged to keep a diary where we recorded daily reflections on self-awareness of four parts of self: the body, the mind, the spirit, and emotions. In somatic sexology as taught by Caffyn Jesse, students are guided through self-pleasuring rituals that explore breath, movement, sound, touch, and thought in relationship to body, mind, spirit, and emotions.

You may want to consider how you experience these four elements—mind, body, heart, and spirit—in relation to yourself. Do you ever find connecting with one or more of these challenging? Is there one you more naturally gravitate towards and feel safer connecting with?

Covey's Four Intelligences

In his work on four intelligences, self-help author Stephen R. Covey says:

> Develop all four intelligences. PQ (physical intelligence), which represents seventy trillion cells that fight disease and digest your breakfast; IQ (intellectual intelligence); EQ (emotional intelligence), the sensing and wisdom of the heart; and SQ (spiritual intelligence) having to do with meaning, purpose, and integrity around your selected value system and your believed source. When combined, they change the world for good.[2]

I appreciate that this framework provides an expansive, multidimensional way for thinking about what we mean by intelligence. Are there any of these aspects of intelligence that you feel you have cultivated well, or perhaps ones that you would want to work on?

The Four Monogamies

In their book *Designer Relationships,* Mark A. Michaels and Patricia Johnson talk about four kinds of monogamy: sexual, emotional, social, and practical. They describe these as the "core structural components of monogamous arrangements that come into play whether the monogamy is true or serial." They go on to discuss the ways that exclusivity in these four components of monogamy can have very diverse definitions and pose essential questions, such as, How is sex defined? Is it only penis-in-vagina sex, or is any kind of genital play included as sexual? What about watching porn? On social monogamy, they write,

> For many couples, autonomous pursuits and outside interests are something to be tolerated but not celebrated, because the contemporary monogamous model teaches us that our spouses should be able to meet all of our needs and that by marrying we're creating a self-sustaining, self-contained universe.[3]

You may want to consider whether you desire more exclusivity in any of your quadrants, and if so, what that might mean for you in the rest of your landscape.

Holistic Health Care for Chronic Illness

It surprised me that the four quadrants also appear in tools for navigating chronic illness. The Visible app, created by researchers at Imperial College London, allows people with long COVID, myalgic encephalomyelitis or chronic fatigue syndrome, and other similar conditions to track their data daily and share it anonymously with researchers. Every morning the app prompts the user to measure their resting heart rate, and in the evening it asks about symptoms during the day, asking for an assessment of how much exertion there was in four areas: mentally, emotionally, physically, and socially.

The researchers ask this because many people who experience chronic fatigue have found that it isn't only physical exertion that can trigger a flare-up of fatigue and other symptoms; emotionally challenging events, mentally stressful experiences, and periods of socializing can also create a significant drain on their body's capacity.

You may find it helpful to think about how you expend energy in each of the four quadrants, and notice if there is one quadrant that takes more energy for you to engage in, or where you find it more exhausting to engage with others. There may be specific ways that you engage in each quadrant that boost your energy.

The Four Quadrants in Practice

As any gardener or farmer will know, not all seeds that you plant sprout, and not all seedlings flourish—and not for lack of sunlight and water, but sometimes it's because something needs to be nourished in the soil. In the relationship landscape, we provide the nutrients in which our relationships grow; working on and nourishing ourselves is required to cultivate a flourishing relationship ecology.

Nourishing ourselves can mean many things, and what it specifically means to you might differ from what it means to another person. Generally, it involves moving towards a positive relationship with ourselves, honing our boundaries with others, attuning to our needs and learning how to meet them, and also doing our best to make sure our energy reserves are not eaten up by things that we do not want to cultivate in our lives. We take a deeper dive into this in chapter 15.

This nourishment of the relationship landscape is a cyclical practice. We nourish ourselves by nourishing relationships in all four quadrants. And when we nourish ourselves, we nourish all four quadrants in return.

In patriarchal monogamy and the nuclear family, it is expected that we will have one person in all four of our quadrants—namely a romantic partner. But with four distinct areas to experience relationships in, you might have post-monogamous relationships that are erotic, emotional, and social but not practical, as in someone you date but don't live with. Or you might have relationships that are practical and social but not erotic or emotional, like a roommate. Indeed, there are infinite possibilities and combinations.

The practical relationships you have with roommates might include shared meals, splitting bills or even streaming accounts, but you might not include them in your emotional quadrant, and you may not want to have an erotic relationship with them. You might have deeply connected emotional and erotic relationships with people you don't live with or share any other aspects of your practical life, such as finances. It's also possible that you develop emotionally solid relationships with people you share common values with, who you then form a practical relationship with, and that these aspects of the relationship continue regardless of whether or not there is an erotic component.

One of the things I love most about exploring all the quadrants is that it invites us to consider all our connections as worthwhile relationships. It helps to decentre sex as the most critical aspect of a meaningful relationship—and when we expand the possibilities of relating, we alleviate the pressures on a single relationship—and person—to fulfil all our needs. Our attachment needs don't have to be reliant on a single person and can be sourced through multiple relationships rather than exclusive ones. Instead of feeling stuck in self-protection modes, we can derive safety from being able to draw on diverse sources without stepping beyond our capacities or calling on others to go beyond their ability to support us.

In mono-normativity, security relies on adherence to a singular model of relationships, but in the relationship landscape, security comes about through its resilience and the flexibility to redefine and transform relationships as the individuals in them change. A friend (social and emotional) might become a lover (emotional and erotic); you might break up and only see one another at social events (social only) and then come back to a friendship and decide to be platonic roommates (social, emotional, and practical). The possibilities are many.

When the way we engage in relationships shifts from a quest for the relationship escalator—where there's only room for two people to ascend at a time—to stepping into this wide-open relationship landscape, where we are agents within our own ecology, there's much greater potential to feel fulfilled in all our loving connections.

9

THE LAYERS OF RELATING

In this chapter, we're adding dimensions to the relationship landscape by exploring its different depths. We take a broad look at these layers before exploring them in more detail in the following chapters, where we dive into how each layer looks in the four quadrants.

Just as relationships can exist in different quadrants of our relationship landscape, so too there are layers within each quadrant, correlating to the proximity of deep knowing someone might have of us. Acquaintances, colleagues, friends, lovers, partners: all these people may relate to us at different depths. Relationships don't have a static or fixed existence in these layers, and the ways we experience them in any given relationship, both in the four quadrants of the landscape and in these layers, can move over time.

Launching into romantic intimacy is often different from starting friendships. Friendships begin when we notice something in common: an interest, challenge, or goal. As we come to know someone, we may desire to spend more time with them or prefer to stay acquaintances. The safer we feel with someone, the deeper we may want to explore. From friends who see each other at parties and social events, we may become friends who hang out one-on-one for coffee, or friends who help each other move, rescue one another from tight spots, and support one another through work turmoil. We may even have the good fortune to make friendships that can go deeper than this and become platonic life partners, emergency contacts, next of kin, and recognized chosen family. The deepest friendships may only form after a long time and many experiences together.

Meanwhile in our romantic relationships—where we've been taught by cisheteronormativity to seek out safety, stability, and life security—we often arrive at connections hungry for depth. Because of this, we may dive right into a relationship with the hope and perhaps faith that we will be able to reverse-engineer our way to the same kind of warmth and depth we have in lifelong friendships. This could result in love bombing, where a person is overwhelmed by positive attention, affection, gifts, and praise from a new partner, or deep attachment to a new connection before there's even really an opportunity to deeply know and become familiar with all the aspects of who a person is. We might fill in the blanks with some wishful thinking only to find ourselves upset at revelations that arrive months into a relationship. When we have rushed into depth, we might see that we've been in a relationship with our projections—a projection-ship, if you will, rather than a real-ationship.

Sometimes this "fake it till you make it" approach can work out, but very often these projection-ships can leave us feeling bound in experiences of struggling to feel fulfilled, lost, and at odds with our fantasies—and sometimes in perpetual cycles of conflict and rupture. It might feel like the more we come to know someone, the more distant we feel from them.

There are four distinct layers that we move through in our relationships: awareness, safety, intimacy, and relationship. I call them layers of relating, but you could also think of them as layers of trust. It can be helpful to consider what layers we're experiencing in our relationships, especially if we're coming up against conflicts or wanting to grow more. As we continue in this chapter, consider what has supported you and your relationships to flourish in each of these layers.

REFLECTIVE JOURNALING
Thinking About the Layers

Who are the people you have only awareness of? For example, someone you see regularly on your commute to work, or at your local café.

Are there people you experience awareness of and safety with? For example, a coworker you get along well with, an extended family member, a metamour, or someone you find yourself on warm and friendly terms with in your community?

Now think about intimacy: Are there people you have come to know, who you have had repeated good experiences around, and who you feel safe enough to be a little more vulnerable with? Perhaps a trusted colleague you can talk to about some of your challenges at work, or a longstanding friend who is a committed confidante?

To be clear, this isn't a rehash of the relationship escalator, that linear and limiting trajectory of relationships that is such a fundamental aspect of mononormativity. This is a way of considering relationships without needing to escalate, allowing any relationship to simply be where it is. Let's explore these layers more.

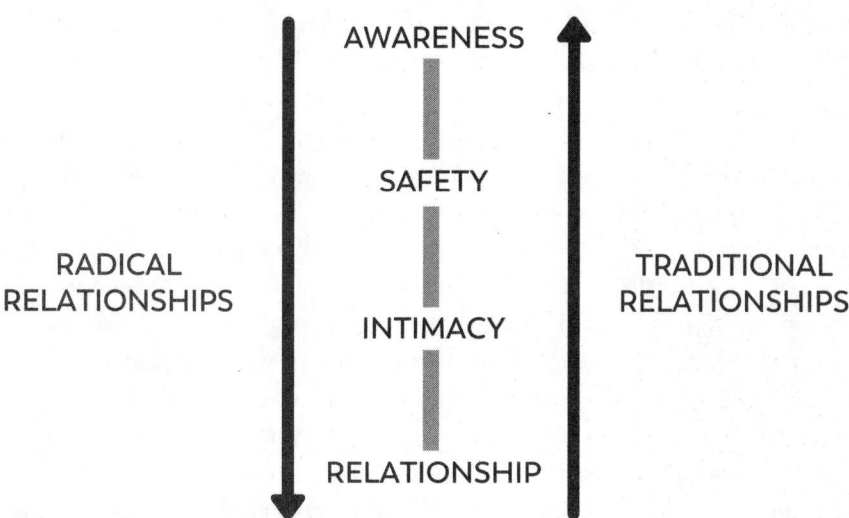

Figure 9.1. The layers of relating

Awareness

Awareness is a layer for exploring orienting, the pillar of trauma-informed relating where we gauge the lay of the land. Awareness helps us begin the relating process based on what *is* rather than what we assume. It is the very start of relating: the acknowledgment of another being's existence and the beginning of understanding how you may affect and impact one another.

To explore the layer of awareness is to be curious. Sometimes that curiosity might feel closer to vigilance: a self-protective response when we fear that a threat is imminent. In a state of sobriety and alertness, there is almost always a part of our nervous system engaging in a level of attunement to surroundings and the people in it. Just as you may be used to checking your rearview and side mirrors often when driving, so too your nervous system is doing frequent safety checks on your environment. The more familiar an environment, the more at ease you might feel. We can also support our nervous system awareness in new and busy environments by slowing down, checking in with our senses, and taking things one at a time. This can help shift us from a fast-moving vigilance into a more open state of curiosity, where we can be both inquisitive and receptive.

Growing our knowledge of who another person is and what they enjoy brings breadth to a relationship. We don't necessarily abandon awareness as we access deeper layers of relating, even though it can be tempting to do so when we feel confident that we know someone thoroughly. There is always more to learn about who we ourselves are, who our loved ones are, how we show up in the world, and who we are becoming.

Take a moment to look around the space you're in. The first time you entered this space, you probably noticed some general things about it: its shape and size, what objects you could use, and what colours there were. But you would not have noticed everything. You would have noticed more the second time you entered this space, and the third even more, and so on. It's much the same with people: The more we spend time with a person, the more we might become aware, if we're paying attention, of who they are, what they value, and what things they enjoy.

Exploring the layer of awareness isn't only about being aware of others; it's also about how you experience yourself when you are around others. Does someone's presence make you feel tense? Or does their warm and welcoming manner help you feel more at ease? We engage in awareness through our curiosity. Here are some things to be curious about when you are exploring awareness in each of the four quadrants:

Emotional: We often begin conversations by asking someone how they are doing today. This is one of the simplest forms of engaging in emotional awareness. You might notice whether you reply to these kinds of inquiries with simple answers or more complex ones. When you ask after others, do you notice if they are emotionally expressive or emotionally reserved?

Social: What things interest you? What activities do you enjoy, and who do you enjoy doing them with? What values do other people have, and do you share any values in common? Often when we meet someone, we will ask them about what they do, what hobbies they have, perhaps what music, films, or television shows they enjoy. If you meet someone at a sports game, you might get curious about what other sports teams they support. If you meet someone at a music festival, you may want to know what other artists or festivals they recommend.

Practical: How does this person take up space? Does this person have any accessibility needs? You might ask if they are comfortable, hungry, or thirsty. We often do this naturally when a friend comes over and we ask if they would like something to drink. Note that engaging in practical awareness can sometimes be more challenging if we have experienced any kind of head trauma, such as a motor vehicle accident or concussion, which can affect our ability to attune to the space around us.

Erotic: Curiosity about someone's erotic quadrant might not be a natural part of everyday conversation, but we certainly notice people we are attracted to, and have many ways of expressing and exploring this. Consider how you ask someone about their relationships. Are they single? Are they available? Do you notice how others engage creatively, or how they see themselves in relation to the world? We engage in erotic awareness when we get curious about someone's turn-ons, as might happen when we are flirting. Think too about your own erotic self-awareness, and how you attune to your own creativity, something that you may or may not have felt permission to explore.

Awareness can also include sensitivity to the vectors of power and privilege someone may or may not experience. This might include an understanding of the access needs someone has, whether that's due to a disability, illness, or neuro-divergence, or the ways that they may have experienced discrimination and stigma because of their age, country of origin, ethnicity, skin colour, gender and gender expression, sexual orientation, relational style and status, economic or class background, profession, education, and more. When we lack awareness of who another person is, we may be quicker to judge them, dehumanize them, bully them, take them for granted, or even shun them.

Awareness also includes understanding. I might know that my friend is alien-ated from their parents, but can I extrapolate what that might mean for them? Putting my awareness into action might look like checking in on them during family-centred holidays or inviting them to my own holiday events. Awareness in action can lead us to the next layer: safety.

If we skip awareness—if, instead of openness, receptivity, and curiosity, we expe-rience being closed, unyielding, and dismissive—then moving into an experience of safety will feel hard indeed. Any relational rupture could kick us back into seeking awareness, and we might feel confused. "Why did my partner do that? Do I even know them? Can I really keep sleeping with someone who voted for that politician?"

Similarly, if we rely on telepathy and make assumptions rather than being curi-ous, we might feel betrayed, misled, or even lied to if, in the process of reverse-engineering awareness, we find that the person we assumed a partner to be is not who they are at all. This plays on what I call the necessary fantasy, which we will explore shortly.

REFLECTIVE JOURNALING
What Makes Someone a Friend?

Think about someone who is a good friend. When you first met them, what did you notice about them? Can you remember what they were doing, wearing, or perhaps something they said? How did that first impression impact you?

What about the second, third, or fourth time you met? Can you recall what it felt like when this person was no longer just an acquaintance but started to feel like a friend?

When did you feel understood by them?

Safety

Safety is about feeling held and supported, a layer we explore through attunement and responsiveness to one another. When I talk about safety here, I'm talking about the internal experience of it, and that internal experience can certainly be supported by external safety measures, but it can also be impacted by past experiences and things we attune to unconsciously. We might think we're safe driving in our car, but wearing a seatbelt is an excellent way to support our safety. Similarly, in relationships, we might look to certain things—agreements, actions, attitudes— as strategies for safety.

When we experience intimate ruptures, we may need temporary "scaffolding" through agreements and other relationship practices to help us restore safety before stepping into intimacy again. We take a closer look at agreements in chapter 17. Some examples of things we do to grow safety in our relationships include:

- celebrating and honouring boundaries, especially any "no"
- understanding our partner's needs
- respecting differences and individuality, bodily autonomy, independent thought
- staying responsive and attuned to others even during conflict
- erotic care and aftercare
- following through on commitments
- arriving on time

In mono-normativity, we often gauge safety based on elements of the relationship escalator, but this framework is never a guarantee of relational safety. Traditional gender roles might also seem to offer safety—but it's a safety conditional on everyone conforming to the expected role of their assigned gender. As our society continues to challenge the expectations of conventional Western binary genders, some feel their safety is threatened because they have relied on the gender binary for safety and don't know how to resource real, somatic safety. Consider the recurring conservative rhetoric that polyamorous, non-monogamous, and LGBTQIA2S+ people and our relationships are a threat. These arguments all rest on an assumption that cis-hetero-mono-normativity is the only possible strategy for relational safety.

Real, embodied safety can feel like ease in our bodies and minds. The sensations of safety are ones of openness, relaxation, presence, and engagement. It is not rushed or lethargic. It is rooted and grounded and invokes a capacity for deep interpersonal connection. Embodied safety helps us access that second pillar of trauma-informed relating: resilience.

While we might mask around strangers, or even people we are still getting to know, we can show up more authentically when safety arrives as an embodied and felt experience. Quite simply, the more we know about a person or space, the greater our sense of whether they may accept us. As we experience more trust, we can trust that it is okay to be ourselves, and those self-protective and defensive responses soften.

The sensations of a lack of safety—the sensations that we often experience as corresponding to jealousy, fear, envy, and so forth—are ones of a nervous system reorganizing itself into self-protective modes: sensations of intense energy, a lack of groundedness, difficulty staying present to our partners, an internal dynamic that alternates between pushing towards and pulling back. Depending on the situation, we may be simultaneously scared and angry, want to run away, puff up and be loud, roll over and surrender to something uncomfortable or unwanted, and feel completely frozen about what to do. In chapter 18 we explore this more.

Self-protective responses in our nervous system might kick in before we even have time to process what's happening and why we feel the need to protect ourselves. In some instances, these self-protective responses can lead to a choice—conscious or unconscious—to drop our masks and be a little more vulnerable as a strategy for reverse-engineering safety. This kind of bid for safety may involve lending or borrowing trust to do this. If reciprocated, we may find it possible to spend more time exploring curiosity and growing awareness. But when we misplace that trust and don't, in fact, create safety as a result, this can lead to relational rupture, injury, and a potential loss of trust beyond an ability to repair.

Safety is not a permanent experience. It is forever in flux. However, the more often we experience safety in a connection, and the more reciprocal trust we feel, the deeper we might go into the layers of relating. Safety makes it possible for us to think about joining someone in connection.

To look at what experiencing safety might be like through the four quadrants, I want to borrow from the work of Tricia Bowler and Michael Haines. Tricia and Michael are two of the most compassionate and kindest people I have known, and I hold deep respect for their work in supporting people to experience safe, nurturing, and nourishing connections in their Being Held gatherings on Vancouver Island. These events weave in elements of somatic-adjacent practices to support healing experiences of connection. Their work has evolved and grown over the years, but I always come back to their original foundation of four pillars of safety because I was struck with how well they correlate with the four quadrants:[1]

Heart safety (emotional quadrant): acceptance of the parts of us that feel unsafe; going to an emotional edge but no further; checking in regularly with one's self and others; accountability and ownership of our own thoughts and feelings; honouring and seeing each other as complex beings with a rich inner emotional life.

Mind safety (social quadrant): co-creating activities through negotiated participation; revealing personal intentions and having transparency about who an action is for; creating clear time frames for activities; debriefing on each activity; holding confidentiality.

Soul safety (erotic quadrant): recognizing the stories our brain creates; cultivating an attitude that there is nothing to fix, we are whole as we are; gratitude for all that is; honouring erotic energy as life energy; maintaining a container of honouring and loving acceptance.

Body safety (practical quadrant): meeting equally in physical connection; defining boundaries for touch; prioritizing comfort; protecting the body; and thanking the "no."

Within Being Held gatherings there is also an ethos of allowing connections to be meaningless, which is to say, just because you experienced something deep and profoundly safe in one moment, this does not mean you need to escalate that experience into anything more. Within the container of the experience, we can experiment, and nothing, whether it was a pleasurable experience or an uncomfortable one, has to be continued beyond the gathering. This helps to lower the stakes, creating greater ease for the nervous system, and allowing more space for playfulness and exploration.

REFLECTIVE JOURNALING
What Helps Create Relational Safety for You?

Take a moment to think about a time you softened into being more at ease and open with another person.

What supported you to feel safe with them? Was the person known to you, or a stranger? Where were you? Were there others present? What do your senses remember about the moment? What smells, textures, sounds, tastes, and colours were around you?

How did elements like integrity, congruency (words and actions matching up), personal respect, honouring of boundaries, and time-keeping factor into your experience?

Intimacy

Intimacy is about connection, and is also profoundly playful. Whereas in safety we are still proactively navigating the formation of trust and finding where our boundaries lie, within intimacy, the sandbox of a connection is clearer, and we experience it as collaboration. Intimacy is the coming together in a field of mutual trust, a meeting point where transactionality is dropped and collaboration begins. We might experience more coregulation—the natural attunement between nervous systems we learn as infants when we coregulate (or sometimes co-dis-regulate) with the adults around us. I find that in spaces of intimacy we develop a sense of knowing the why behind the needs, desires, and behaviours of loved ones. Experiencing intimacy can feel nurturing, nourishing, and even healing—the third pillar of trauma-informed relationships.

Intimacy is defined as having a close affectionate relationship, a deep understanding, a quality of being comfortable and familiar with others. In intimacy, all parties feel seen and welcomed. We may feel an impulse towards playfulness, perhaps even greater curiosity. We come together in a synergistic dance that might include emotions, desires, thoughts, an ability to navigate conflict and difference, and how we explore and express affection.

Some experience this as a state of flow, while others describe it as feeling like they are in sync. Some find that in an experience of intimacy, they have established awareness and safety so well that they can let go of conversation and words, while others find that conversation becomes much more accessible, engaging, and enjoyable.

Intimacy might not always feel pleasant and pleasurable. Think of the intimacy of a long trip with friends where you go through many ups and downs as you adventure together. Or think of the intimacy of being part of a team with your peers as you prepare a presentation together. The synergy of intimacy can include friction, sparks of difference, and sometimes conflict.

I'm of the generation who came of age online, and who have navigated the confusing waters of virtual intimacy: connecting in deep conversations through online forums and finding camaraderie in common interests—and later in online dating, where there is ample room for projection and wishful thinking to take hold. Many xennials and millennials have expressed feeling challenged around intimacy, with repeated experiences of disappointment when they've thought there was depth and intimacy to a connection, only to find that they are ghosted. We might step into *faux intimacy* thanks to the perceived safety that the virtual world offers, along with the ability to disconnect from that intimacy at any indication of friction. I invite you to be curious about how the speed of connection facilitated by online mediums has impacted your experience of intimacy.

Intimacy can be grown and supported by things like:

- sharing a meaningful experience, for example, going to an art gallery, watching a movie, attending a concert or festival, going on vacation

- safe and trusting vulnerability

- consensual physical touch, for example, massage, foreplay

- playing together, for example, music, video games, board games, sports

- taking a class or workshop together

These moments of shared experiences can enhance trust, continuing to nourish awareness and safety, and in turn making intimacy all the more richer. However, when we experience a disconnect or loss of trust after crossing the threshold of intimacy, that loss can be as painful and dysregulated as any real, physical injury, and just as challenging to recover from. When we feel a loss of intimacy or feel ourselves falling out of sync or flow, the following things can happen:

- We get louder or more forceful with our story. This can lead to anger or acts of oppression against others, either physical or emotional-mental. We might even become controlling.

- We surrender our power and agency, feeling helpless and unable to take action.

- We self-silence, try to pretend we are someone else, convince ourselves to keep calm and carry on or that we have a different story from what is really true for us. In doing so, we lose connection to our authenticity.

For some, this can harden self-protective and self-defensive ways of being. We might find it more challenging to stay present to our innate curiosity in new relationships, and instead feel a pull to rush our way into intimacy as we seek out what we have lost. We might pull away from intimacy altogether, or we might feel it challenging to regain safety and trust in relationships, isolating ourselves further from connection. In short, a loss of intimacy can leave us feeling like it's either not okay, or not possible, to make connections in which it is safe to truly be intimate. This can be a painful and isolating experience.

Intimacy is the quality of connection many of us yearn for, but the kind of intimacy that matters most to us can be different from our loved ones. In nonmonogamy, one partner might prioritize erotic intimacy, while another may prioritize emotional intimacy, and yet another may prioritize practical intimacy.

Intimacy helps us grow that experience of resilience, which we've explored as one of the pillars of trauma-informed relating: knowing that there is a steady supply of nourishing connections supports us through all kinds of stress. Here's what this might look like in the four quadrants:

Emotional intimacy might feel like being able to engage with more softness and empathy. It becomes easier to be vulnerable when there's strong emotional trust. Sharing with an open heart may feel easy, and we may find such sharing to be emotionally nourishing. It feels easy to be emotionally present when a partner is expressing emotional vulnerability.

Intellectual intimacy might include stimulating conversation, a flow of ideas, and a sense of excitement. It could involve playing a video game together, discussing a social cause, or even playful (perhaps *pun*-ishing) banter. It feels easy to stay engaged in communication centred on sharing thoughts and ideas with a partner.

Erotic intimacy may feel intoxicating, synergistic, and creative, shaking off shame around sexuality and sensuality. It can also include creative collaboration, such as improv comedy, playing music together, or sharing a massage. It feels easy to share creative, sensual, and erotic space with a partner.

Practical intimacy might look like greater ease in navigating space-sharing, for example cooking together, camping, or coworking. It can also include inviting a partner to keep a change of clothes at your place, planning a vacation together, or having a platonic sleepover with a friend. It feels easy to spend time in one another's company, whether engaged in activities or at rest.

In experiences of intimacy, the edges of our own being can feel less defined. It can be common to mistake intimacy for Relationship. Intimacy can feel like a timeless, expansive experience, and so we might assume it to be the same as the deep-rooted nourishment of a relationship. However, intimacy is more transient than Relationship. To get to the layer of Relationship, we first have to grow comfortable with conflict. We look at conflict intimacy in chapter 19.

REFLECTIVE JOURNALING
What Opens the Door to Intimacy?

What is your experience of sharing intimate moments? How playful and connected have they felt? Have they been momentary or long-lasting?

What has supported that experience of intimacy?

What has shaken you out of an experience of intimacy, or when has accessing intimacy felt challenging for you?

Relationship

Relationship is about anchoring into a more embodied and resilient experience of connection. I'm using a capital *R* with *Relationship* here to signify that I'm talking more specifically about a depth of connection, rather than a small-*r* relationship that could refer to any kind of connection.

While many may be content with intimate experiences, the ruptures we experience with any loss of trust can impede the movement to Relationship. Indeed, sometimes we grow distrustful of Relationship, conflating it with the relationship escalator, codependency, and loss of autonomy. I invite you to expand the possibilities of what Relationship can be.

Contrary to the fairy tale that once we achieve intimacy we will live happily ever after, we instead experience ongoing challenges and differences in our relationships, and that isn't necessarily a bad thing. This does not mean that we have to seek out conflict in order to deepen our relationships, but rather that as we learn how to stay connected and intimate even when there is conflict, and hold the grief and discomfort of differences tenderly, we can move from intimacy into Relationship.

We look more at social relationships in chapter 12, but it's worth mentioning here that many communal living setups struggle to make this transition. Even in intentional communes and decentralized communities, the capacity for holding conflict, and indeed trauma itself, requires the ongoing support of every

Figure 9.2. The layers of relating depicted as the roots of an ecosystem (illustration by Joan Trinh Pham)

participant in that community. Some can make the transition from communal intimacy into communal Relationships, and they are exceptional. I hope that these practices and frameworks can help more communal Relationships flourish.

There is an energetic difference between intimacy and Relationship. Intimacy can feel a lot like merging. Just as when we are infants who don't yet have a sense of our own boundaries, and so naturally coregulate with adult caregivers, whose presence hopefully supports us to find our boundaries, sometimes in intimacy we drop our sense of boundaries and find ourselves energetically merging into our partners. This kind of enmeshment can lead to codependency and loss of self. It can feel functional for a time, but only as long as there is never any conflict, difference, or mismatch of needs, desires, and capacity.

On the other hand, Relationship is a disentangling from this enmeshment and a reclaiming of selfhood while staying in connection. This layer marks a maturing of our nervous system in relationship to the nervous systems we coregulate with, and we do not surrender to the point of being consumed. Relationship includes intimacy, but here it is more like joining side by side than merging into one. We can maintain a sense of individuality while simultaneously having a deep sense of knowing who we are in each of our relationships, and understanding what that relationship is.

If our nervous system was under-supported in childhood, then we may be hungry for deep nervous-system connection, and it may feel very hard not to merge, in which case we might benefit from doing work to develop more nervous-system skills and boundary awareness. A nervous system prone to merging might also find it helpful to cultivate multiple deep connections that put no pressure on moving from the experience of intimacy into Relationship, as this may help the nervous system experience broader support in coregulation and refine the ability to self-regulate.

We can have a small-*r* relationship with many people, even when doing non-monogamy or relationship anarchy, and we might have a big-*r* Relationship with only a select few. A relationship might be profound and lifelong, or deeply meaningful yet short-lived. A relationship isn't necessarily about longevity but is more about the quality of connection. It could include entwinement or joining life paths, but it doesn't need to. It is a connection that is deeply mutually nourishing.

Whereas intimacy might be compared to what is often referred to as new relationship energy (NRE), Relationship is more akin to what some in the non-monogamous world might call *established relationship energy*. This is a very different experience from how we attempt to fake it till we make it in projection-ships under the influence of NRE, where we may assign a label to a relationship based on assumptions and desires and hope to reverse-engineer our way towards safety and then awareness.

For example, in the Relationship layer of the emotional quadrant, we go from being emotionally present to being emotionally available. We don't just see and understand the emotional experience of another, nor do we exist in the emotional flow with them only when we spend time together. We begin to share in an emotional life where we experience our own emotional responses alongside our partners, and not only in reaction to their emotional state. A sense of deeper knowing and care means we feel emotionally engaged even when not with a person. This might look like a natural and reciprocated impulse to check in on them, share about your day, and ask them for their thoughts. You always maintain your individuality, your sense of being a separate person from your loved ones.

REFLECTIVE JOURNALING
Presence Versus Availability

Think about these two contrasting experiences: being emotionally present versus being emotionally available.

What is it like to be emotionally present for a partner or a friend? Listening to them share emotionally vulnerable things about themselves and their lives can give you a sense of ease. Do you notice yourself responding with a desire to soothe, support, and allow them to feel comforted?

How is this different from being emotionally available: being part of an emotional experience with a partner or friend? You might think about a time you were in a shared stressful situation, such as being stuck in traffic for an event you were attending together, or shared grief, such as the loss of a pet. What was it like to have your own separate and unique emotional experience alongside another person's emotional experience, which may have been different from yours?

It's okay if the difference is subtle. I encourage you to become curious about it as you explore these layers more in your relationships.

We explore more about what Relationship looks like in each of the quadrants in the following chapters. In understanding these layers, we also have to understand the necessary fantasy and how it affects our experiences in the layers of relating.

The Necessary Fantasy

The necessary fantasy is a strategy for nervous system safety that helps us feel safe enough to stay engaged and invested in a new relationship when there is still so much to learn about who a new partner is and what our relationship could be. As much as we want to move through the layers in order, when the chemistry is good and the possibilities seem potent, we might jump straight into acting as if we are already in a Relationship. We may have an assumption about who the other person is, formed from hopes, desires, and assumptions. This fantasy keeps us engaged.

Imagining ourselves with someone in our lives can be exciting—and highly motivating! We might label a relationship or explore the mutual fantasies of where the relationship might go and what it might include. The fantasy is a kind of scaffolding, holding the shape and form of the future structure while the structure is being built.

Over time, as we work through the layers of relating, that fantasy will be replaced with reality, and hopefully it is a reality that is not too different from the fantasy. When that happens, the glow of new relationship energy settles into a deep love of established relationship energy. The necessary fantasy inspires us, gives us hope in times of hopelessness, and encourages us to bravely lean into exploring something new and unknown. It offers our nervous system something to attach to as we step courageously into novel experiences with a new person.

There is nothing wrong with having this fantasy. Without it our nervous system may feel unsettled, and we might quickly exit a new connection. In some instances, the fantasy provides us with an ego boost, inspiring visions of a future together with a person, or enticing possibilities of what could be explored within the connection. With the necessary fantasy, we get enough safety for our nervous system while we figure out what the relationship really is. Ideally, we're aware of this process and can temper ourselves, slowing down so that we can continue the process of growing from awareness to safety and intimacy before arriving at Relationship.

However, most of the time we think that the fantasy is reality, and then, as time goes by, we run into conflict when we realize that the way we see the relationship is different from how the other person sees it. When we aren't able to move through the fantasy, we might get stuck perpetually looking for confirmation of our fantasy and possibly even resenting our partners when they fall short of it.

When we lose the necessary fantasy, we feel grief. This can manifest as anger, aggression, or resentment. Sometimes it can manifest as denial, or we may try to bargain and change reality. This grief can feel particularly devastating if we've grown deeply invested in the fantasy.

Slow Dating Equals Radical Relating

Radical Relating starts with slowing down our relational pace so that we can move more gently between fantasy and reality. We learn how to navigate relationships as a landscape, a rich ecology within which to situate ourselves, and we nurture the soil so that all things may grow in time.

Building on this process of slowing down, we bring our work with boundaries, communication skills, self-regulation practices, and connection activities—and all the trauma-informed skills no one ever told you you'd need.

This approach doesn't mean you can't have spontaneous and enriching connections that happen in a short time. A one-night stand, a spontaneously formed friendship, or even a moment of connecting with a stranger in need might still include a micro-journey through some of these layers of relating.

10

THE EMOTIONAL QUADRANT

To love without knowing how to love wounds the person we love. To know how to love someone, we have to understand them. To understand, we need to listen.

—THICH NHAT HANH[1]

The emotional quadrant is all about our heart and relates to our feelings and emotions and how they live within our nervous systems. Your relationship to your emotions, including your comfort with and awareness of your feelings, will significantly influence the relationships you experience in this quadrant.

When we feel emotionally fulfilled, seen, and understood, we may experience greater capacity for empathy. It may seem easier to sense what others are feeling even without them telling us, and we may find that we can better differentiate our own emotions from those of our loved ones. When we don't feel like there's space for our emotions, or that others are not emotionally engaging with us in the ways we desire, connecting emotionally might feel more challenging. We might behave more rigidly, have a harder time being compassionate for others, and even feel irritable.

Emotions are a lot like water: fluid and changeable. Like water in a river that flows to meet the ocean, emotions are at their best when allowed to flow and change. If you've grown up with a sense that emotions are hard for you to access or identify, or you've felt like your emotions might be too big to express safely and you've felt pressure to control them, know that some of the perspectives and activities we cover in this section may be particularly useful for you.

Emotional depth arises from a longing to be seen and understood. We might experience emotional depth as a marker of relational safety, security, and stability along with a deep-felt sense of ease in our nervous systems. The quest for emotional depth is one of the biggest drives in relationships, yet many of us may have experienced wanting to avoid the vulnerability that comes with it because being vulnerable can feel scary.

When we've been privileged to enjoy emotionally safe relationships with adults in our childhood, we may seek to replicate that closeness with our partners. If that closeness wasn't safe, or included unwelcome emotional experiences, we might prefer emotional distance. Conversely, if we didn't have emotionally available parents (for whatever reason, be it their own intergenerational trauma, a lack of emotional availability, or otherwise), we may be hungry for deep emotional connection and go into relationships with significant emotional expectations and porous emotional boundaries.

Sometimes a desire to protect ourselves from emotional depth can lead to a pattern of avoidance. In monogamy, this might look like short-term recreational relationships or serial monogamy. In non-monogamy, emotional avoidance might look like diving deep into one relationship, then feeling scared and escaping deep into another relationship, then feeling scared and escaping to another, and so forth. The emotional belonging we crave can only come when we have taken the time to build emotional safety in our relationships, and rushing into escalation and enmeshment are poor strategies for this.

Expectations in the Emotional Quadrant

The emotional quadrant is often oriented around connection and a desire to experience being emotionally understood. Once we feel nourished and affirmed in our internal emotional experience, whether from a partner, friend, or therapist, or even reading something that feels emotionally validating, we may find more capacity to be present with the emotions of others and have greater access to empathy in ourselves.

On the other hand, if we don't feel met in our emotions—if the emotional quadrant feels barren, overgrown with weeds, or otherwise tumultuous, or if no one seems to understand our experience—our capacity for empathy diminishes. We may be more likely to feel disconnected from our own emotional awareness. We may even emotionally dissociate, shutting down our hearts and withdrawing from emotional availability.

As we explored in chapter 1, the monogamy hangover tells us that we have to be able to be everything for our partner, and acts of self-sacrifice are the means to demonstrate love and commitment for someone. If you fail in any way, if you aren't fully aware of everything going on for them, don't understand their feelings, or your needs and desires conflict with your partners', then you are an imperfect partner. Wanting to be perfect partners, we put aside our needs to prioritize others. These tendencies and habits towards self-sacrifice often hang out in the emotional quadrant.

Emotional labour is emotional attention we give to support one another. To be clear: There is nothing wrong with doing emotional labour for a loved one. This is an essential part of being in an emotional relationship. Supporting someone with emotional presence is a kind, nurturing, and nourishing act. It is also a form of emotional validation that is a natural, loving thing to do. It could look like listening to a rant or helping someone sort through a difficult decision. Often, in relationships, we offer our emotional labour to affirm that we understand our loved ones.

However, our capacity to show up for emotional labour can vary depending on our emotional capacity and resilience, and in patriarchal monogamy, there is a power structure based on gendered expectations. Traditionally, in Western cultures, it is girls and women who have been socialized to do the burden of emotional labour, while boys and men are generally not encouraged to develop the same emotional skills and may feel less capacity to hold space for others' emotions as a result. Whatever our gender experiences, when we try to hold space for emotions in others that we are either unfamiliar with or uncomfortable with in ourselves, we may find that our nervous system struggles, and we may try to shut down the emotional expression of our loved ones because of our own discomfort.

Emotional labour can become challenging when our partners are the only source of emotional support. We might try to turn a partner into our therapist or coach, and visa versa, and look to them for solutions to our problems, or think that it's up to us to fix our partners' problems. This can lead to us turning to our partner to fulfil the role of a parent or elder, asking them to help us understand ourselves and explain our emotions to us, much like a child looks to an adult to help them understand their world. Many of the ways we seek emotional connection in our intimate relationships can be connected to the experiences of emotional connection we had in childhood, or the lack thereof.

There is a difference between being able to be emotionally present and doing emotional labour, and being emotionally available to share an emotional experience. Emotional relationships can be profoundly validating, supportive, and healing. Our hunger for that healing experience may cause us to rush into emotional depth before building the foundations of safety and leave us feeling scared of emotional connection, with hearts so knotted that while we might be able to feel emotionally present, we struggle to be emotionally available.

As the one doing emotional labour, it might feel safer and less vulnerable to hold space for another while revealing little or nothing of your heart. Emotional availability, on the other hand, is about joining someone in their emotional experience. There is more empathy, and emotions arise within us in response to what our partner shares about theirs. Being emotionally available is a collaborative experience, a flow-like state where we can be emotionally open, present, and vulnerable, yet boundaried. We aren't just witnessing someone's emotional journey; we are in it with them.

Obstacles in the Emotional Quadrant

In the fairy tales of monogamy, we believe we will be understood, met, and emotionally cared for by our one true love, and that we will also be the ones who understand, meet, and care for them. That's not to say this isn't possible; many relationships are formed on a foundation of deep emotional connection, and there's an undeniable compulsion towards partnership when we feel seen, heard, and understood in our feelings, especially in the most vulnerable parts of our emotional self. But reliance on a single partner for this emotional well-being is strewn with risk and fragility: If the single person we rely on is unavailable, to whom do we turn?

There is no guarantee that our partners will understand the things that matter to us. When we expect that our partners will implicitly understand everything that is part of our life experience, not only are we burdening them with a tremendous amount of emotional labour, but we're also setting them up to fail. No one can comprehensively understand all the nuances and textures of another's emotional experience. In other words, boundary-less emotional labour in which one person is expected to carry the emotional weight for a loved one is a recipe for eventual emotional overwhelm and resentment.

Self-sacrifice in the emotional quadrant might leave you believing that emotional vulnerability carries high stakes, and you might be wary, and possibly even avoidant, of creating depth in the emotional quadrant. Unprocessed grief about how much we've sacrificed to try to make a relationship work can manifest in denial: convincing yourself that everything is fine while ignoring red flags and behaviours in partners and metamours that might be concerning. Denial often wants us to keep a fantasy of perfectionism alive and avoid the pain of realizing that no relationship or relationship structure can ever be perfect. Self-denial and emotional bypassing—denying jealousy and frustration, trying to fake it till you make it, or even minimizing and gaslighting partners about their feelings and reactions—can lead to deceit and emotional harm in any kind of relationship.

Sometimes the biggest obstacle in the emotional quadrant is unfamiliarity with emotions: Many of us have been socialized to keep our feelings small and sometimes repressed. This means that when a strong emotion does show up, the stimulation it brings into our nervous system may be so much that we become overwhelmed and feel a pull to repress or shut it down. This can also show up in our capacity to engage with the emotions of others: If a loved one is expressing an emotional experience that is unfamiliar to us, the unknown of their emotions can feel scary, and we may feel less safe.

True emotional depth in relationships is found by moving slowly, gently, and without pushing or rushing; it grows at its own pace, with compassion and care, allowing for opportunities to get familiar with the emotional body of another. We can practise this by becoming more familiar and compassionate to our own hearts and emotional state.

Queering the Emotional Landscape

Queering the emotional landscape is about divesting from our obsession with the emotional quadrant as exclusive to one person or exclusive *at depth* to only one person. This is to say, we can have many different kinds of emotional connections, and experience those emotional connections in any or all of the different layers of relating.

In Greek, love is a multidimensional experience: *agape* (unconditional deep affection), *eros* (erotic passion), *philia* (friendly affection), *storge* (familial empathy), *xenia* (welcomingness), and *ludus* (playfulness). In Sanskrit, love can be a transcendent experience: *prema* (unconditional love), *sneha* (tender affection), *kama* (longing and desire), *rati* (sensual pleasure), and *bhakti* (devotion).

Expanding our awareness of what love can be invites us to explore what it might be like to expand our awareness of other emotions too. Anger and sadness can both be aspects of grief, and disgust a flipside of fear. The ways we engage emotionally can be singular—we may only be interested in emotional relating with happiness and joy—or we may have capacity and willingness to engage with a full spectrum of emotions. Let's take a deeper look at emotional connection in each of the layers of relating.

Emotional Awareness

Attuning to how emotions can impact our behaviours can feel challenging for some. In Western culture, where the bold expression of emotions is often shamed, being present to our emotions can initially feel unsettling. This is true of warm and positive feelings like joy and excitement as much as rougher feelings like shame, hate, and fear.

Witnessing our own emotions can be a powerful experience, and witnessing the emotions of others can help us grow more comfortable with them. It helps us to know we aren't alone in feeling our feelings. Witnessing the emotions of others can expand our awareness of what it is to feel. This is especially healing if you or someone you know has been raised to repress your emotions or limit your emotional range of expression.

You might find yourself experiencing emotional awareness of others at a group therapy session or with your metamours, in-laws, a coworker, or even a stranger in distress. Maybe your parent calls to tell you that your sibling is having a hard time: You've now gained third-party emotional awareness! In emotional awareness, you're not necessarily showing up to be emotionally present yet, but you're orienting to an outline of someone's emotional state.

SOMATIC PAUSE
Emotional Self-Awareness

Let your body rest somewhere comfortable. You can lie down or be seated.

Breathe in and out. Notice how the air moves through your lungs as you breathe in, as if it is caressing your heart space. Notice how, as you exhale, you can let go of tension and feel ease in your chest.

Breathe this way, noticing how your breath flows around your heart for a few minutes. You may want to close your eyes, or you might prefer to keep your eyes open and focus on something that reminds you of someone who has given you loving support.

Take some time to write or speak the answers to the following questions:

- What is alive in your heart right now?
- What has brought your heart comfort in the past year?
- What does your heart yearn for now?

Emotional Safety

Emotional safety arises when you feel comfortable enough to open up and share your emotional reality with someone else. In this space, we might selectively share specific emotional experiences with others, or engage in specific emotional experiences with others.

While you may have been taught that the only appropriate places for emotional safety are in romantic partnerships, and that you must keep them closely guarded otherwise, finding emotional safety with friends, family, colleagues, and community members will significantly benefit your emotional health.

People you might have an experience of emotional safety with might include:

- newer partners
- a mentor
- a confidante
- helping professionals, such as a therapist or coach
- online friends

When we experience emotional safety, we begin to feel seen and understood for who we are.

Emotional Intimacy

Recurring and consistent experiences of emotional safety can lead to emotional intimacy. Instead of occasionally sharing about our experiences, we join together in an open field of empathy and start having emotional experiences together. Empathy is a somatic experience arising through the coregulation of our nervous systems with each other. This is similar to how a parent or caregiver finds themselves emotionally attuned to an infant. We might experience this in our adult relationships as pulling us to merge with or join someone in their experience to feel more connected with them.

When we don't feel safe, or don't yet have an experience of being comfortable with emotional vulnerability, we might keep our distance and hang out more in sympathy and spaces of emotional safety. Indeed, sometimes keeping distance from another person's emotions, what some might call "emotional avoidance," could be a perfectly reasonable self-protective response to emotions we are unfamiliar with or fear being overwhelmed by.

This means that our ability to engage in empathy will be inhibited if we are not in an emotionally grounded space, such as when we're vigilant, scared, or frightened. Emotional intimacy requires resilience skills, and if we struggle to be present and aware of our own self-protective and defensive responses, then any experience of emotional intimacy will struggle to transition into an emotional Relationship. We'll explore this more in chapter 18.

Emotional Relationship

The threshold between intimacy and Relationship lies in the spaciousness we find when we can retain our individuality while joining someone in an emotional connection. Rather than the merging sensation of responding to someone's emotions as they feel them, we can move in and out of their emotional experience while also being present to our own.

This might sound counterintuitive—after all, isn't the romantic ideal of an emotional relationship one where we merge and two become one? While that kind of emotional merging is crucial when we are infants and have not yet had a chance to develop our sense of self, as adults in relationships we have to allow our nervous systems to mature and reclaim our sense of individuality in order to grow a healthy emotional Relationship. The experience of emotional depth does not need to equate to relationship escalation or enmeshment. Likewise, enmeshment and escalation are not required for deeply emotional experiences in a relationship—and emotional depth does not necessitate emotional exclusivity.

An emotional Relationship holds deep compassion: Seeing and understanding one another can bring a sense of flow, ease, and understanding. We aren't occasional participants in one another's emotional landscape, nor are we joined at the proverbial hip in our emotional bodies. We participate in a shared landscape, and also in our own independent landscape. We maintain our own separate emotional body, joining in a chorus of hearts and nervous systems singing together in harmony.

Platonic Love
A Story of Friendship

I realized I loved Xianny the day we were bouncing up and down on a double stack of mattresses in my East Vancouver bedroom on Christmas Day. As the only two roommates home for the holidays, we'd gotten high and decided to clean the whole house, moving a mattress left behind by one departed roommate into my bedroom. We spent hours laughing in a way neither of us had laughed in a long time.

We had met in 2013 through the closely woven networks of the East Van polyamory scene and discovered we were neighbours. In 2014, when my landlord gave my then-roommate and I notice that he was going to move family members in, Xianny invited us to move into two rooms that had become available in her large multi-family "Vancouver Special." As roommates, our friendship deepened. At first, we bonded over being outsiders in Canada: I'd grown up in Kuwait, she had grown up in Singapore, and we'd had similar schooling experiences. But as we grew to know one another even better, we began to find more in common in our values, how we looked at the world, how we navigated relationships, and *how we felt our feelings*. We would swap clothing and also swap stories of our various dating escapades and experiences. It was Xianny who coined a term I've used often and that I now sometimes see show up in the polyamorous lexicon—date zero: referring to that first date when you aren't really sure if you're interested in dating a person and are just getting a feel for the vibes. But the most remarkable thing we had in common was a willingness to love our friends deeply.

We were roommates for two years, and even after I moved out, we remained fast friends. When she and her then-partner moved to Vancouver Island during the COVID-19 pandemic, they ended up living a twenty-minute drive from me. We "bubbled" together, sharing weekly walks, and I joined her and her partner in building their vegetable garden, sharing in its bounty. I picked all the berries and turned them into jam for Xianny to enjoy through the winter. I remember her partner being surprised by how openly we would say "I love you," bring each other gifts, and do traditionally romantic things for one another.

When Xianny broke her ankle and had an extended stay in the city for medical care, I spent several days assisting her with tasks she couldn't do alone. In my early days of learning to manage life with long COVID, Xianny would video-chat with me and keep me company while I slowly chopped vegetables and prepared food for myself.

When Xianny's work took her to California, I found myself grieving the loss of our regular connections, but we continue to hold our friendship dear. We still experience *agape* (unconditional and deep love), *philia* (friendly affection), and *ludus* (playfulness). We have been there for one another through multiple break-ups, life changes, and some serious curve balls. Even though there is now more physical distance, we remain emotionally available to one another: rejoicing in one another's celebrations, feeling the sadness and grief of each other's sorrows.

We explore more about how to expand our capacity for empathy in the next section. For now, remember: Deeply ingrained and socially developed habits take time and persistence to fully break free from. Once we begin to recognize where we are slipping into self-sacrificing and ignoring our emotional boundaries, struggling to know our feelings, or struggling to be with the feelings of others, we can start to bring ourselves back and grow more capacity for relationships in this quadrant.

I invite you to practise honouring and recognizing your emotional capacity. Notice, in your emotional relationships, when you feel energized and when you feel emotionally drained. Sometimes this is more subtle, and sometimes it is more obvious. As you become more aware of what drains versus what energizes, making choices to engage in what nourishes you will become easier.

True emotional depth is found by moving slowly and gently, without pushing or rushing; it grows at its own pace, with compassion and care. The emotional belonging we crave can only come when we have taken the time to build emotional safety in our relationships, and rushing into escalation and enmeshment are poor strategies for this.

REFLECTIVE JOURNALING
Who and What Is in Your Emotional Quadrant?

Take a moment to think about your emotional landscape:

- Who is in your emotional quadrant?
- What do you enjoy doing and sharing with others in your emotional landscape?
- What do you not enjoy?
- What would you like more of in your emotional quadrant?
- Is there anything that you would want less of in your emotional quadrant?

11

THE SOCIAL QUADRANT

To belong is to rest into the collective, to be woven into the all. It's the feeling that the group has found meaning and usefulness in your presence.

—PRENTIS HEMPHILL[1]

The social quadrant is all about our mind, thoughts, values, and beliefs and the people we share them with. The beliefs and values we inherit from our family of origin aren't necessarily the ones we stick to. Knowing what your own values are, without any social pressure to conform to someone else's, can be a lifelong journey, and the friendships we form along the way can in turn influence our personal cosmology: how we relate to the world and the beings in it (everything we can see and can't see), the values that guide us, and the systems of relationships, commerce, and politics that we subscribe to.

Relationships in the social quadrant represent shared values, interests, and cosmologies, whether it's a shared love of a specific fandom, common spiritual beliefs, or a political allegiance. These relationships often greatly influence our overall joy and satisfaction. With a vibrant and healthy social quadrant, we may feel inclusion, acceptance, and a sense of belonging.

When we struggle in the social quadrant, we might feel isolated, rejected, and othered. Some may make do with romantic connection as a substitute for social connection, but as social creatures, we fundamentally need diversity in this quadrant to thrive. If you feel pressured to fulfil a romantic partner's social needs, you might eventually feel burned out or have reduced capacity to tend to your own social landscape.

Expectations of the Social Quadrant

Being social beings doesn't mean forming social relationships is easy, or that it comes naturally for everyone. Maybe you know someone who seems to make new friends wherever they go, even when they aren't even trying, which isn't necessarily a sign that they are great at being a friend; or perhaps you have known people for whom forming friendships seems very hard. For many of us, maintaining social relationships can be a struggle, even once we have found them.

We may want to find our people, but people are complicated and confusing at the best of times. If we experienced any disruptions during childhood, like moving frequently, growing up neurodivergent, living with suppressed or repressed queerness, a lack of support at home, or even as adults have struggled to adjust to living in a new community, then building social connections may feel harder. On top of all this, political polarization can make people reluctant to share their social values, for fear of ostracization, or lead some to dismiss connections without complete 100 percent political agreement. We may lean on social transactionality—"You did something nice for me, so at some point I'll do something nice for you"—which can leave social connections and community spaces feeling like spaces that try to control through obligations and spoken or unspoken rules and etiquette.

Generally speaking, folks who got to be part of clubs, societies, after-school activities, and sports teams in childhood and adolescence, all of which often require some degree of privilege, tend to have an easier time making new social relationships. If you had the privilege of access to something like this when you were growing up, as an adult you might have more social capital: an ability to make friends and network with ease. But if you didn't have access to this as a kid, this does not mean you can't make friends and find community as an adult. As adults, friendships are strengthened by shared values and interests. We might make new friends through work, our spiritual or ethnic communities, our hobbies and volunteerism, or attending events focused on arts, music, politics, or fandoms.

Obstacles in the Social Quadrant

The social quadrant is a space for experiencing *belonging*. Speaking about this experience in her book *Braving the Wilderness,* Brené Brown writes: "True belonging doesn't require you to change who you are; it requires you to be who you are."[2] But being who we are in order to find belonging is easier said than done. If we aren't white, cis, heterosexual, monogamous, able-bodied, and neurotypical, then we may face judgment, stigma, and even exclusion when we try to be ourselves and engage socially in a world that orients around privilege and values laid out by white supremacy culture. Systemic barriers may even prevent us from finding others like ourselves. As a result, we might become guarded around strangers and lean into the support of familiar people, which often means family and partners. We might also feign agreeability when engaging with people we perceive as holding more social power than ourselves, and attempt to squash our discomfort to maintain a harmonious relationship with someone we depend on for safety and security.

For queer people of colour and immigrants, community spaces organized along cultural and racial affinity might not translate to spaces that also have capacity for queerness. For us who are polyamorous and queer, our family of origin may not be a source of belonging. This can contribute to leaning more heavily on romantic partners for social connection.

Mono-normativity encourages us to prioritize dyadic partnership and enmeshment at the cost of other social relationships. Friendships with someone of the same gender as your partner are still often considered a potential threat. And how often have you heard of someone seeing less of a friend after they started dating someone new? In mono-normativity, to be on the escalator romantically means we are expected to de-escalate how we engage with our friends.

Indeed, the nuclear family model of monogamy disrupts our connection to community, a connection that is essential for resisting the external forces that might seek to subjugate and control us. Is it any wonder, then, that European colonialism has so often imposed monogamy as it has asserted dominance over Indigenous populations, or that the nuclear family was glamorized in media propaganda as Western politics sought to counter the rise of socialism? Perhaps it is also not surprising that grass-roots community movements, like the Black Panthers, whose People's Free Food Program in Oakland, California, ensured that 150 school children were fed breakfast before every school day, have prioritized social support that isn't reliant on governments or institutions.

When it comes to the experience of belonging, discerning how communities and friendships handle issues like bigotry, discrimination, and conflict can be helpful. Anyone who experiences marginalization or othering in their everyday life is more prone to marginalization stress when engaging in spaces that don't have processes for addressing harm and supporting repair.

Put simply, marginalization stress describes the stress experienced by being part of any kind of minority. This could mean gender, for example, for women, trans, and non-binary people, as well as ethnicity, orientation, ability, and many other possible vectors. If you've been marginalized by dominant society, it is far more likely that you will experience a consistent level of stress in life that is beyond your individual ability to change. Imagine if you were somewhere no one spoke your language and where you knew only a few words in the local dialect. You would experience daily stress just attempting to express your needs and navigate fundamental interactions. This is an experience many immigrants and refugees have when they arrive in a new country, and this translates to other experiences of marginalization, such as the daily stress a trans person might have about being misgendered.

Many who step away from traditional compulsory monogamy, whether through break-up, divorce, or practising some form of consensual non-monogamy, report experiencing forms of marginalization stress, including the challenges of being accepted by family and friends, and facing obstacles and possible ostracization in the workplace due to having no partner or multiple partners. Stigma and judgment about our relationships, especially singledom and non-monogamy, can weigh heavily on hearts that just want to be open and loving.

Finding like-minded people to form community with helps foster resilience against the impacts of minority stress, and many polyamorous, open-relationship, and relationship-anarchy spaces have excelled at creating opportunities for meaningful community and connections to form. However, not all these spaces successfully take into consideration the many possible intersecting vectors of minority stress and oppression. Not all alternative relationship spaces are anti-racist or welcoming of people of colour or consider accessibility needs for people with disabilities. Just because a space welcomes one aspect of you doesn't mean it will welcome all of you.

Despite the image that may prevail in the media of open relationships equaling open-mindedness, there are still some exploring non-monogamy who adhere to fascist right-wing ideologies. You might encounter incels, misogynists, and people who are casually transphobic, homophobic, or racist. Some may be less aware of their prejudices, but others may be overtly so, and even proud of them. Some might even appear like allies to the queer community, doing ally-like things like attending pride events, but despite this, they might fetishize trans people, much like someone may claim they aren't racist because they have a Black friend. Perhaps you or someone you know has unwittingly harmed through unconsciously othering a person in non-monogamy spaces by doing something like this. If so, know that it's never too late to start learning about how to show up as a true ally for folks who are marginalized. Simply put, just because two people reject monogamy doesn't mean that they are compatible, and the values behind the rejection of monogamy might reveal much more about what their social, and indeed overall relational, compatibility might be.

Even within the non-monogamous world, there can be lateral violence that leads to marginalization stress. As a young woman in my early thirties and new to the polyamorous scene in Vancouver, I encountered stigma about my solo-ness. Some saw my lack of desire for a primary partner as threatening. Even when I found people who understood and accepted my solo-polyamory, the spiritual beliefs I had been raised with and practised saw me judged in other ways. I also encountered racial prejudices, being gaslit about my ancestral ethnic identities and traumas, and felt a massive gap in cultural understanding even in some of my intimate relationships. And, sadly, I'm not alone in this. The lateral violence in the form of judgment and othering from one polyamorous person to another that I have witnessed in the non-monogamous world is genuinely heartbreaking.

When you hold a marginalized identity, engaging in spaces where you know you might encounter hatred and discrimination is exhausting and overwhelming, which makes it potentially traumatizing. And yet, many of us tolerate it because we so desperately crave a space where we can be safe to talk about our non-monogamous experiences.

Let's remember that not all social relationships go deep. We might believe that to maintain social connections, we must avoid discomfort and conflict. Indeed, divisive social dynamics can activate our self-protective responses. We feel we need our friendships to survive, and so we avoid social conflict. Many of us go through life with mostly surface-level social relationships that stay in the layers of awareness and safety. You may be fortunate enough to have true social intimacy in a handful of friendships.

You may have learned that your social quadrant is transactional and that self-sacrifice is required to achieve social inclusion. Perhaps you've had an experience of a friend inviting you to be part of something they are doing, celebrating a birthday or attending their wedding, for example, but to participate requires considerable effort on your part. Perhaps there is a cost involved, or a need to take time off work or away from your loved ones. Sometimes this cost feels reasonable, and other times it may feel disproportionate or unreasonable. We may grow habits of tolerating unpleasant behaviour from friends because pushing back could put the friendship at risk. This does not a resilient social quadrant make.

We all need a community to grow security, stability, and anchoring in our lives, not just as an emergency survival strategy but as a long-term approach to nurturing our whole landscape. We each deserve to find communities of friends and lovers who will respect our independent spirits and hold us steady through rough times. The longer we tolerate relationships that don't feed and inspire our spirits and hearts, the more weighed down we feel.

Queering the Social Quadrant

Rather than making social inclusion the goal of your social quadrant, I want to encourage you to think about how you form your own social network. There may be different layers of proximity in your personal social network—people you hold close and people who are further away. Let the quest for belonging turn from seeking a space where you feel like you belong to instead being about the people you feel the different parts of you can *belong with*.

Social relationships that begin with deeply held values centred on compassion towards our fellow humans (and our nonhuman relations) have the power to disrupt the status quo of social transactionality and resource hoarding that so much of colonialism is anchored in, and the potential to bring about incredible change across many relational landscapes. In non-monogamous spaces, what is called a community is often more like a scene, a socializing space where people come together for a limited time. This might take the form of a discussion group, a social meetup, a book club, a board game night, a play party, or otherwise. It's a temporary collection of humans. Outside of non-monogamous spaces, social scenes might include ecstatic dance, conscious intimacy or sexuality groups, hobby-based clubs, fandoms, and more. Social scenes tend to be open to most and welcome diversity. Still, unless it is a focus, scenes tend to lack awareness of how internalized misogyny, racism, ableism, and other isms can impact and harm. They may offer incredible experiences for individuals but rarely lead to any meaningful systemic changes.

In the social quadrant, we also need to examine the intersections of power and privilege. The social capital you hold in any space can be influenced by what you do, how you show up, and also how others perceive you to be. When we do occupy social privilege, it's essential to consider how we might use that power for good. This could look like supporting organizations that help marginalized people, either through monetary donations or donating your time. It could also look like lending and sharing your resources with those who don't have sufficient resource access, practising democratic and servant leadership models at work, and creating more space for those with marginalized experiences to be supported in being understood and honoured.

As we explore the social quadrant through the layers of relating, I will use some dancing analogies. This is partially because I love to dance—but also because dance is a universal social practice. As you read this, I invite you to consider how other social experiences parallel these four layers in different ways.

Social Awareness

We might think of our connections in this layer as acquaintances: the people you nod to in the coffee shop or the elevator because you see them daily, the folks you often run into at the park or out partying. You may know their names or have had little incidental conversations. Perhaps you've added them on social media and like each other's memes. There may be people in your relational network who fall into this label of acquaintance: perhaps a metamour you haven't spent much time with, or the person you went on a single date with but who has some polycule overlap with you. You might even feel this level of connection from interactions on discussion forums and meeting people in conferences and workshops.

I think of social awareness as being a lot like formal dancing from the 1800s. We circle around the space of knowing one another, exchanging pleasantries and light banter, and perhaps share some time dancing one-on-one in a practised style that observes social etiquettes, enjoying the chance to get better acquainted with one another. Of course, in the 1800s, a dance like that might lead straight away to a marriage proposal, but today we can explore it as just the first step towards growing social safety.

REFLECTIVE JOURNALING
Cultivating Social Awareness

Consider these questions:

- What values are important to you?
- What is your personal cosmology: What morals, ethics, and beliefs about the world do you subscribe to? What values and behaviours in others help you to feel safe with them?
- What influences and guides you when you are at decision-making points? For example, do you follow cultural or spiritual practices that support your decision-making? Do you adhere to the wisdom of a respected teacher or elder?
- What aspects of your life do you like to involve others in, and where do you desire more spaciousness?

Social Safety

Social safety is about camaraderie; for many of us, this is where our friendships start. It's a comfort in connection where we can kick back, laugh, and unwind together. We might nerd out about a new superhero show or play tabletop games together. We might find social safety in the connections we make in virtual or in-person discussions, book clubs, and social events that centre on non-monogamy and alternative relationship styles.

The qualities of social safety are often ones of ease and flow. There may be a sense of growing connectivity and playfulness. I think about one of my first experiences at a blues and fusion dance class. At first I was very nervous about letting someone else lead me in the dance, but the more we danced, the more I felt like I was able to trust them, and I began to relax and have fun.

Growing safety in the social quadrant requires a lot of attunement, listening, and giving space when needed. Just like in any kind of dynamic partner dance, such as swing or blues, there are little indicators at the edges of our connections that help us dance together with greater harmony as we learn to understand them.

Social Intimacy

Remember that we are not a monolith when it comes to finding community and belonging within non-monogamy and alternative relationships. There are atheists who practise non-monogamy and there are new-age shamans. There are socialists, communists, Marxists, and capitalists. There are environmentalists and deeply spiritual people doing non-monogamy, and there are people who don't recycle, and people who ridicule spirituality. There are scientists and artists whose work has influenced how we experience the world, and there are also people who don't believe in science and reject art as bourgeois. There are vegans and vegetarians and there are hunters. There are individuals of all backgrounds, BIPOC, LGBTQIA2S+, and there are also alt-right fascists and white supremacists. Non-monogamy attracts all types.

The plural nature of polyamory lends itself well to growing networks through interconnected and interweaving relations. This can be healthy and empowering if the network is one where everyone is engaging in self-awareness and growth and celebrates individual diversity. It can be potent and liberating if the community embraces consent, compassion, empathy, and forgiveness. However, if a community is mired in draining, limiting, fear-based behaviours, or if it lacks cohesiveness in shared values or tolerates abusive behaviours, it may start to feel like a place where we can't be safe. It's easy to feel small when trying to be part of a space that isn't safe, and we might experience depression or anxiety as a result. In short, if we are ever sacrificing ourselves to feel like we belong in a community, it's worth asking ourselves if that community relationship is worth the cost.

To extend the dancing metaphor, intimacy in the social quadrant is akin to the revolution of disco, a decentralized dance movement that changed how people socialized. When New York DJ David Mancuso started hosting dances that didn't require a partner, but where everyone came together on the dance floor as equals, he echoed global pre-colonial dance practices that fostered community rapport and social intimacy.

Movements, which typically bring people together for action, be it on a small scale or large, can evolve, grow, and change shape and form as the people within them get curious about how to make life better not just for themselves but for others as well. Movements are more community-oriented and forward-focused, in contrast to the social scenes we sometimes think of as community.

Activism-based movements tend to include accountability, social values, diversity, equity, and inclusion, and they often have a strong sense of what social justice means. Membership in a movement may be formal or informal, but people are usually vetted somehow. In non-monogamy, movements support education, advocacy, and legal change. The people in non-monogamous movements are often keen to explore non-monogamy as part of a larger vision of countercultural, decolonizing, anti-racist, and deeply feminist ways of living. Just as dating doesn't necessarily mean you're in a relationship, being part of a movement or a scene doesn't mean you're necessarily in a community. Many of us in non-monogamy may mistake our local community spaces as being a real community when they are actually scenes or occasionally movements.

The joy and delight of finding people with enough common ground to form a collective or a movement can often be mistaken for a deep sense of belonging and an indicator of social Relationship. However, many movements have a singular focus and may struggle to expand beyond that. For instance, the Canadian truck rallies in 2022 brought together many different demographics, including both libertarian white Canadians, who objected to the perceived loss of privileges under COVID mitigation rules, rallying alongside First Nations peoples, who protested vaccine mandates that felt reminiscent of government-endorsed medical experiments on First Nations children and adults in the 1960s. They shared a common goal to remove vaccine mandates, but they didn't actually share values. Months later, during criminal prosecutions, the leadership of the trucker movement was shown to have ties to violent and racist white supremacist organizations.

Finding a personal alternative relationship community can be a process. Non-monogamous spaces usually offer a mix of education, advocacy, and socializing with the potential for meeting new dates. Surprisingly few have clearly articulated core values, guidelines, or processes for accountability. Organized social spaces with clear guidelines and protocols are often safer, but the intimacy only comes when we feel secure enough to connect with those same people outside of that contained context. Real alternative relationship communities are few and far between, and the ones that do exist tend to be intergenerational, diverse, aligned in core values, consent-based (for example, with cooperative decision-making), and have organic restorative processes for repairing from harm. Look for communities that clearly outline their values and what behaviours are and aren't tolerated in the space.

As we live through a time rich in global change, where social scenes struggle to adapt and new social movements emerge, it's worth remembering that a movement can, over time, give birth to a community. If you are part of a social movement today, whether it's related to non-monogamy or not, what can you do to more deeply nurture the relationships with your comrades to grow a future community? If you hold a minority or marginalized identity, what has helped you feel safer to participate in community spaces?

Affinity and Belonging
Sharon's Story

Sharon moved with her family from Trinidad to the United States when she was three years old, sponsored by her uncle, a Vietnam War veteran. In Trinidad, she had been part of a close-knit community where everyone was deeply connected. There was no sense of who you were related to and who you weren't; everyone was somehow family. Even after immigrating, Sharon's grandparents and aunt lived downstairs from her and her parents. They frequently hosted newly arrived immigrants, and the sense of community was so strong that Sharon never realized others lived any differently.

As a teenager, under pressure to excel academically, she focused on her studies and felt the pangs of social isolation. She dropped out of school and in her twenties left home to seek out what was missing. She threw herself into a romantic relationship that introduced her to sex positivity but still didn't meet her craving for community. When that relationship ended, she found herself at a crossroads and returned to Trinidad. There, she was reminded of the strength and warmth of her extended family's community. "A light went off inside me that I thought had died," she shares. "So many of my mental health struggles seemed to be about not having community."

But Trinidad lacked the sex-positive spaces Sharon had begun to value. After a few years she returned to the United States and moved to the Pacific Northwest, eager to find a sex-positive community. A friend introduced her to some new-age spaces that talked about community, but she didn't feel aligned with them. She eventually turned to dating apps, where she met someone involved in sex-positive spaces in Seattle who was also working on building intentional community. That connection led her to Star Community, a collective inspired by the Tamera healing biotope in Portugal, a multi-generational intentional community. The people at Star approached life a little differently. Unlike others who often overlooked Sharon's story of being an immigrant, one of the residents showed genuine curiosity, wanting to see and understand her. Sharon started spending more time getting to know the Star Community.

In 2016, Sharon moved into Star House and began exploring polyamorous relationships while staying curious about what path was right for her. Within a year, however, she began to encounter the community's limitations. Star House was part of a larger network called New Culture, and in the Pacific Northwest, the group was predominantly white. At a July retreat, Sharon was one of only three Black attendees. During the July 4th weekend, hopeful that the openness of the community would be able to hold space for what she was experiencing, Sharon shared her struggles as an immigrant and her feelings about the legacy of slavery and violence against African Americans. But her words made some attendees uncomfortable, and tensions around social justice began to simmer in the following months.

When Sharon suggested that the community explore taking social justice training, one of the core members expressed concern, fearing that a focus on social justice would cause division, and told her, "Black people have a victim mentality." At that moment, Sharon realized the community wasn't equipped to address systemic injustice—at least, not yet.

Sharon moved back to the East Coast to finish her education and spent several years living in cities with large Black populations. As she left Star House, one member admitted they would likely stop discussing social justice without her presence. On the East Coast, she found a sense of comfort and ease, free from the many microaggressions she had faced in Seattle. Being surrounded by people who shared a social justice mindset was healing for her. Though she had left, she remained in touch with friends from Star House and New Culture.

In 2022, some New Culture members from California invited Sharon to participate in workshops focused on decentering privilege and fostering inclusion. In one of these spaces, Sharon had a breakthrough: Allowing herself to feel the grief she had carried from trying to find a sense of belonging at Star, she saw a renewed capacity to engage in the community in a new way. She was soon invited to help organize a summer camp themed around affinity and belonging, the AB Camp.

The planning for AB Camp brought together people of colour, LGBTQIA2S+ individuals, and allies to build a radical, intersectional community vision. The goal was to create a space where people who had felt rejected by New Culture could feel included, safe, and welcome. It was envisioned as a disruptive space where Black, brown, queer and trans bodies could come together as allies to create meaningful change.

The summer camp of 2024 was perfect in its imperfections. Sharon felt a sense of homecoming as she walked the land where the retreat was held. Courageous conversations took place to address microaggressions in the moment, and community resilience was nurtured in meaningful ways. On July 4th, one participant sang Negro spirituals, another gave a presentation on slave narratives, and discussions flourished about the history of the holiday. Magic happened: Participants stayed in touch after AB Camp, creating new workshops and feeling inspired to bring new projects into the world.

Sharon is now looking ahead to the next wave of affinity and belonging camps. Having finished law school, she is helping to set up an organization to sustain this work. No longer feeling alone in her values, she has found deep, interwoven connections that align with her beliefs. "It feels very healing," she shares. "I think about the sacrifice my uncle made for our entire family to come to this country. This camp, and what I'm feeling here, this magic—it makes me feel like his sacrifice was worth it. Maybe we can do something to heal this country."

Social Relationship

Social Relationships are where we find the experiences of belonging: showing up fully as we are, with all our values, beliefs, and dreams, without taking away any part of ourselves. In my experience of contact improvisation, a free-style form of dance with little formal structure that relies on principles of movement and connection, there is a deep sense of ease and rapport. Two or more bodies may have drastically different abilities and ranges of movement, yet they may be able to come together in an organic flow. Contact improv dance maestro Martin Keogh has compared the form to the murmurations of starlings he observed flying over the botanical gardens in San Miguel de Allende in Mexico. There is no single leader; the flock shifts organically. It is a visible social form that is decentralized and dynamic. In his essay "101 Ways to Say No to Contact Improv," Keogh speaks to the importance of boundary work and individuation to arrive at community:

> Being in a group of dancers and doing this ongoing work of clarifying boundaries is like inhabiting a rock tumbler—those containers you fill with stones and spin for days so that the stones polish one another. As we learn to sense and

express our boundaries, we tumble and rub and hit against others physically and figuratively. It can hurt as our sharp edges get rounded, but over time we become polished, slowly revealing the precious gems we carry. Through this process we begin to treasure the living entity called "community" that helps us develop a greater capacity for yes—in our dance and in our lives.[3]

Many of us experience a degree of stress in social connections, especially if we are divergent or nonconforming. One way to think of a social relationship is as a stress-reduced space. A social relationship doesn't need to be a connection where we align in all ways, but it will be a space in which we hold deep respect and honour for the ways in which others are different, and we feel welcomed and included in spite of our differences.

I've had plenty of experiences of confusing social intimacy for social Relationship: I remember feeling a sense of community around creative, alternative-lifestyle folks only to feel excluded as they poked fun at my spiritual practices, which they didn't understand. I've also gotten into deep layers of loving friendship only to find that my access needs as a disabled and immunocompromised human aren't respected. One of the metrics I've come to use personally is to gauge how people engage with my vegetarianism. The people I'm able to have long-lasting social relationships with are either vegetarian themselves or respectful and supportive of my values about this. The metrics that make sense for you will of course be personal for you. For example, maybe for you, it's about how people relate to others' health and safety, or how they treat the unhoused.

Finding truly meaningful social Relationship may not be easy. It may require extensive self-reflection to identify what deeply matters about the people we share social time with and build communities with. It may even feel harder to stay in these relationships with a loving and compassionate heart, since communities are inherently complex. But it is so worthwhile to put in this effort. Writing about how we learn to love one another in *Radical Dharma,* Reverend angel Kyodo williams says,

> The sheer weight of the task of unravelling a massive social habit pattern of an addiction to violence and injustice cannot be underestimated. It comes with the requisite and convenient forgetfulness about historic transgressions of such enormity and persistence they boggle the mind.[4]

To develop social relationships—meaningful social bonds that last and can withstand the roller coasters of life, politics, climate change, and economic upheaval—is a massive task. We cannot ignore the impacts of marginalization or harm, and yet we have to find ways to continue to love and support one another as beings sharing our existence on this beautiful planet.

We all ultimately want social connections where we can feel that we belong. Whether through community, intimacy, family, friendships, activist groups, or otherwise, we long for a social relationship landscape that feels stable and safe for us to flourish within.

REFLECTIVE JOURNALING:
Who and What Is in Your Social Quadrant?

Take a moment to think about your social landscape:

- Who is in your social quadrant?
- What do you enjoy doing and sharing with others in your social landscape?
- What do you not enjoy?
- What would you like more of in your social quadrant?
- Is there anything that you would want less of in your social quadrant?

12

THE PRACTICAL QUADRANT

The metamour who shows up with food when you're in the hospital so your part-
ner can continue supporting you; partners who trade off caring for an ill partner
and for their kids; co-parents providing backup for moments difficult and beau-
tiful, whether or not they're romantically entangled with you—these are all kinds
of chosen family that our society is pretty quick to dismiss as less than.

—LAURA BOYLE[1]

The practical quadrant is about how we care for our physical form and the physical forms of others. This can include practical self-care like staying fed and bathed and keeping a living space clean. It can also include the work we do to feed and house ourselves and our loved ones. It might also include a relationship to our physical health, and can expand to encompass our financial commitments.

When we feel fulfilled and nourished in the practical quadrant, it's usually an indicator that some of our most basic survival needs are met. We might feel ease in our bodies, find it easier to breathe, and feel more grounded. When we don't feel fully nourished in this quadrant, we might experience deep anxiety, a preoccupation with practical survival, and an urge to rush, push, or hustle in our relationships.

Attaining security in the practical quadrant is one of the core motivators of traditional monogamy. Political and strategic alliances between landowners and rulers were historically cemented through marriage. Families tied their fortunes together through bonds of wedlock. The expression "to marry up" was a common way of saying that someone had a spouse who came with greater financial and practical security, and by assumption, positional power, than they did.

Even in post-monogamous relationships, when we aren't engaging in relation-ships for the purpose of financial security, we still need to think about how we explore relationships that do exist within the practical quadrant of our relationship landscape.

Expectations of the Practical Quadrant

We cannot talk about the practical quadrant without also talking about the impact of capitalism, specifically late-stage capitalism. Capitalism as a philosophy is based on the management and trade of resources. There was a time when it was seen as a means to liberate resources from hoarding by feudal overlords and to empower the masses, but in the context of colonialism, and within the corporate economic climate of the last two hundred years, it has increasingly become about resource hoarding. Large corporations now take the place of feudal lords, controlling the majority of resources, hungry to extract more from the earth with little to no thought as to sustainability, exploiting both workers and consumers to maximize profits. Marketing algorithms ensure that grim news is often juxtaposed with advertisements for products that promise to enhance how one feels, and we are encouraged to engage in a kind of commercial bypassing: spending more money to ignore or forget any existential dread this economic dystopia brings.

In this paradigm we've learned that practical relationships are transactional. I pay my landlord rent, and in turn they permit me to have a home; I spend money at the grocery store and then have food to eat; I buy new clothes so I can be suitably presented at an interview and get hired for a job with a wage that I hope I can afford to live on. We may internalize this transactionality and apply it in our friendships and familial relationships too. Perhaps you have believed that a romantic relationship would only continue for as long as you were "paying into it." And while not contributing anything to a relationship wouldn't be the best strategy for sustaining it, hinging this on actual financial and monetary contribution erases the many other ways that we can exist in practical relationships with one another.

We are, after all, co-existing on a planet going through ecological change, and we face shared challenges around water supplies like floods and droughts, famines, desertification, forest fires, rising sea levels, storms, and other environmental disasters that further impact our economic reality. These circumstances cannot be readily overcome through individualism or by existing in isolation. We need one another to survive all of this. Even if non-monogamy isn't your thing, challenging the status quo around resource hoarding and expanding the ways you relate in the practical quadrant in the midst of all of this just makes sense.

Obstacles in the Practical Quadrant

We face many obstacles to expanding our experiences of practical relationships, for example:

- Government systems and insurance policies generally only allow for a single partner or next of kin.
- In many jurisdictions, limits are placed on the number of unrelated adults who can share a dwelling.

- To co-purchase a home with someone you aren't related to often involves a costly legal process.

- Smaller cost-sharing measures are frowned upon and penalized by corporations; for example, sharing your TV streaming passwords with a partner you don't live with, or passing your grocery store points card to your roommates.

Furthermore, we are often told that discussing the money and resources we have is boasting and prideful, meaning that in an emergency we may not know who has the resources to help us. We are also shamed for wanting help, and even the government systems designed to support those experiencing hardship often fail to recognize where the actual poverty line sits.[2] In many places, disability benefits are hard to access, and those with them may face a loss or reduction of benefits if they marry or cohabitate with a partner who has an income. To avoid hardship, many of us feel that we have to push ourselves hard when it comes to the practical quadrant. We can find ourselves living in ways that might be detrimental to our relationships, unsustainable for our physical and or mental health, just to keep our financial health stable. It doesn't have to be this way.

My Experience of Collective Living

In my journey as a solo polyamorist, saying no to getting on the relationship escalator with any of my partners meant that I was either going to live alone (which is expensive) or live with roommates. For a decade I did the latter, at first sharing a home with a friend and then moving together into a six-bedroom collective home of mostly non-Canadian queer artist types in East Vancouver that we lovingly called the Cinnamon House. From there I moved into a two-bedroom garden suite with an ex-partner (we did our escalator in reverse). When I left Vancouver, it was to move to another collective home, a four-bedroom house nicknamed Wood's End on Vancouver Island, owned by a friend who filled it with queer polyamorous folks. All of these shared living experiences were very different, but they had in common a foundation of shared values around how to co-exist harmoniously. One house agreement I proposed each time I moved was "no shame about sex noises." This was always popular and welcomed.

I was living at Wood's End in 2020 when the COVID-19 lockdowns arrived. Two of the five roommates were partners, two of us had dated in the past but were now firmly platonic friends, and one was non-monogamous with a spouse working abroad. Apart from the one established couple, there weren't any other romantic dynamics in the house, but we were able to apply our experiences in multi-party relationships to living together harmoniously through the first year of lockdowns.

As a household with multiple at-risk individuals, we navigated the pandemic with regular house check-ins to ensure that everyone could feel safe and supported in their needs. While we waited to find out what financial support would be available for those unable to work, one roommate put our shared groceries on his credit card for all of us. We took on projects to improve the house, expanding the vegetable garden and repainting the dining room and kitchen. We had regular movie and board game nights and shared meals with our extended bubble. We took our polyamorous practice of clear and transparent communication about sexually transmitted infections (STIs) and applied it to communication about COVID risks and potential exposures—or at least, we attempted to.

Just as sometimes happens in romantic relationships, communication broke down as time wore on. Different ideas about what vaccination meant led to the house disbanding, with three of us eventually migrating to living situations that would better meet our needs. Despite this, I remain incredibly grateful for the experiences I shared with all the different roommates there through the years, and it remains the longest I have yet lived in a single home during my adult life.

Queering the Practical Quadrant

Queering your practical quadrant doesn't have to mean that you start a commune, but it might! You might already have some experience challenging the status quo in this quadrant: car-sharing, tool libraries, co-parenting arrangements, and collective housing with friends. The changing economics of the last twenty years have meant that many of us, out of necessity, are already exploring ways to diversify our practical quadrant.

To queer the practical quadrant is to get creative about how we resource and task-share. This might look like living in a multi-generational household with friends, joining buy-nothing groups, or growing your food and then sharing the excess produce with friends or a local food bank. You might even pool your resources together to make larger food purchases at wholesale costs. Maybe you create a free library in your neighbourhood, or even a people's library to support counterculture spaces. Knowledge sharing allows for overlap between practical and social quadrants. Support groups for chronic illnesses, for example, offer spaces for people to receive validation about their experiences and also to learn more about how others are navigating the same or similar conditions.

To queer our experience of the practical, we also need to be clear on our values and boundaries. To what extent are we comfortable sharing spaces and resources, and with whom? To be clear, I am not saying that you need to turn over your life savings and assets to a poly-commune bank account; in all my communal living experiences, my finances stayed independent. What I am inviting you to do is consider what it might be like to lessen the internal grip that late-stage capitalism has on you, and welcome the possibility of resource hoarding a little less.

This could look like clearing out your kitchen cupboards regularly for donations to a food bank so that no food expires. It could also look like working with your partners to create schedules that work for everyone's complex time-management needs rather than one or more people feeling consistently left out. It might also look like hosting regular potlucks with friends or organizing collective work days when someone in your circle has a big task they need help with. It includes meal trains for new parents and those recovering from injury and illness. It can also involve creating shared spaces to enjoy together, even if they are just temporary, such as a birthday celebration or a camping trip. I invite you to get curious: What could you share if you didn't need to hoard your resources or be exclusive in all practical matters?

Practical Awareness

The journey of practical awareness starts with knowing our own needs and understanding the physical spaces we exist in. This can feel challenging if we've had accidents that impact our ability to physically orient. Whiplash, concussions, paralysis and partial paralysis, and specific trauma experiences or conditions that affect the inner ear or any of our other senses can sometimes make its hard to actually know what's going on in our relationship with the space around us.

Being in practical awareness with others could be as simple as noticing where something exists, such as remembering where you parked your car. We engage in practical awareness when we look outside and check the weather forecast before deciding what to wear for the day. We also explore practical awareness when we practise conscientiousness about accessibility needs, recognizing what might affect or support different bodies with differing abilities.

If you find yourself having a hard time tuning in to awareness of your practical quadrant, I invite you to explore this Somatic Pause activity:

SOMATIC PAUSE:

Exploring Practical Awareness

You can do this activity standing or seated. If any part of this movement feels inaccessible for you right now, you can visualize or imagine yourself doing it.

Gently tap across any part of your body you can reach: your knees, thighs, belly, shoulders, arms, neck, or face. When that's done, stretch your limbs out as far as they can go, like a four-pointed star. Imagine there is a sphere all around you.

Starting with your right arm out as far as it will stretch, take your left hand and trace an imaginary line from the right, over as far to the left as your left arm will stretch. Then trace that line down to the ground, and stretch away from you to the front of your body.

Having traced the line forward, explore tracing the line backwards. Now explore all the other dimensions this sphere might have for you. Reach up high, crouch down low, extend one leg to the left, extend an arm to the front.

This is known as your kinesphere, your personal bubble of space.

Explore the flow of space around you, and revel in the dimensions your body can experience.

If staying aware of your body is challenging for you, you can practise this by focusing your gaze on something external: raindrops on your window, the sound of birdsong outside, or even the textures and colours of your surroundings.

Consider: How do you welcome and include someone into your physical space?

Practical Safety

Practical safety is practising good citizenship: treating all as equals, with kindness, and doing what we can to support those in need. When we practise these qualities, others feel safer with us. We can also support the experience of safety in the practical quadrant by being more open and direct about our practical needs, for example, if you have a particular allergy or dietary requirement, or you require accessibility support to attend an event. To be able to do this may mean working through any shame we've internalized about being too much or too needy; we talk about this more in chapters 15 and 18.

Practical safety can also include maintaining integrity with what we've said we will do, such as honouring the plans we've made for a date, following through on commitments, and communicating any changes in a timely manner. If time management and scheduling is challenging for you, whether because of unpredictability in your life or because that's how your brain works, you might want to think about how else you can demonstrate reliability and practical safety. You might consider, for example, how you engage with the practical needs of your partners. Do you consider your loved ones' capacity when planning activities? Can you accommodate your friends' or partners' dietary needs and access needs? In what ways can you support your loved ones to feel welcome when they are sharing space with you, whether that's in your home, your vehicle, or somewhere else? I know some who keep notes on the practical needs of partners and loved ones so they don't need to rely on their memory for everything.

Growing up, I always marvelled at how well my aunt was equipped to welcome guests, and would feel immediately at home when I visited her, thanks to the offerings of mini hotel toiletries, towels, and fresh sheets on the guest bed. I've endeavoured to welcome friends, partners, and lovers to my home with similar hospitality: There are always new toothbrushes in the bathroom cabinets, spare toothpaste and other toiletries, sanitary napkins, and guest towels available.

Practical Intimacy

Practical intimacy is an exploration of collaboratively existing. We aren't just hosting someone else, we are mutually surviving, and hopefully, thriving! This is a common experience within close friendships, where we may have shared meals, celebrations, or vacations together. It's also represented in romantic relationships when we have regular sleepovers, perhaps leaving some of our belongings, such as a toothbrush or change of clothing, at a partner's home.

Collaborative existence invites us to explore mutual aid. Mutual aid can be a formal or informal structure for voluntary sharing and trade of resources and services that benefit others—often a whole community, but sometimes focussed on a specific individual or family in need. Mutual aid usually addresses socio-economic inequities that governmental and infrastructure systems fail to. If you've ever participated in a meal train for new parents, or donated to someone's GoFundMe to support them through a time of crisis in their life (or had someone do that for you), you've experienced mutual aid.

Mutual aid invites us to step out of constraints created by resource hoarding. Instead of holding that someone must perform a task or activity to earn our support or money, we send our support as an expression of love, care, and compassion. And we don't have to wait until a crisis or significant life event to engage in it, nor do we have to be flush with finances or personal resources to be part of a mutual aid network. Volunteerism, philanthropy, and participating in social action groups can also be part of community-level mutual aid.

Asking for, and being able to receive, practical support can feel vulnerable. The hyper-individualistic conditioning of modern Western culture can cause us to feel shame when we are unable to provide for ourselves or our loved ones. We may feel pressure to provide for others yet need nothing for ourselves, or we might feel like we are undeserving of support, or that we haven't done enough to earn someone's support. Remember that to collaboratively exist means we have to be willing to be a little more vulnerable about our physical needs and limitations, and also might invite us to reframe how we measure the worth of what we can offer in support to others.

When we shift into a more collaborative state of surviving and thriving, we may find more capacity for resisting the powers that create division, poverty, and oppression. In *Joyous Resilience,* Pakistani American therapist Anjuli Sherin connects the dots between self-love and honouring, with the capacity to show up for others with love as part of resisting social inequity and injustice:

> Radical self-love simply means we begin to see how this love that will fill us up and make our lives so much easier and fulfilling cannot stop within our own hearts or the hearts of those who look like us. Radical self-love is the birthright of each beautiful being (plant, animal, human) on this planet. It means loving ourselves so well that we begin to love others and strive for them to have the same opportunities and freedom we want for ourselves. We do more than wish for it; we are active.[3]

On a more personal relational level, exploring practical intimacy asks us to consider many things we may take for granted. As Laura Boyle highlights in *Monogamy? In This Economy?,* it's important to understand how we all engage with our physical space:

> Are you a family that gathers and spends time in traditionally public rooms? Does everyone gather in kitchens, around the table for homework and dinner and cooking, and with a bustle and hum of different activities for much of the day? Or is your polycule's kitchen table actually the living room?[4]

We can extend this to think about the meaning we make from sharing space or mutual support. With the ethos and values I was raised with, doing something nice for a friend going through hard times, such as dropping off a meal for them, is a practical expression of love and care. But for some that gesture may land as rude, unwelcome, or even insulting. Similarly, I might think nothing of having a partner spend the night or asking them to water my plants while I'm away, but to them these acts might hold deep significance, and even be seen as markers on the escalator.

Practical Relationship

While we may traditionally think of having a practical Relationship with only a few people over the course of our lifetimes, I invite you to consider how you can expand this. Think about how you share space with the people you live with, be they partners, roommates, or family members.

In a practical Relationship there's an implication of continuity. You aren't just leaving a change of clothes; you've got a wardrobe, or you're moving in. Practical Relationships aren't just about nesting. They include co-parenting arrangements, financial agreements, starting a business together, being a listed next-of-kin or emergency contact, being in someone's will. If you've experienced any of these in any of your relationships, you probably know that they can feel incredibly fraught. The stakes of entwined finances and entrusting your life to another are high, and higher stakes can carry greater emotional weight.

Coming Home to Nest
The Phamazons Story

The year 2018 is when everything changed for the Pham sisters. Joan, the eldest of three siblings (and the illustrator who created the gorgeous artwork for this book) ended her marriage of a year and a half and moved back home to live with her parents and younger sister, Janine. A few months later, their father passed away, leaving Mama Pham a widow. With their brother living away from home, the household became a matriarchal haven that would prove to be healing and nourishing for all of them.

Mama Pham was a first-generation immigrant who came to Vancouver as a refugee from Vietnam. Like many marginalized immigrant women, she was tough as nails and candid with her children that getting married and having children was her survival strategy. Between their father and the support of the local Vietnamese Catholic community, she was resourced in a way she had never experienced growing up. She made it clear that she expected her daughters would also one day get married and move out, and worried that Joan and Janine would compete over boys. She encouraged the girls to adhere to an ideal of submissive purity.

Joan moved out while she was at university and ended up living solo for a decade, slowly developing an independent life and exploring her bisexuality and eroticism through burlesque, BDSM, and eventually non-monogamy.

Meanwhile, after being the wild child of the family, Janine attempted to move in with her boyfriend for three months. It was a disaster that made clear for her that she wasn't interested in conventional relationships, and she moved back home.

Working at a government call agency, she heard many stories of women in states of despair due to financial dependence on their partners, and she swore she would never let herself be in a similar position.

With dramatically different personalities, the sisters hadn't been close as children, but as they matured, they became closer. Joan inspired Janine to join her in burlesque classes, and the two found camaraderie in the shared journey of unpacking the narratives their mother had handed them about relationships and sex.

When Joan moved home after her divorce, she never intended it to be long-term, but the loss of her father and the support needs of their mother brought her and Janine together in a whole new way. They started having open conversations about sexuality, love, relationships, and more. Mama Pham exclaimed that it was a joy to walk around the house naked, knowing it was only her daughters around.

In 2019 they formally decided that Joan wouldn't move out again. Joan migrated from her childhood bedroom to the semi-independent suite on the ground floor of the house, while Janine lived upstairs with their mother. Joan and Janine started to refer to one another not just as sisters but as nesting partners. Maintaining the family home, rather than struggling to buy their own places, was a huge relief. It felt profoundly settling to know they could plant roots there.

One of Joan's realizations during her marriage was that even when she had a primary partner, she kept going back to Janine for emotional support, care, and camaraderie. Since they decided to stay as nesting partners, they've both found that their romantic relationships have had more ease, less stress, and a lot less pressure. Both non-monogamous and actively dating, they are often attracted to similar types of people and can cross-compare their matches on dating apps, but find that their very different personalities mean that the same people are not often attracted to both of them.

Folks have told them that they make it look easy, but the sisters affirm it has been a journey to get to where they are. Today they say it feels like a radical, empowering partnership: They are platonic nesting partners. They say there's something ancient and radical about their sisterly power dynamics, and it feels like they're part of a lineage of women who defy traditional expectations.

Over the last 150 years, Western culture has experimented with returning to communal living. From cult compounds to spiritual ashrams to intentional villages, the results vary. One common pitfall for these communities has been how they address conflict.

As a teenager I had the good fortune to spend many summers in a yoga ashram in upstate New York. Founded on traditional principles and with a clearly outlined code of conduct, the teaching hierarchy maintained and role-modelled a discipline that, while it adapted to modern Western trends, was still rooted in a deep sense of spiritual study and discipleship. In the rare instances when conflict arose, it could usually be resolved by reaching out to one of the community elders for support and mediation. However, this kind of reliance on hierarchy and rules doesn't feel comfortable for everyone.

In the archives for the Kerista Commune, the poly-fidelitous group credited with coining the word *compersion* and who owned several group houses throughout the Bay Area of California in the 1970s and 1980s, you can read numerous accounts of how the group leader abused his positional power by imposing his own will when there was conflict. This group followed strict rules: To avoid favouritism within the multi-partner heteronormative relationships, rotating sleeping schedules gave each woman her own bedroom, but each night she spent time with a different man in her house pod. One of the common practices used in Kerista was a communication process called gestalt-o-rama to help its members create community transparency and resolve issues. A combination of peer support and radical honesty, it had eighty-four principles to follow, which were codified in the early 1980s.[5]

Around the same time that Kerista was exploring how to navigate the complexities of long-term communal living in the United States, over in Germany an intentional community called ZEGG was developing something known as Forum, also inspired by group gestalt processes. Note that my mentioning the ZEGG community is not an endorsement of it. Drawing from principles of self-reflection and collaborative, creative interaction between a patient and therapist, the ZEGG Forum was a theatre for promoting awareness, communication, and trust.[6] In Forum, the community gathers to witness one another. Anyone with something to share can move into the circle to share their joys, sorrows, frustrations—anything. The facilitators of the Forum may offer provocations or challenges to the speaker to support them to say more. These could include invitations to physicalize or vocalize instead of speaking, or offer catharsis by welcoming other community members to support the speaker through a deeper exploration. After a speaker has shared, they can receive reflections from the community, where those who have witnessed them can share what they saw, heard, and felt. These "mirrors" never give advice or try to problem-solve. Their purpose is to help the speaker know they have been held with exquisite attention and care. This Forum practice can now be found in various communities worldwide, such as the Tamera healing village in Portugal, and at events hosted by Network for a New Culture in North America.

The ZEGG Forum is not for everyone, and I've found that its efficacy depends very much on the skills of the facilitators. Having been in the facilitator's chair myself, I know it's a position of tremendous power and requires a vast capacity for space-holding and compassion. To be a witness in a Forum circle also asks a lot of an individual's emotional capacity and empathy. Forum can feel like having empathy on tap for folks who have felt starved of empathy. For others, it might be too much for their nervous system. I've learned that stepping back from group processes that don't support one's nervous system or a healthy relationship to one's self or community is sometimes necessary.

What I learned from my own shared living experiences is that there is tremendous potential for community living to support and nurture resilience, and also, while being in a residential community has many practical benefits, you don't necessarily have to live together. When I have felt part of a community with loving and kind humans, I am grounded and more regulated in my nervous system. Living with others, there was always someone to bounce ideas around with, to share in the joys and lows of the day, and to have a spontaneous cooking party with. In many ways, the platonic roommate relationships were far more enriching than anything I had experienced when I was married and living with my husband, and they have met my needs for social consistency while not being complicated by a sexual or romantic component.

I invite you to consider what kinds of practical relationships you would be open to having. Would you ever want to navigate the dynamics of a large group or communal living situation? Are you happiest when you live solo, and if so, in what ways do you resource your practical quadrant so that you aren't carrying all the practical burdens of life alone?

REFLECTING JOURNALING
Who and What Is Part of Your Practical Quadrant?

Take a moment to think about your practical landscape:

- Who is in your practical quadrant?
- What do you enjoy doing and sharing with others in your practical landscape?
- What do you not enjoy?
- What would you like more of in your practical quadrant?
- Is there anything that you would want less of in your practical quadrant?

13

THE EROTIC QUADRANT

If you live your life orgasmically, your death will also be orgasmic.

—DEBORAH TAJ ANAPOL[1]

Despite what traditional monogamy might think, the erotic quadrant isn't just about sex. Yet whether you are a sexual person, asexual, or find yourself somewhere in between, you're bound to have absorbed some of the culturally dominant stories about what being sexual is supposed to mean. You might have internalized an idea of what "being sexy" looks like and sounds like, and the kind of behaviour it involves. Patriarchal, white supremacist, or colonial ideas about bodies may have influenced your aesthetic attraction to others. These stories may in turn have impacted how you experience your own sense of worthiness. However, these things do not need to define eroticism, and your experience of the erotic does not need to be limited by them.

At its core, the erotic quadrant is about the ineffable essence of who we are. Some may call this spirit; others may refer to it as energy. Our own relationship with the erotic can invite us into openness, curiosity, and non-judgment, in spite of the social messaging that the erotic must be kept private, never talked about, and shamed. Erotic liberation doesn't only mean enjoying sexual freedom or fulfilment, just as sex positivity doesn't mean having sex frequently. Instead, it's about shaking off the limitations that have been placed on how we explore and experience the erotic quadrant, challenging our internalized notions of what attractiveness is, and expanding upon our conceptualization of what sensuality and eroticism can be, beyond just sexual, and diving into exploration of our innate creativity.

When we experience fulfilment in the erotic quadrant, we might feel empowered and free. There can be a sensation of expansiveness, of growing to be greater than the sum of our parts, and a more profound sense of connection to all things. Sometimes we may engage in our erotic quadrant as a strategy for either processing or, in some instances, bypassing intense emotional experiences. When our erotic quadrant is neglected or dismissed, we may experience shame, self-loathing, isolation, and a sense of smallness.

SOMATIC PAUSE
Creative Resourcing

The erotic quadrant is a vulnerable space. It can feel fiery and intense. As you read through this section, notice any strong emotional or physical responses you feel. I invite you to be curious about these.

If the material feels overwhelming at any point, pause and honour that feeling. Don't push yourself to continue until you're feeling ready.

Practice a pause right now by engaging in a creative activity of your choice. This could be music, art, movement, or something else. Explore how the energy of creative inspiration can support your body in moving through any intense, fiery feelings that arise.

Once you can move through any strong sensations and feel grounded and present, you can continue reading.

Many of us carry shame related to our sexuality. Maybe you've experienced shame about enjoying your own sexual pleasure, or you've been afraid to voice an erotic desire. Perhaps you've felt judged for wishing to explore erotic experiences that are non-sexual, such as sensual, artistic, or creative expressions, or to have sexual experiences that forgo genitals or any kind of penetration. The suppression and limitation of erotic exploration is, I believe, one of the great harms in modern Western culture. Given the conflicting messages about sexuality that we receive, developing a relationship with your own erotic quadrant can feel a little intimidating.

Our human ancestors were not so suppressed about sex and sexuality. In ancient Egyptian beliefs, the universe was formed from the swallowed and spat-out semen of the God Atum.[2] In Tantric traditions, sexual energy is seen to be the same as creative energy. Within some branches of Tantra, the goddess Kundalini Shakti, who rests coiled at the base of the spine, is said to govern not just procreation but also the very creation of the universe itself. It is said that every being retains a piece of this creation essence of the universe, and having a relationship with this goddess is believed to support one's spiritual growth. In this cosmology, erotic energy and creative energy are one and the same.

In scientific terms, we're still understanding what an orgasm is and why it happens, but what we do know is that orgasmic potential exists in the nervous system. The stimulation of sensitive tissues within many nerve clusters can support orgasms that move through both our sympathetic nervous system and our parasympathetic nervous system. It is the same nervous system communication energy that sparks in the brain when inspiration strikes. Whether you call it Kundalini Shakti or vital nervous system energy, it allows us to experience pleasure in so many more ways than sex alone.

We can make our life orgasmic through connecting with pleasure in every sensation. Pleasure doesn't have to be solely an experience for those sensitive clusters of nerves around our genitals. Our nervous system is stimulated through all our senses, and the sensory nerves all across our body hold the potential to support arousal.

If you are someone who struggles to feel at ease in erotic connections, even with yourself, I want you to know that you are not alone. Not everyone has an erotic quadrant that centres on their sexuality, and even for those that do, sex can be an experience that carries with it complex memories, difficult feelings, fear of unwanted consequences such as unplanned pregnancy and STIs, and so much more. Know that when we talk about the erotic here, we are not limiting this to sex: The erotic includes our creativity, our sensual pleasure, and whatever means we have to support us in connecting to that which is greater than ourselves. We might even consider a different relationship to orgasm: that orgasmicness isn't just about a sexual climax but might actually be about connecting with that ineffable essence of who we, and our partners, are.

Expectations of the Erotic Quadrant

You may have experienced the pull to forge lifelong partnerships with someone after a significant sexual encounter and then discovered that good sex wasn't the most stable foundation for relationships after all. Let's be clear: Satisfying and fulfilling sexual relations are important to many people, but when we prioritize them over the social, emotional, and practical connections in our lives, we might find ourselves falling into the trap of expecting sexual intimacy to lead us into other dimensions of intimacy too—and that's not necessarily the case.

Patriarchal monogamy would have us believe that the value of relationships is directed by our sexual or procreative activities. It used to be that a Christian marriage could be annulled if it failed to produce an heir, and lack of a sexual relationship is still considered by many legal systems as reasonable grounds for divorce.

Cultural stories around the importance of sexuality are tied to our internalized notions of what it means to be a good partner. Stories like: As long as you perform sex, then you're fulfilling your duties, and as long as your partner performs sex with you, then you have no reason to want for anything else.

And yet, at the same time, we live today in a quandary of polarizing attitudes to and mixed messages about sex in the West. Religious purity culture exists right alongside the glorification of sexuality in the media, and we can see the tensions of this come to the forefront in the politicization of issues related to sexuality and reproductive freedoms. Men may experience being celebrated for sexual prowess, while women who claim their sexual agency are labelled as sluts—and non-binary, trans, and gender-nonconforming folks are portrayed by conservatives as perverse and dangerous.

A double standard about sexuality exists: We are expected to be sexually alluring in our bodies, and we celebrate those who have alluring bodies by elevating their social status, and yet we are simultaneously expected to be chaste, fidelitous, and private about our sexuality. Furthermore, sexiness is equated with youthfulness and vigour, fuelling industries that cater to body modifications that promise to youthen a person's appearance. In Western culture, cis women's bodies are often considered sexier if they have small waists and hairless bodies, whereas cis men may face pressure to achieve unrealistic degrees of musculature to demonstrate hyper-masculinization. Trans people who choose to transition may experience pressure to conform to these expectations. And achieving this youthful allure costs money, meaning that sexiness becomes a symbol of privilege—and in turn, those who do not meet the social expectations of youthful allure are often seen as being less worthy. Anything and anyone who differs from culturally accepted norms faces shame, ostracization, and potential violence.

The openness of sexuality that we experience in modern times is a fairly recent development, and in much of the world, it is still considered inappropriate for men and women alike to expose too much of their bodies in public. Sex education, if it exists at all, is often limited, and still frequently based on abstinence rather than on understanding biology and pleasure. Sometimes there is just straight-up misinformation.

Perhaps in a world without birth control and without medicines to treat STIs, fear of sexuality was a form of preservation of community and population control. Maybe it helped with managing limited resources. But today, ample access to STI treatments and management of diseases once thought to be unsurvivable, such as HIV, as well as improved access to birth control and improved social advocacy— whether that education is grass roots–based or at an institutional level—means we no longer have to remain in a paradigm where sexuality, sensuality, and eroticism are considered taboo.

In mono-normativity, the practical and erotic quadrants are often conflated: A great sexual or sensual experience with someone can compel us to bring them deeper into the practical aspects of our lives. Stepping onto the relationship escalator following a fun sexual experience may make sense for some, but when we're consciously working on undoing unhealthy relationship scripts, it's prudent to pause and examine what we really want to be experiencing in these areas.

Furthermore, when sex is held as the primary measure of a relationship's health and success, any partner in that relationship may feel pressure to perform sexually as a strategy for maintaining the relationship—and that if they stop being sexual, the relationship will end. This can lead to sex feeling more performative rather than embodied, and as a result, it might feel less connected and less enjoyable for those involved. And a sexual dynamic that is purely performative might indicate that one or more partners have a nervous system teetering between fawn and freeze.

REFLECTIVE JOURNALING
What Does Sex Mean to You?

What significance have you put on needing a sexual relationship with someone you're romantic with?

Do you feel pressure to cultivate a particular erotic persona because of your gender, age, appearance, ethnicity, or relationship status?

Have you ever seen sexual relationships as needing to be transactional? For example, "My partner did something nice for me, so I need to do something nice for them in return."

Have you found yourself trying to become more deeply enmeshed in the emotional, social, and practical aspects of life with someone you were very incompatible with in those areas—but the sex was incredible?

What have the most satisfying sexual or sensual relationships looked like for you?

What kinds of non-sexual erotic experiences have brought you joy, and what has detracted from those experiences of joy?

Obstacles in the Erotic Quadrant

Not everyone experiences erotic connection as being pleasurable. Many centuries of patriarchy, sexual stigma, masturbation shaming, and lack of sexual education mean that a pleasurable sexual experience is, for many, the exception and not the norm. In modern times, there are some who have sought to harness the allure of eroticism as a means to control others, usually resulting in harm and abuse. Add to this the pressure we may feel to perform a sexual act not out of pleasure but as a strategy: for procreation, to affirm a relationship, to soothe a partner, or to feel self-worth.

While sex is important for many, incredible sexual chemistry doesn't necessarily translate to a strong emotional relationship, nor does it guarantee a lifelong one, and a lack of sexual desire doesn't mean that all is doomed. Sex can often be used to Band-Aid emotional struggles, differences in beliefs, mental health challenges, and as an often effective strategy to diffuse tensions instead of directly addressing them, like make-up sex, which isn't always the healthiest approach. We may fall into believing our sexiness and the sexual merit of our partners is determined by things like stamina and insatiability. Fixating on the erotic might obscure other ways in which a relationship is struggling or where there is incompatibility.

We may be quick to conclude that an enjoyable erotic encounter is a sure sign of a new lifelong partnership, but what if it is only an indicator of erotic compatibility? We may, through lack of knowing alternatives, believe in stories about sex that erase queer sexualities, such as "Men are always sexual pursuers," and "Women are the gatekeepers of sex." Even when we come to understand the importance of consent, we may engage with it more as permission-seeking than collaboration. Many of us find the erotic quadrant to be the most vulnerable space to build connections, and the obstacles we face include:

- terror, hesitation, and self-protection from past experiences where body, psyche, or heart have not been honoured, respected, or held with care
- religious doctrine-based shame or fear, for example, purity culture
- erotic armouring: self-protective responses that settle in the body and nervous system and block erotic arousal and joy, which can sometimes be interpreted by a partner as sexual disinterest, or even erotic abandonment

In addition to these, any kind of life stress can pull us away from our connection to the erotic.

I want to say more about the role of purity culture. It is a product of a desire for control of pleasure as a means to control humans. I didn't grow up anywhere near the evangelical purity cults of the United States, but I've experienced similar iterations of purity culture: suppression of creative expression, shaming of inherent sexuality, fear rhetoric about intermingling between genders and segregated seating areas, defunding of the arts, the repression of sex and intimacy education. Unpacking sexual shame is for many a strong motivator for exploring non-monogamy, and cultivating daily pleasure and sensuality can nurture the agency, personal choice, and joy that purity culture has prohibited.

Queering the Erotic Quadrant

The erotic is a measure between the beginnings of our sense of self and the chaos of our strongest feelings.

—AUDRE LORDE, "USES OF THE EROTIC"

To queer our experience of the erotic can mean to explore our sensuality, our creativity, or even our spirituality. It might include holding curiosity about sex that decenters genital penetration or virile performance and ejaculatory orgasms. It may challenge us on our own internalized ideas of what embodying eroticism and sensuality looks like or feels like, and may even shift the gaze through which we notice our attraction to others. It might mean an approach to erotic connection that's a lot less performative and a lot more collaborative.

Queering the erotic quadrant is a practice of actively choosing pleasure as a radical act of agency, and it is a rebellion against cultures that seek to shame and control pleasure. As we orient to pleasure that inspires and uplifts, and that is not limited to sexual intimacy, we may find an enhanced experience of orgasmic delight in all aspects of our lives.

In her essay "Uses of the Erotic," Audre Lorde describes the erotic as "a resource within each of us that lies in a deeply female and spiritual plane, firmly rooted in the power of our unexpressed or unrecognized feeling." She goes on to define it as "the sensual—those physical, emotional, and psychic expressions of what is deepest and strongest and richest within each of us, being shared: the passions of love, in its deepest meanings," and as such a bridge to the spiritual.[3]

Whereas organized religion has often politicized and policed human sexuality, I hold that eroticism as spirituality has the potential to liberate us from social binds and oppression, and support us in reclaiming an experience of embodiment. That is, we can aspire to be engaged and integrated with the sensations of our nervous systems and whole bodies as well as connected to that which is beyond ourselves—be that other people, nature, or unseen energies and forces in the universe.

Cultivating a culture of erotic pleasure doesn't have to mean hedonism or escaping into sensory excess. It can be about feeding our senses and becoming more attuned to and aware of our bodies, our minds, our hearts, our spirits. It can be about paying attention to our desires and listening to the whispers of our souls' yearnings for delight, sharing joy with others, and imbibing the creative abundance that others share with us. It might also be about slowing down and savouring each loving relationship and every moment of bliss.

Erotic Awareness

Erotic awareness can begin with knowing what awakens our own senses and brings us pleasure. It may include expanding our awareness of what can be pleasurable for others, such as listening to different music, visiting an art gallery, or learning about traditional practices for pleasure and creativity from other cultures. You might expand your erotic awareness when it comes to sex and sexuality through watching queer pornography. You might attend public sexuality-related events such as swingers clubs, kink nights, or even conferences that showcase sex toys, bondage equipment, and educational workshops. Even just paying a visit to a sex-toy store and asking the sales associate for information about anything there you do not understand can help enhance your appreciation for the vastness of possibilities that the erotic quadrant can hold when it comes to sexuality.

You can also expand your erotic self-awareness through art and creativity: going to the theatre, visiting art exhibits, listening to different types of music, trying new kinds of cuisine. Exposure to the creativity of others can spark our own erotic selves in fascinating ways, opening the doors to new paths for creative exploration.

When it comes to exploring your erotic awareness of others, you might think about what it is you attune to when you first notice an attraction. Perhaps there are subtle hints of the scent of someone's pheromones, a widening of the iris in their eyes, a flushing of skin, or even a change in the pace, timbre, or pitch of their voice that generates an arousal response within you.

Erotic Safety

Just as enjoying art doesn't make one an artist, arousal alone doesn't mean circumstances are ready for intimate contact. We first have to establish erotic safety. In the erotic quadrant, safety is supported when we are able to trust that our vulnerability will be held and honoured. This isn't just the vulnerability of being naked, though it might include that; it's also about finding greater capacity in our own nervous system to feel safe enough to expand our internal, felt sensation through-out our being.

To attune to all the sensations we experience at once may sound like an over-whelming prospect. It's not something we often do, and if we hold any experi-ences of physical dysphoria, physical pain, or have been shamed about our bodies, it may not be easy to trust that it's safe to explore all these sensations. This is true of both creativity and sensuality. Masterpieces are never rushed.

Erotic safety needs to be explored gently; rushing through can lead to injury, either physical or somatic. We may feel the urge to hurry through a sexual situ-ation and perform as a safe erotic space for a partner as part of an unconscious strategy to mask our anxiety about being seen. This might indicate a state of high stimulation in our nervous system that leads us towards a fawn response.

In erotic safety, we can let go of how others may judge or shame us. The threat of rejection or ostracization is gone, and our erotic self shines. We may feel safe to share our creative expressions, and we may feel safe to share a sexual experience. This liberation from shame is essential in our sexuality since the ner-vous system plays such an important role in how we access pleasure. This also applies to our creative self-expression. When we feel safe for our art and creative expressions to be witnessed, we may grow more open to experiences of receiv-ing and pleasure.

Erotic safety can look like talking about our sensuality, establishing boundaries and a foundation for collaborative consent, and figuring out the proverbial sandbox that we will co-create in. It might also look like inviting a friend to read a poem you've written or take the form of attending a spiritual ritual that opens you up to a more personal connection, whatever "spirit" means to you. Erotic safety can feel like a softening in the nervous system, and it can beautifully ease us toward erotic intimacy.

My Journey Back to Erotic Safety

I want to share a personal story about my journey to recover from a sexual assault. I won't be talking about the details of what happened during the assault itself, but rather I'll focus on what happened to my experience of sex and eroticism afterwards.

In the early 2010s I was experiencing a sexual liberation I'd never dreamed possible. It wasn't easy being demisexual, having unaddressed trauma from past relationships, and taking my time to feel into a sexual connection. But in the midst of great sexual joy, I experienced an intimate violation. I was so in shock after this experience that for a time I blocked it from my conscious memory. Instead I became haunted by nightmares and flashbacks, particularly when I was having sex with my partners. I even started to dissociate the moment intimacy was initiated. Sometimes I would fake it (a fawn response), pretending to enjoy myself because I didn't want to disappoint anyone.

Over time, I noticed that just the mention of sexual activity would trigger anger and fear in my body. I felt an irrepressible impulse to escape, yet I couldn't. Unable to flee the resurfacing memories of the assault, I began to escape through anxiety medication and alcohol—but that didn't help. Safety felt elusive, and I constantly feared another attack. I didn't realize it at the time, but looking back, I can see that trying to force myself to be sexually engaged when I hadn't addressed the trauma yet was actually retraumatizing me. The relationships I had began to struggle. Partners either lost interest when I became less sexually available, or they struggled to understand what I was experiencing—probably because I was struggling to understand it myself.

Relief finally came when I started dating someone who was asexual. With no pressure to be sexually engaged for the sake of the relationship, I got to experience, for the first time, what it was like to grow a deep connection without any script. Dating them gave me permission not to have to push myself somewhere I wasn't ready to go, which helped me slow down in my other relationships too. To this day, they remain someone I share deep love with.

Around this time, I had my first experience of a sensory deprivation float. Floating in the tank's Epsom salt–rich water, my body felt safe for the first time since the violation. I began to feel like recovery of my eroticism might be possible. I continued going to sex parties and orgies, with a self-agreement that my underwear would stay on. I also started going to therapy and doing Somatic Experiencing, healing on many fronts. Through exploring a mix of kink and spending time with partners who could honour my pace, I started to reclaim some sexual agency.

I wanted to grow a more enriched experience of my erotic quadrant, and began to explore my sensuality and creativity through dance and art. I started dancing weekly and eventually learned how to DJ, offering ecstatic dance sessions. My synesthesia helped me collage sounds together, which became a healing expression of my erotic self. In the embrace of the bass beats, I could feel an expansive sense of safety moving through my whole being.

Almost a decade later, and after years of somatic work in my erotic quadrant, I had an opportunity to explore a sexual activity that I'd avoided for a long time because it reminded me of the ways my body's agency hadn't been respected in the past. With a very different relationship to my own eroticism, I felt fully and safely embodied in my sexuality. I was able to touch that ineffable essence of my own self and share it without fear. Parts that had felt disconnected for years began to come online again, and I was able to once more engage in my erotic quadrant with courage and joy. Over the months that followed, I discovered an increased capacity to experience confidence in my sensuality and even in my non-erotic creative expressions.

Erotic Intimacy

For all the emphasis that pop culture puts on sexuality in our relationships, we often overlook the importance of an experience of intimacy in our eroticism. An erotically intimate experience could be hours of sensual lovemaking, but it can also be an enticing and exhilarating kink scene with a play partner that never involves genital contact, or it might be enjoying a hot tub together under the stars.

Erotic intimacy arises from mutually enjoyable experiences of pleasure that we engage in together. This might include cooking a meal, painting art together, massaging one another, or co-creating in any form. There is a reciprocity to this: Having built a foundation for collaborative consent in erotic safety, we can now explore this collaborative energy through many means of co-creation.

Think of the creative eroticism of musicians playing together, or singers in a choir creating harmony. If you are musically inclined, you may have experienced this firsthand, but even if you haven't been the person co-creating music, you have probably witnessed it. There is a sense of connection: The musicians know their parts through practice, refining their musicianship skills and rehearsing with other musicians. In a truly great musical performance, the musicians may seem to be moving together. Indeed, one of the most mesmerising aspects of orchestras is their ability to move as one.

Haylee's Story
From Performative to Embodied

Haylee is a trans grey-ace lesbian in her late thirties who has been actively polyamorous for almost two decades. With a background in theatre and music, throughout her twenties she found herself at odds with her relationship to her sexuality and to the erotic quadrant.

At the time Haylee was still presenting to the world as a man, and as a man she was considered aesthetically handsome and attractive, receiving a lot of attention from straight and bisexual women. But as an asexual person, sex felt like a utilitarian thing that had to be performed. She enjoyed it, but only as an act of creation, and as someone with a background in the arts, was no stranger to putting on a convincing and enjoyable performance. But she found that many of her partners didn't quite know how to engage with her and felt that they had to centre her gratification. But Haylee didn't have sexual desires seeking to be met, and sex wasn't how she tapped into her creative flow.

At a time when most of her peers were hyper-sexual, Haylee found her erotic joy in the arts because it satisfied her need for creation and self-expression. Actively polyamorous, she would put on a sexual performance for her partners, only to find that they were left wanting more—something more she couldn't authentically give. Sex for Haylee was a practical experience.

During the COVID-19 pandemic, she began her transition and started to date lesbians. She found it liberating to be with partners who had no expectation of a set end point to sex (a climax) and to have sexual experiences where pleasure was being co-created rather than her pleasure being centred. It was a time of sexual awakening: sex as an act of shared creation, sex that would be different depending on who was part of it, what their bodies wanted or needed, and what kind of aftercare was desired. Even though she still felt aligned with grey asexuality and not necessarily motivated by sex right away, she found she could access responsive desire through being with partners who deeply respected and understood that she was never going to be the instigator and that she wasn't someone who would want to have sex daily.

It's like my sexuality has been decommodified. My pleasure today comes from intimate stimulation: mind, heart. . . . Since my transition, my experience of the erotic has felt more natural and attuned rather than transactional . . . and maybe something about novelty. Self-understanding has created newness out of something familiar. It's like reading a really well-written book the second time through, when you're catching all the foreshadowing, and you're seeing the seeds of the character's triumph or downfall from the way that they're behaving in the beginning of the book. The veil lifts and you're experiencing the same thing with a different perspective. Exploring the familiar with a new perspective gives me pleasure.

As she's made her journey through transition, Haylee has been able to connect to her own authenticity, and in so doing has found more authentic ways of engaging in the erotic. Haylee recognizes that for her, this shift in her relationship with the erotic began with her transition. Before that, she had felt bound by the social expectations of performing masculinity and all the patriarchal sexual narratives included under that umbrella. She holds that men don't necessarily need to trans their gender to divest from patriarchy and access the erotic in a new way, but it was the path that was right for her. As long as she was performing masculinity, which wasn't who she ever was, she was unable to connect to that ineffable essence that eroticism offers.

Erotic Relationship

Moving from erotic intimacy into erotic Relationship requires so much trust. In the process of crossing that threshold, we must erotically disentangle ourselves from the fantasies we hold that may be rooted in colonial and white supremacist narratives. We have to learn to let go of the assumptions about what eroticism should look like, feel like, or behave like and come into the deep presence of sharing an erotic journey together.

An erotic self-relationship might be an erotic or spiritual discipline: practices of creative self-expression that we engage with for ourselves and seek to enhance our skills with. Within this, there are practical arts like cooking, sewing, graphic design, and writing as well as private art, like poetry or drawing, that we may never share publicly, or only with a few select friends.

Whereas intimacy brings union, erotic Relationship allows for spiritual and creative differentiation and dynamism. The erotic stagnancy experienced by couples who have been long monogamous may find relief through the expansion of the erotic quadrant, whether through new sexual connections or via creative endeavours, and potentially even deepen the erotic relationship that they already share.

I am reminded of the words of a wise teacher: To be a musician, it is not enough to be a lover of music; you must serve music. I expand this and invite you to ask, if you wish to grow a luscious erotic quadrant, how is it that you can serve, support, honour, and enrich the erotic, creative, and orgasmic experiences of everyone who wants to join you there?

An erotic Relationship is playful, easy, dynamic, and deeply satisfying. It does not have to centre around sex, but it can absolutely include it. The experience of collaborative co-creation can find expression through art, shared projects, and sensory adventures, and the orgasmic quality of connection is sustained over the course of time. You may experience many different kinds of erotic Relationships during your life.

REFLECTIVE JOURNALING:
Who and What Is Part of Your Erotic Quadrant?

Take a moment to think about your erotic landscape:

- Who is in your erotic quadrant?
- What do you enjoy doing and sharing with others in your erotic landscape?
- What do you not enjoy?
- What would you like more of in your erotic quadrant?
- Is there anything that you would want less of in your erotic quadrant?

PART 2 SUMMARY

In this section, we've discussed the challenges we face when we move away from culturally ingrained relationship norms and considered how the philosophies and practices of **anarchy** and **queerness** might support us.

As an alternative to the mono-normative relationship escalator, we have the **relationship landscape,** which consists of four **quadrants: emotional, social, practical,** and **erotic.** Similarities between this four-quadrant framework and other cultural, spiritual, and somatic practices, both ancient and modern, can be found.

We've also looked at the **layers of relating,** which can reflect the depth we experience within our relationships. We've explored in more detail what each quadrant can hold within the layers of relating, building a three-dimensional model of the relationship landscape that can help us better understand our individual **relationship ecology.**

You may find it helpful to look back and reflect on the journaling activities and notice if there is one or more quadrants that stand out to you as being more important to you in your landscape today.

How

Having a map to help you understand and situate yourself in your relationship landscape is only the start of the work of Radical Relating. In this third section we explore how to relate in this ecology, including key skills to support you in your journey of shaking off mono-normativity and embracing a post-monogamous paradigm. We focus on four key themes:

- relationship to self
- relationship to others
- disconnection from self
- disconnection from others

We will consider the joy of **letting go of perfectionism** and explore **self-partnership, boundaries, agreements, consent, conflict intimacy, dissociation, and compersion.** Each of these topics could be a book unto itself, and what I present here is just an introduction. It should not be taken as a complete thesis on each topic.

Within each chapter you will find practical guides and exercises you can do solo or with loved ones. You may want to bookmark the activities in each chapter to have on hand when you're navigating specific challenges in your relationships. These activities can help with letting go of our inner perfectionist, cultivating self-partnership, understanding the dynamics of multi-partner relationships, creating relationship agreements, working with shame, and courageous communication.

14

EMBRACE THE MESS

Perfectionism is the conditioned belief and attitude that we can be perfect based on a standard or set of rules that we did not create and that we are led to believe will prove our value. Perfectionism is the conditioned belief and attitude that we can determine whether others are showing up as perfect and demand or expect that they do so. . . . As long as we are striving to be perfect according to someone else's rules, we have less energy and attention to question those rules and to remember what is truly important.

—TEMA OKUN[1]

While the practices in this book are designed to be gentle, it is important to recognize that the journey of post-monogamous relating can be confronting. It asks us to become more aware of what's happening in our bodies, minds, hearts, and spirits, which can potentially bring awareness of traumas, buried memories, and tender parts of our psyche that we haven't touched in many years. In addition to this, we're learning new skills that may feel clumsy at first. It can all feel a bit messy—and I want you to know that that is okay. Messy doesn't necessarily equate to dysfunction in relationships.

Here's the thing: Perfectionism is not embodied, despite white supremacy culture trying to convince us otherwise. Perfectionism fuels division and the disruption of relationships because it implies that some people are worthy and others are unworthy. Breaking free of perfectionism invites us to hold compassion and see the messy, and sometimes harmful, behaviours of others not as personal failings but rather as consequences of systemic issues and being immersed in cultures that perpetuate harm and separation.

I felt like I had failed so badly at monogamy that when I arrived in polyamory, I was terrified of doing something wrong. The fear of messing up was overwhelming, and when I turned to discussion groups in search of a compassionate community, I discovered so much rhetoric focused on what the "one true way" to be polyamorous was. I felt like there was no room for mistakes, and I became afraid of talking about my struggles. Thankfully, the conversation has shifted in the decade since then, and polyamorous spaces tend to be more forgiving and compassionate. But within the heat of things, and the overwhelm of new relationship experiences, hurt feelings are still conflated with harm, internal messiness leads to external ostracization, individual trauma might be pathologized, and social rejection abounds.

Nobody does relationships—monogamous, polyamorous, or otherwise—perfectly, though some might like to think that they do. The idea that there's one true way to do things comes straight out of the patriarchal colonial handbook and white supremacy culture, holding humans to impossible standards of perfection and embracing black-and-white thinking that has no room for nuance or compassion. To be liberated from these internalized limiting and traumatic cultural scripts, we must cultivate compassion for our messiness and seek repair rather than retribution.

I used to think that repair and healing were things I had to do independently of others. I thought I had to be tough. I thought that healing my heart meant no longer feeling so profoundly affected by emotions. Instead, I discovered that healing is a journey best taken with a community of loving support. There's only so much we can heal, and integrate the wounds from relationships, if we avoid new ones. I learned that healing one's heart means we feel so much more, so much more profoundly, and that feeling so much so deeply doesn't have to be scary.

Many of us can think we've messed up in our past relationships and feel terrified of doing something wrong, especially if monogamy hasn't worked out for us. And so we are keen to be ethical, fair, honest, and respectful in how we conduct ourselves. We may seek out podcasts, books, blogs, social accounts, influencers, coaches, and more, hoping they will guide us to our vision of relationship perfection. That internal voice of perfectionism fears that acknowledging any messiness might imply that we're just not cut out for alternative ways of relating, or would validate the people who cautioned us against questioning the status quo. Some may feel pressure internally, or externally from others, to prove that they are as or more competent than their peers who have stuck to the nuclear family.

Remember that the unfamiliar often feels unsafe to the nervous system, which interprets familiar patterns, even unhealthy ones, as safe. As we step into new relationship dynamics, our nervous system may trigger self-protection responses, which can be compounded by a fear of loss. Alongside this is the fear that these changes won't satisfy, creating concern that we may have disrupted our lives in pursuit of something that might not actually fulfil us. Our perfectionism can create a fear of messing up, making us wary of harming partners or falling short of someone else's standards, which may prevent us from openly addressing and learning from our mistakes.

Perfectionism, and the pressure to get it right, can feel like a straitjacket when it comes to our relationships. For some it's like a litany. When we're succeeding, it feels ecstatic and joyful, but when we fail or fall short, that litany turns into a dirge, a funeral march that may feel like it condemns how we show up in partnerships. Rather than treating ourselves with kindness, compassion, and leading with humility, our own internalized sense of what being a perfect partner means, and the pressure to achieve and maintain that, can sometimes contain such lofty and perfectionist ideals that it leads us to being hard on ourselves, and even impatient with others. It might also make it hard for us to own it when we make a mess of a situation, making repairing trust much harder.

This isn't to say that people who deliberately behave in harmful ways get a pass. Accountability is always important for healthy long-term relationships, and it requires humility, empathy, and a willingness to do the hard work of repair. We must all learn to undo our internalized notions of perfectionism to create the tender space needed for meaningful accountability.

If we feel overwhelmed by the pressure of our inner perfectionist, this can manifest in our relationships as anxiety or even panic. It may be accompanied by the urge to seek reassurance from partners, or it may look like completely shutting down and avoiding them. This experience can be less overwhelming as we become more familiar with how our inner perfectionist shows up and the many facets perfectionism can take. The more we grow a relationship with our inner perfectionist, the easier it becomes to feel like it has less hold on us.

When we embrace vulnerability, the perfectionist in us melts. I invite you to find the perfection in the imperfection and rest in the knowledge that none of us has all the answers. This sense of humility and vulnerability offers us a perfectly imperfect way to have relationships because it permits us to show up as our genuine, imperfect selves and maybe even be loved for who we are in the moment rather than an impossible ideal we desperately try to become.

REFLECTIVE JOURNALING
Your Litany of Good Partnership

What do you think it takes to be a good partner? What are the things you've been told by others—parents, elders, community leaders, influencers, peers, and even your partners—that constitute a good partner's characteristics and behaviours?

Consider: How do you measure yourself against these expectations? Is there a spectrum to how you measure yourself, or is it an all-or-nothing situation?

Are there aspects of this litany of good partnership that, when you've fallen short, have made you feel shame or disgust at yourself, or that you have been hard on yourself about?

Working with Perfectionism

If we've had many struggles in life, or lived with systemic oppression or intimate abuse, we might feel used to almost always being in a state of panic or anxiety. We might feel like we do have capacity to engage with our relationships amid anxiety, even when we don't. Our inner perfectionist may hold us back from being able to admit to ourselves when we are struggling.

Our inner perfectionist can also show up as minimizing discomforts about other relationships our partners have, or specific dynamics in our relationship landscape. We mistake our agreeableness and our capacity for people-pleasing as an expression of love. We may even pride ourselves on being self-sacrificing or overly generous with our partners and experience an enhanced sense of self-worth the more accommodating we are.

We explore this more in the coming chapters, but remember that people-pleasing is almost always a self-protective or self-preservation response. Having a self-protective response doesn't mean the relationship or partner isn't safe, although that is certainly a possibility. More often it's a reflection of feeling overwhelmed. It arises from anxiety about abandonment or harm and is often an indicator that we aren't feeling safe, that we aren't fully grounded in our self-relationship, or that our nervous system is not as regulated as it could be.

When we ignore, deny, or dismiss our fears, they have more control over us. However, when we acknowledge them and talk about them with our partners, peers, therapists, and mentors, we learn more about them, and the fears become less scary. When we can relate to our fears, actively seeking to understand what lies at their root and explore ways of soothing and assuaging them, they have less influence in our intimate relationships. Over time, fear holds less grip.

Instead of trying to have a tidy, perfect relationship landscape, which can leave us pretzelling our way through minefields of emotions guarded by rigid rules and fear of making mistakes that might hurt others, we might benefit from cultivating a practice of loving the messes when they happen: holding compassion for everyone's experience, taking responsibility for how we impact others, and learning how to navigate the pathways of repair and maintenance of deep, loving connections.

Messy situations in non-monogamy can sometimes benefit from external support: community, elders, and helping professionals like counsellors and coaches. They can be turned into incredible opportunities for growth, understanding, and transformation within the relationship. And that is infinitely healthier than constructing complex rules and agreements aimed at some imaginary idea of perfection of polyamory.

If you notice yourself experiencing any distress around this, and feeling like you're failing to live up to your own standards of perfection, I invite you to note it in your journal. Ask yourself: Is this something I can delve deeper into now? It is important not to push yourself into exploring something you don't feel ready or resourced to dive into. Doing so can run the risk of overwhelming the nervous system. It is okay to skip any activities in this section if they don't resonate with you or don't feel accessible right now.

A truly radical relationship is one in which there is space to be messy and take responsibility for one's own mess without fear of punishment, abandonment, or reprisals.

15

SELF-RELATIONSHIP

Caring for myself is not self-indulgence, it is self preservation, and that is an act of political warfare.

—AUDRE LORDE[1]

In this chapter, we explore what it means to be in a loving and caring relationship with ourselves and how this creates a foundation for loving and supportive relationships with others. We also explore what self-partnership entails and the critical work of understanding our core values, needs, and boundaries as well as creating self-agreements.

This is an invitation to take everything that helps you in friendships and partnerships and apply it to yourself—including honouring your capacity for being with others, identifying your core values, and creating direction and vision for yourself. Everyone's relationship with themselves will be unique, which means there's no single pathway. You get to discover what works for you.

Mono-normativity suggests that loving someone means becoming one with your person. To resist the mythology of "one true love" and self-sacrifice as a love language, we have to get rooted in ourselves. This work invites us to mature not just emotionally but somatically. That is to say, we invite our nervous system into a dramatically different experience of safe and healthy relating—starting with feeling at home in our own bodies.

We are multifaceted creatures filled with desires, longings, aversions, preferences, dreams, and possibilities. Your experience of self may not be singular, and you might have many different versions of yourself, with aspects that come forward for specific occasions, for example, your work persona, or you may notice subtle shifts depending on whose company you are in, such as with different partners. Self-relating can deepen our understanding of all the ways we show up.

Self-relationship doesn't mean being alone or refusing connection with others. Rather, it's a personal practice that supports our nervous system in growing greater capacity for connection and relationships. As we get better at knowing, understanding, and honouring ourselves, we naturally increase our capacity for knowing, understanding, and honouring others.

Self-relationship also doesn't mean dominating and controlling others. The urge to control, manipulate, or manage others can come from not feeling safe enough, and sometimes from a sense of not feeling sufficient within ourselves. Bulldozing the boundaries of others, trying to manage your partners, or even laying down stern ultimatums for loved ones can all be self-protective and self-defensive responses to feeling powerless. If you've found that you lean more towards taking up more space, I invite you to consider how nourishing your self-relationship may support you in cultivating an internal sense of safety and security that frees you from the impulse to seek control over situations and power over others.

When I was fresh out of my marriage and working on reclaiming my agency, committing to being in a primary relationship with myself—being self-primaried—was a liberating choice. I knew I wasn't looking for a new spouse, and fostering intentional commitments (including self-agreements, which we look at in this chapter) helped me to create a secure base within myself from which I could enjoy relationships without the stress or anxiety of seeking a relationship escalator.

Self-Relating Is Radical

To love ourselves as we are, instead of shaming ourselves for failing to live up to some impossible privilege-ridden standard set by patriarchy and colonialism, is radical. When we approach self-relationship as a practice of countering the external messages given to us by patriarchal, colonial, and other culturally oppressive practices, it becomes a practice of internal anti-oppression: a tool against the dominant cultural narratives that limit and undermine worthiness. As we liberate ourselves internally, we also liberate our relationship with others from these oppressive narratives. I invite you to consider how healthy self-relationships create more space for nourishing relationships, and even community, to flourish.

REFLECTIVE JOURNALING
Taking Up Space

In what ways have you made yourself small in relationships, in workplaces, in family, in your life?

In what circumstances do you feel you have to make yourself bigger? Are there situations where it feels easy to take up space?

Do you ever notice yourself taking up space in a way that others pull away from you?

Are you ever fearful of taking up too much space?

Is there a way of showing up in your relationships, workplaces, family, and friendships that you aspire to?

Here are some key practices to explore as you engage in self-relating, which we go through in more detail through the rest of this chapter:

- knowing yourself
  - identifying your values and living in integrity with them
  - identifying and expressing your needs and desires
- honouring yourself
  - identifying and embodying your boundaries
  - understanding and honouring your capacity
- actively loving yourself
  - taking up space
  - self love through asserting and caring for your needs
  - respecting yourself through self agreements

Knowing Yourself: Identifying Your Values

Many of us were taught that fidelity, pleasing our partner, and staying together at all costs are key values in relationships. However, in a post-monogamous paradigm, other values such as honesty, collaboration, authenticity, agency, pleasure, family, diversity, and inclusion may become more relevant. Your values also extend to your relationship with the living world, animals, the environment, and even the dead. These values shape how we handle conflict, embrace new friends, respond to injustice, and set priorities as our needs change. Being clear on your values helps guide your choices, free from limiting narratives or societal expectations.

REFLECTIVE JOURNALING
Identifying Your Values

Consider the following questions:

- What matters to you?
- Are there religious or spiritual beliefs that have informed your personal sense of morals and ethics?

- Are there particular political or social movements, ideologies, or leaders that inspire you?
- What rights would you defend if someone tried to take them away? Does that include rights that don't directly impact you?
- How do you decide who to include in your life, and who to exclude?

As you contemplate your answers, are there particular themes that you see emerging? What are the top three or four values?

Practice articulating these verbally or in writing and sharing them with others. Notice how it feels to share them.

Knowing Yourself: Needs and Desires

Knowing what you need, and how you desire to fulfil those needs, is core to knowing yourself.

Needs are essential and include physical (food, shelter, touch), social (community, connection), emotional (love, care), and spiritual (purpose, meaning). When our core needs are met, we have more capacity for relationships. Conversely, unmet needs can make it challenging to engage with others, like how hard it is to focus when you're hungry and tired compared to when you're rested and nourished.

Desires, on the other hand, are the preferred strategies we have in mind for meeting our needs. For example, wanting dark chocolate isn't a need, but the underlying need might be physical (a sugar craving) or emotional (comfort). If chocolate isn't available, you might find an alternative like candy or tea to meet that need. We can sometimes fixate on specific strategies and feel frustrated when they aren't available, like craving only dark chocolate and believing nothing else will suffice.

Understanding the difference between your needs and your desires—the strategies you use to meet your needs—can help you explore more possibilities for creating meaningful connections in your relationships.

Try this Relational Toolkit activity, which I call the Desire Dive. It's inspired by Nonviolent Communication, as created by Marshall Rosenberg.[2] I've adapted it to support my endlessly inquisitive mind, and I love using it to identify my core needs and find alternative strategies for meeting them.

RELATIONAL TOOLKIT

Desire Dive Exercise

On a piece of paper or in your journal, write down one thing you want.

I WANT . . .
For example, "I want dark chocolate."
Ask yourself, Why do I want that thing? What need is it meeting? Maybe you are craving sexual pleasure, or you need a reprieve from stress, or you are tired of cooking at home and want to be cared for. Write down whatever comes to mind.

BECAUSE . . .
"I want dark chocolate because I am tired."
Then dig! Why does that reason matter? When you have obtained this thing or experience in the past, how has it affected or changed you?

WHEN I GET THIS . . .
"I want dark chocolate because I'm tired, and having a piece gives me a boost to get through the rest of my day."
Dig deeper. What would happen if you don't get this need met? How might you feel? This gives us clues to deeper unmet needs. Keep engaging with the inquiry, until you have gone as deep as you feel you can go.
"If I don't get this dark chocolate, I might feel tired, or sad, and I might have a harder time being patient with my kids before dinner."

THEREFORE I NEED . . .
"I need something to help me stay kind and focused until dinner."
Once we identify the core needs driving us, so many more possibilities of strategies and desires open up. Brainstorm some other actions that could meet your newly discovered core needs, and as you brainstorm, consider who you could engage with to join you in these desires.

TO ADDRESS THIS NEED I COULD ALSO . . .
"I could have something else as a snack: some fruit, a cup of tea, heat up some leftovers."
"I could also leave work early."
"I could explore other techniques to support my mood, like dancing, calling a friend on my way home from work to catch up, or taking ten minutes to listen to a guided meditation while on the bus."

There's no finite end to this exercise. What matters is taking the time to dive deeper and identify what we want—what we really, really want—because that becomes the gateway to a path of radically more authentic, honest, and compelling intimacy.

As the saying goes, knowing ourselves is half the battle. Sometimes we might find that what we desire feels at odds with the values we hold dear—or at least seems to. Reconciling our needs and desires with our values could be lifelong, especially as values and needs can change over time—and that's okay.

Carrie's Story
God Doesn't Want Me to Be Afraid

Carrie grew up in a traditional working-class Protestant family where the trajectory laid out for her was that she would get a degree and then get married. Her mother role-modelled that life as a woman was about making sacrifices to make others happy to keep a family together.

After graduating from a Christian college, all her friends were getting married, and Carrie didn't want to disappoint her family, so she married the boyfriend she had been living with. But the cold feet wedding jitters never settled down, and she never felt comfortable. She eventually had an affair with a married man, Samuel, and went on to divorce her husband.

A year after the divorce, she reconnected with a high school friend, Tom. He made her laugh, and they fell in love. Eventually they moved in together. Despite both feeling ambiguous about marriage, after five years together they got married. Fertility challenges impacted their intimate relationship, and as the pressure to perform became a source of stress, the interest in a sexual relationship waned. Carrie leaned into her social life, developing small crushes on friends.

One day Samuel called her up. The emotional affair between them was rekindled. When Samuel was in a minor car accident, Carrie realized she loved him. She was confronted with the realization that she loved both Tom and Samuel, and was confused. She started to search online for information about how people deal with loving more than one person. When she found polyamory, she realized, "This was me, this had always been me, suddenly everything made sense!"

The timing was divine: She had just started training as a Lutheran deaconess, a journey of self-discovery and connecting more deeply with her faith to enter a ministry of service, and was wrestling with how she would be able to have a ministry if she was having an affair.

As she began to learn how to navigate jealousy, new relationship energy, and be with her feelings, she started to feel more comfortable sharing her truth. She shared openly with Tom about where she was at and that she desired to love more people. Tom felt that they should divorce. It was an amicable divorce, and they stayed close friends. Carrie started going out on dates and reconnected with Samuel. During the COVID-19 pandemic, Samuel opened up his relationship with his wife, and he and Carrie began dating openly. Despite the divorce, Carrie still has a loving and practical relationship with Tom. They see one another regularly and are still listed as one another's emergency contacts.

Today as a solo polyamorous Lutheran deaconess, Carrie shares openly about her queerness and her non-monogamy. She realized that it was never her faith drawing a line; it was the institution. She came to the realization that her sexuality was a gift: "God doesn't want me to be married in a monogamous relationship where I'm not having sex and not having fun. I think God wants me to be happy. I'm not hurting anyone. I believe that we're meant to love one another and be happy and try to make it better for the people in our path." As an independent deaconess, Carrie's openness and courage in discussing open relationships has supported others in her church to come out.

I think there's so much in the conservative and evangelical church that is based on God's wrath, which keeps us in fear. I can't believe that God wants us to walk around being afraid. We pray for forgiveness from our sins, and rather than asking for forgiveness for loving more than one person, I can pray for forgiveness for my inherent racism, or misusing my privileges. It's so silly when I think about it: asking God to forgive me for not being able to limit my love.

Now in her early fifties, Carrie broke free from the self-sacrificing patterns and limiting beliefs about love, marriage, and family that she was raised with and found a path to live in her truth, without abandoning any part of herself. She has found that being openly polyamorous and being of service has brought her tremendous joy. She has become the safe person for younger family members and people in her faith to talk to about sex, queerness, and relationships, to feel validated and liberated from shame.

Honouring Yourself: Boundaries

Boundaries define how we engage in relationships. They can be physical, emotional, psychological, or even energetic. They can range from rigid, making connection difficult, to porous, making it hard to pull away. Healthy boundaries strike a balance—flexible enough to adapt when needed, but still clear about our limits and capacity.

As infants reliant on adult caregivers, we may not have had a sense of our individual boundaries. We were hopefully encompassed by the protection of loving adults, and as we grew we may have adopted and adapted their boundaries or lack thereof as our own. If we had the privilege to experience nervous-system coregulation with multiple adults, we may have had multiple role models for boundaries.

A healthy boundary has the strength of a tree: deeply rooted in what is nourishing, strong, and stable, yet it doesn't break when the wind blows. It can dance with the seasons and weather the storms. Healthy boundaries are not about trying to control others. They are about recognizing and honouring our core needs and developing strategies when what we need is less of something. In other words, a boundary marks out what I say no to in order to make space for my yes. Asserting boundaries can be a way to mark out what we have control over in our personal experience of life, which means they can also be a way to hold close the things we do want to experience.

Boundaries themselves are not a negotiation with others, although how you allow others to interact with them can be. Nor are they an excuse to impose your will on another, although sometimes another person's boundary that prevents you from connecting with them feels like an imposition. There are many reasons why someone might not express their boundaries: fear of negative consequences, trauma, distraction, desire for something that requires ignoring one's own boundaries, and lots more.

When the nervous system experiences struggles through stress, trauma, injury, illness, or neurochemical differences, knowing and asserting our boundaries gets harder. Think about what it's like to choose an activity for a date when you are stressed out, or decide what to have for dinner when you're exhausted, or how it's much easier to become irritated by others when you feel unwell.

REFLECTIVE JOURNALING
Boundaries

What are some boundaries that you have right now in your life?

Write down one boundary in each quadrant of your life: practical, emotional, social, and erotic.

Some examples you might consider:

Emotional: "I make sure I have regular appointments with my therapist."

Social: "I want more friends, so I say yes to many event invitations."
Practical: "I don't let strangers sleep over."
Erotic: "I get my STI testing done every three to six months, no matter what my sexual activity has been."
Consider: How rigid or open are you in these boundaries?
What makes it more challenging for you to share your boundaries with others?
What is it like when your boundaries feel respected?
Are there ever circumstances in which you're willing to reach a compromise about your boundaries?

At the edges of our boundaries is a space of willingness, where we might feel okay about compromising without discomfort. For example, I might not be into superhero movies, but I might be willing to watch one because it's what my partner wants to do. Being clear with what we're willing to be accommodating about is every bit as helpful as knowing where our boundaries lie and can help us maintain our personal capacity. We explore this more shortly.

Ideally, our boundaries maintain a degree of flexibility and resilience. However, if we feel scared, insecure, or fearful that we may lose a relationship, our boundaries might become rigid—stubborn, control-seeking—or more porous, malleable, and accommodating to the whims of others.

Honouring Yourself: Knowing Your Capacity

How do you know when you've been too accommodating in your boundaries? I use the analogy of walking with a pebble in your shoe. You've probably had a pebble in your shoe at some point; I often get them on trails in the forest, or sometimes at the beach. Noticing a pebble in your shoe is a choice point. Do you stop walking, take off your shoes, and shake it out, or do you keep going?

It may not be convenient at that moment to take off your shoes. There may be nowhere to sit and relace them, or maybe you're in a rush and cannot delay. You might think, *This pebble isn't so bad; I'm not walking too far,* or *It's not too big a pebble; maybe it will just work its way out,* so you just keep going. If you never stop to remove the pebble, you do eventually get used to it, and your nervous system learns to ignore it. But, as you keep walking with that pebble in your shoe, day after day, the sole of your foot might develop a callus to protect the skin from damage, or your skin might even blister.

We do the same thing in our relationships: tolerating discomfort beyond our capacity leaves us with emotional blisters that are every bit as painful as physical ones. When we tolerate something uncomfortable to the point of blistering, trying to engage emotionally can feel increasingly painful and may even sting.

If knowing your own boundaries has been challenging for you, and you think you've been walking with blisters in your shoes, I invite you to be gentle with yourself. Many elements can interfere with your ability to recognize your boundaries, including illness and injury, pressure from others, trauma, and even hormonal changes.

RECOGNIZING THE EDGE

Capacity is not just about our boundaries but also about recognizing limitations beyond our control, such as physical injuries, mental health, emotional recovery, or logistical constraints like time. We might desire something but cannot pursue it: wanting a winter vacation but being unable to take time off work, or wishing to see a partner more frequently but having other commitments that make it difficult to schedule quality time.

When we consistently push ourselves beyond our capacity, profound exhaustion can occur. In the workplace we might call this burnout. Emotionally, mentally, and physically, this can feel like trying to walk with painful blisters. Staying connected to loved ones becomes increasingly challenging, and maintaining relationships can feel even more complex and draining. When we're trying to sustain multiple intimate relationships, it can be tempting to write metaphorical cheques that we don't have the capacity to cash. For example, we make promises to our partners about valued time that ends up being cut into by work, sickness, or other obligations. This is especially common when we are under the influence of new relationship energy.

Capacity is a somatic experience, not an intellectual one. Recognizing on a somatic level how much we can hold, how much we can engage with, and what internal resources we have to share in our relationships allows us to navigate multiple loving relationships and stay grounded at the same time. Understanding capacity—yours and others'—helps to build sustainable relationships.

The greatest lesson I've had about capacity came after I developed long COVID and chronic fatigue syndrome. As anyone with either of these conditions will know, pacing is everything. With chronic fatigue, flu-like symptoms can flare up when you overdo any activity, and it doesn't matter whether that activity is intellectual, physical, or emotional. To avoid the post-exertion crash, I pace out my day with generous breaks between clients, and space out strenuous activities during my week so that I have plenty of time to recover if my symptoms do flare up.

Similarly, if your capacity in relationships is wearing thin, you might be able to replenish it by creating more self-time or some time with no relationship stimulation. This could look like taking longer gaps between dates, or reconfiguring some of your relationships so that your loved ones can more accurately know what you're available for.

When you are experiencing blistering or moving beyond your capacity, your self-protection responses will engage. Often we don't notice them until they hit an extreme when we freeze and feel emotionally shut down or numb. You might notice this for yourself as difficulty listening to or recalling what's been said, or you might feel more tired. It's also possible to cycle through being highly energized then collapsing, then resting until you kick back into high energy again and repeat. This might include putting all your energy into engaging emotionally for a partner while abandoning yourself as a people-pleasing response. If this is the case, maybe you notice yourself feeling deflated when a partner or loved one is unavailable, or the slightest change causes you to respond defensively.

Consider this example: Your partner was late home from work again. You're upset and giving them the silent treatment (the freeze response). They notice and try to engage you in connection, trying to make amends for the thing you're tolerating. Receiving this engagement helps you come out of freeze and access more connection to your emotions, but in doing so you are overcome by a wave of emotions that you don't know how to stop. Maybe you yell or break into tears. Your partner tries to offer reassurance, but now you can't engage with them because you are in self-protection mode. Feeling like this isn't working for meeting your needs for safety, and perhaps wanting to get away from the overwhelm of feeling your emotions, you agree to what they say (fawning) and go back into a state of blistering. In these situations, we might be tiptoeing at the edges of our capacity. We touch on this again in chapter 18.

REFLECTIVE JOURNALING
Noticing the Pebbles

What are some things that might be pebbles in your life right now?

Take a page in your journal and list ten things that you find mildly frustrating, annoying, or exhausting. This could be anything from a squeaky floorboard to difficulty with a coworker.

Consider: What do these things you are tolerating tell you about your capacity? Are there any benefits to tolerating these things?

Notice: What does it feel like to list these out?

What would you do to proverbially shake out your shoes and remove these pebbles before you blister?

Loving Yourself: Taking Up Space

Many of us have experienced making ourselves small in our relationships. We may have learned this as a survival strategy in childhood, as a way to avoid physical or emotional harm from adults or other children. We might have felt like a burden to a struggling parent, been bullied by siblings or peers, or experienced humiliation from a teacher or other elder.

For anyone growing up minoritized or marginalized, putting our needs aside and learning to go with the flow set by others may have been a way to avoid drawing attention to ourselves and our differences. We may also have been shamed when we expressed our feelings, desires, and boundaries—and become hesitant to share them.

These early habits of playing small can continue to show up in our relationships as adults, especially in moments when we fear the loss of a relationship, or we have come to rely on the relationship for our survival. And if we've been in abusive relationship dynamics, we may have been coerced into ignoring our own needs, desires, and boundaries. In close relationships, we might navigate insecurities about ourselves, or about the stability of our relationships, that brings us back to a strategy of making ourselves small for the sake of a sense of safety and stability and survival. This could look like anything from:

- not expressing how you really feel

- avoiding conflict

- telling your partner that something is fine when it really isn't, but you're too tired or worn out to talk about it more

- always putting the needs of partners before your own, even when you're exhausted

- not doing enough of the things that bring you joy, nourish you, or re-energize you

REFLECTIVE JOURNALING:
Permission Slip

What do you want permission about to take up more space in your life?

Make yourself a permission slip or create some other form of affirmation for this.

You can use this template to create a permission slip for yourself:

This hereby affirms that [insert your name] has permission for/to [insert the thing you want permission for].

You can sign the slip yourself, or ask someone you admire to sign it for you!

Some examples of how you could take up more space in your own life could include resting when you are tired, allowing your hair or other aspects of your appearance to reflect your ethnic heritage, wearing clothes you feel comfortable in or empowered by, setting boundaries, and saying no.

Loving Yourself: Taking Up Less Space

Conversely, sometimes we take up space so well that we take away from others. It feels empowering and even validating to grab the attention of everyone around us. It may even feel comforting to know that we can command the attention of specific people. But if we're doing so at a cost to others' ability to take up space, we risk our relationships with them.

Taking up a lot of space can be a self-defensive response. If you've had repeated experiences of being dismissed or minimized, self-assertion is self-preservation. If so, somatic and trauma-informed practices can help you develop an inner sense of safety that counters the impulse to take up space from others. The work of self-relating can support this by honing a deep internal sense of confidence, where you do not need to take space away from others to feel you can be in a relationship with them.

Attuning to how others might take up more space can sometimes help us to be aware of it in ourselves. Maybe you know someone who talks without ever pausing, and struggles to listen or read the room. Perhaps you've had a chance to observe business leaders and politicians. These people are empowered to take up space because of the positional power they hold, but at times they take up so much space that they create relational separation from the people they are theoretically in those positions of power to support.

As you grow your self-relationship, you develop greater capacity for resilience. You might find it easier to orient to or situate yourself amid challenging circumstances without sliding into either a flight or a fight response. Emotional wounds may soften, and over time you might feel more like the person you had perhaps once dared to dream you could be.

Cultivating a healthy self-relationship can be a powerful tool against anything like individuals or institutionalized systems of dominance that seek to subjugate others. Being self-primaried helps you navigate intimate relationships with healthier boundaries and more loving attention so that you do not succumb to unhealthy self-sacrificing behaviours or codependency with multiple partners.

Loving Yourself: Radical Self-Care

Self-love asks for profound self-care: doing kind, nurturing things for ourselves, but not as consumers or waiting to earn the right to love ourselves, instead cultivating an ongoing loving relationship with ourselves. This could include going to bed by the time it feels good or waking up at the time that feels right. It could be consuming foods and drinks that are kind to our bodies. It could also look like not putting ourselves through unnecessary endurance.

Self-love can also invite us to change the ways we talk to ourselves. For over a decade I've kept a regular journal as a way of conversing with myself. Putting my inner dialogue into form as ink on paper helped me see where I was being unkind to myself and others. Over time I was able to start shifting the tone of that dialogue, inviting my inner voice to be a cheerleader more than a critic, and what remained of the critic eventually softened to a gentle and engaging inner coach. Many spiritual and expressive practices can support this kind of self-love, including meditating on a higher self, singing, movement and dance, and art. We humans have been seeking to know and love our innate goodness and worthiness for millennia.

REFLECTIVE JOURNALING
Self-Love List

Write up a list of little and big things you can do any day to be kind and loving to yourself but that you don't currently do regularly.

This list can include simple things you can do at home, like making your bed after waking up, enjoying a warm morning beverage, reading a book, or folding laundry. It can also include activities involving others, such as spending time in nature with a friend or meeting up with someone for a catch-up over tea, or activities that you do solo outside of your home, such as going for a walk or picking up groceries.

Once you have your list, know you don't have to do everything.

What if you start by doing one of these things each day?

Once you can consistently do one of these things for three weeks, see if you can start doing two, and then work up to three.

Remember: You don't have to do everything every day to be loving and kind to yourself!

Loving Yourself: Self-Agreements

Even before we make agreements with our partners, we can also make agreements with ourselves. These can be about how you commit to showing up for yourself and in your relationships. For example:

- I commit to nourishing my body and staying hydrated.

- I will put my devices away at least an hour before bed.

- I will journal about my day every day.

- I promise to pace the way I move into new relationships.

- I will address it when I feel like a partner is disrespecting me.

- I commit to showing up for difficult conversations.

- I will work on challenging my judgments of others.

- I won't lash out at my metamours if my partner is doing something that upsets me.

Self-agreements aren't about re-creating perfectionism; they're about how we commit to showing up for ourselves in alignment with our values. Think about how you can craft them to be compassionate towards yourself, and within parameters that honor your capacity. They can help us cultivate a deeper relationship with all the diverse parts of ourselves and set the foundations for the agreements we create with others. Consciously setting intentions and commitments to honour our needs, values, and boundaries can create more space for all the different facets of ourselves to flourish.

Cyrus's Story
A Journey Towards Celebrating Self

Cyrus was born in Tehran, in pre-revolution Iran, in the late 1950s. The country was grappling with Western colonial influences and a rapid pace of industrialization that threatened traditional ways of life. Cyrus, the only son of a multiethnic interfaith family composed of Persians, Kurds, Jews, Muslims, and Bahais, felt constant pressure from their father to be a man. They spent their adolescence rebelling—skipping school to play drums in a rock band, trading with hippies on their way to India for blue jeans and vinyl records, and exploring their sexuality with other boys.

At sixteen, Cyrus moved to the United States by himself. The family joined him five years later, just before the Iranian Revolution. Their mother and sister, who had been involved in feminist activism in Iran, continued their activism in their new home. Cyrus found the radical movements liberating, offering a refuge from the rigid patriarchal norms they had grown up with. They worked as a journalist, translator, and radical organizer throughout the 1980s and 1990s, working with Marxist-humanist and anarchist movements.

In the 1990s, Cyrus returned to school to study communication and performance studies. On campus, the queer movement was thriving. Though they didn't yet identify as queer, Cyrus's lifelong rebellion against traditional masculinity made them a natural ally. Though they were still working with internalized patriarchy, they were drawn to the idea of relationships where women didn't have to submit to men.

By the 2000s, Cyrus sought new ways to challenge the status quo, both in life and love. They discovered cuddle parties, where they encountered someone who identified as solo polyamorous. This meeting sparked a curiosity about non-monogamy, which aligned with Cyrus's ongoing search for alternative ways of living.

Though they had always questioned masculinity, it wasn't until more recent years that Cyrus, by now a drama therapist and college professor, began exploring gender fluidity. Teaching students who were challenging gender binaries, both on campus and in a prison setting, opened Cyrus's eyes to the possibility of expanding feminism to include new understandings of gender. Coming out as queer became a way for Cyrus to reflect both their pansexual relationships and their own queering of gender.

Cyrus has now been openly queer for the past decade, embracing a gender identity that exists beyond the binary, and embracing a queerness that is not only about sexual experiences but also a broader political challenge to societal norms. They define themselves as solo non-monogamous rather than solo polyamorous, as they challenge prescriptive norms of monogamy while nurturing deep intimate friendships that are just as meaningful as romantic or sexual relationships. These friendships have sometimes caused tension with romantic partners, who felt threatened by the closeness. They shared:

> Monogamy is a powerful force. The way you show you care for someone is constantly tested by monogamous ideals. I have travel partners, intimate partners, and close friendships that a monogamous partner might find threatening. I don't need to give up my values to prove my commitment. In fact, I can be even more committed in non-monogamous relationships because I stay true to my principles.

No longer holding themselves back, they now embrace playfulness, question norms, and build a sex-positive community of relationships that reflect their authentic self. As an openly queer, solo, and non-monogamous immigrant in their sixties, Cyrus feels like their whole life has been a process of becoming who they were always meant to be.

Self-relating is a full-spectrum experience that is about much more than self-care. We are more than our physical bodies, and we need to engage in self-care for our hearts, our minds, and our spirits as well.

For some, self-relating is a practice of prioritizing pleasure, desires, and needs. For others, it's a commitment to showing up responsibly and with integrity. Self-relating isn't the same as self-indulgence; it's about self-recognition. It's about knowing yourself and loving what you find, even if that's uncomfortable sometimes. It's about embracing the mindset that not everything needs to be tolerated and endured, and that asserting boundaries and taking up space can be a radical act of love.

People with strong self-relationships often have dynamic and nourishing relationship landscapes. Communities of empowered individuals who come together for a common purpose and values can create, sustain, and flourish. Intimate relationships between self-partnered people can often be healthy spaces for diving into deeper relational healing work in ways that don't involve trauma bonding or codependency.

16

THE META-MODEL
OF RELATING

In a world that revolves around dyadic relationships, we have relatively few templates for multi-partner relationships. Lacking a map through this unknown terrain, we might default back to the well-trodden path of thinking dyadically—even when we aren't monogamous.

As we consider queering our relationship landscapes and potentially growing relationships with more people in one or more quadrants, we also need a framework to understand the dynamics of these relationships. This invites you to think multidimensionally about your relationships and explore frameworks that can help you orient towards the complexities inherent in multi-partner relationships.

To help us navigate this, let's explore a simple framework for understanding multi-partner dynamics. This model is easy to learn, and you can apply it to include and encompass multiple relationships. I arrived at this model when trying to pinpoint why and where my relationship struggles originated. Was it me? Was it something in my partner's relationship with themselves? Was it to do with how my metamour was relating to our relationship? I now use this model when I'm working with my clients as a way to help me decipher what relationships need tending.

I will use some very simplified examples in outlining this model, but this is not intended to minimize or overlook the complexity you may encounter. Non-monogamy is complex, but that doesn't mean it has to be complicated. There are many moving parts, but what we are doing doesn't need to feel chaotic or unruly. Once we understand that we're dealing with complexity, and find the order in the chaos, we can choose which relationships we track, engage with, and more deeply invest in. It does ask for more emotional and mental energy than dyadic relating, but for many non-monogamists, the benefits are worth it. And, for those in single-partner romantic relationships, this model can offer insight and support for friendships, complex families, and more. In other words, if you are someone seeking to expand your relationship landscape, I encourage you to apply this model as one of the tools to help you orient.

Understanding Your Anarcule

In the polyamorous lexicon, a network of non-monogamous relationships is often called a polycule, a play on the word *molecule*. Some may draw out their polycule, showing the different kinds of relationships between its members. Some illustrations look like an elaborate seating chart, others resemble constellations, and some, like mine, may look like a picture of tangled yarn.

As someone who leans towards relationship anarchy, I've often found it challenging to map out my polycule. Some of my relationships defy definition: How do I label the three-decades-long friendship with my first high school boyfriend that, although long distance, continues to include friendship, creative collaboration, light kink, and open communication about our sex lives? And leaving my significant platonic friendships out of that map feels disingenuous, both to me and to those friends who enrich my life in so many ways that are deeper and longer-lasting than most dating connections.

I coined the term *anarcule* as an anarchist's alternative to polycule, describing a relational structure that defies the nuclear family. An anarcule can include all significant relationships, including friendships and communities we have strong ties with. It's a map of the landmarks in your relational ecology, defying conformity and offering fluidity and adaptability. Orienting to the complexity of anarcules helps us navigate expansive landscapes while supporting our nervous systems to feel safe, secure, and supported.

The Meta-Model

Let's start by looking at the dynamics among three people: Ali, Bea, and CJ. I'll use the gender-neutral pronoun the singular *they* to describe each of them. In any dyad, we are likely tracking five relationships: the relationship each person has with themselves, the shared relationship they create together, and how each person relates to that relationship. For example, Ali may feel insecure about their ageing body and mind, whereas Bea may have a positive self-relationship and feel confident. The two of them may share a vibrant relationship where they both delight in laughing at the same corny jokes and volunteer together in their local spiritual community. Ali may love what they share with Bea and think everything's grand, but Bea may have anxiety about the relationship with Ali and feel uncertain about its future. All this grows in complexity when Bea starts dating CJ. CJ and Ali aren't dating, but they still have a relationship as metamours: people who share a mutual partner.

If we're tracking five relationship dynamics when just relating with one other person, relating with two other people means we begin to track many more relationships. This grows exponentially the more people are part of our non-monogamous network, and tracking these dynamics can help us feel less overwhelmed by them.

In fact, among three people, there can be nineteen relationship dynamics at play, and struggles in any one of them can have a ripple effect on the others. Here are all the relationships happening in the diagram in figure 16.1:

Ali's relationship to self

Bea's relationship to self

CJ's relationship to self

Ali and Bea's relationship

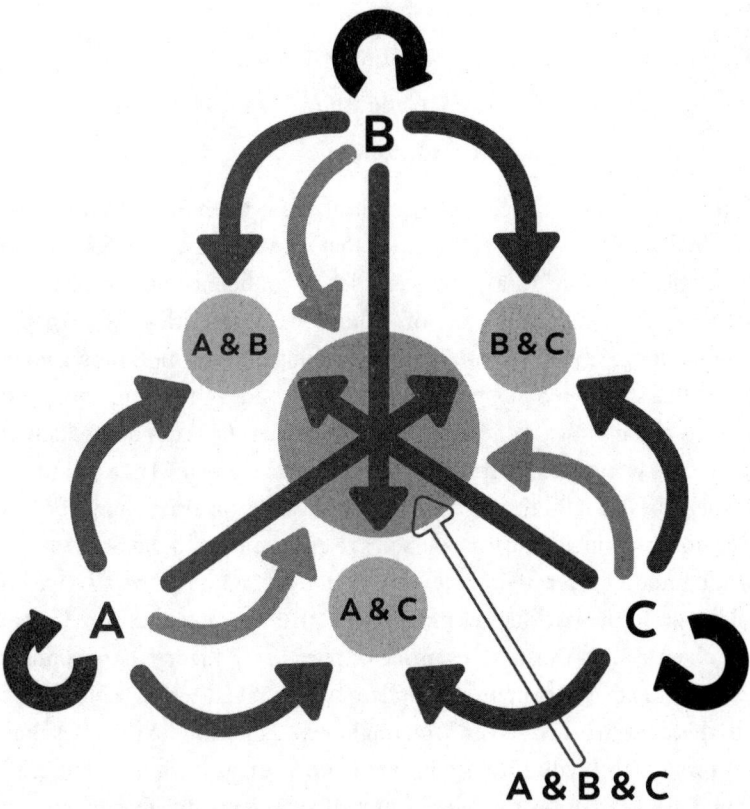

Figure 16.1. The Meta-Model of Relating, showing nineteen relationship dynamics

Bea and CJ's relationship

CJ and Ali's metamourship

Ali's relationship to their partnership with Bea

Bea's relationship to their partnership with Ali

CJ's relationship to Ali and Bea's partnership

Bea's relationship to their new partnership with CJ

CJ's relationship to their new partnership to Bea

Ali's relationship to Bea and CJ's new partnership

CJ's relationship to their metamourship to Ali

Ali's relationship to their metamourship to CJ

Bea's relationship to Ali and CJ's metamourship

Ali, Bea, and CJ's shared relationship

Ali's relationship to the shared relationship

Bea's relationship to the shared relationship

CJ's relationship to the shared relationship

It's complex, but it doesn't need to be complicated. Let's consider what this complexity might include: We've already imagined that Ali and Bea have a well-established vibrant relationship that Ali experiences a lot of confidence in, but that Bea feels anxious about the long-term future of. When Bea starts dating CJ, perhaps CJ is in awe of the longevity of Ali and Bea's partnership and is a bit intimidated by Ali. Over time, Bea starts spending more time with CJ, and CJ begins to develop strong love feelings towards Bea. When they are all together, CJ seeks desperately to feel more included, while Ali feels frustrated and uncertain about CJ as a metamour and blames them for Bea's distance. If conflict were to arise, the origin might be in any of these relationships, including each person's relationships with themselves.

To add another layer of complexity: As individual human beings, we are not often singular. In the last chapter I mentioned that we can tap into an inner critic or inner cheerleader. This is an example of plurality, a theory that proposes that even as individuals we contain multiplicities. Anarchist writer Emmi Bevensee refers to this as networked selves.[1] You might experience this in the ways that activated trauma brings you into a mindset from your past, such as feeling like a frightened six-year-old, or a rebellious thirteen-year-old. In certain trauma-related conditions, such as dissociative identity, you might *become* that frightened six-year-old for a while. But not all plurality is experienced in this way.

Even in a dyadic relationship, you might relate to several aspects of a single individual, and two plural individuals might experience multiple relationships simultaneously with one another. This adds additional complexity that is beyond the scope of this book, but I invite you to consider how you can apply this concept of plurality to understanding your own relationships.

REFLECTIVE JOURNALING
Mapping Dynamics

Practice mapping out the Meta-Model dynamics between you and two trusted friends on a piece of paper or in your journal. You can start with a triangle and put your names at each corner.

What elements impact each friendship?

Consider: What kinds of activities do you do with each friend? Do you ever do something with one friend and not the other?

Do you know how each of these friends feels about one another? Do you know how they feel about their friendship with you?

You might also reach out to these friends to ask them about how they relate to your friendship.

How This Model Helps Us

This model can offer us a better understanding of group dynamics. The dynamics of any anarcule are a blend of individual and collective relationships, with each pair developing its unique connection while also having a relationship to the other relationships in the group.

When relationships become this complex, tracking how everyone is doing at any given time can become overwhelming. It's a Sisyphean task, so I don't recommend that you attempt to track all these relational dynamics all the time. Rather, when you find friction, misunderstanding, disappointment, jealousy, or any other challenges, I invite you to be curious about which relationships may need tending. And when it comes to tending to your relationship landscape, you may want to consider how your relationships may impact and interrelate with one another.

TRIANGULATION

In family systems theory, an approach to understanding relationship dynamics, triangles are the most stable form of relating. We seek out a third party to triangulate with because it brings stability to dyads. We can do this in supportive and empowering ways or in damaging ways that diminish ourselves and others, such as projecting blame onto a third party. We can do triangulation consciously or unconsciously, but it is always a strategy for stabilizing dynamics that feel unstable.

Triangulation is often unconscious, the work of our psyches during times of conflict as we seek additional anchor points in people and relationships that affirm our identity, experience, or story about ourselves or situation. We explore dramatic triangulation in chapter 19. Right now, let's look at healthy triangulation.

There are many healthy examples of triangulation: seeking a third party to mediate a dispute, such as a counsellor or therapist, for example, or asking a trusted friend for their thoughts and input about a challenge you are having with someone else. Healthy, conscious triangulation, where dynamics are openly acknowledged and discussed and where projections are addressed and expectations checked, can be a really great thing, and consensual non-monogamy offers lots of opportunities for this.

As a word of caution: In engaging in the broader ecology of relationships, we must also consider how to do so while still honouring values of consent and collaboration and respecting the boundaries and capacity of others. If the third party is an ally and supporter of the relationship and the people in it, for example a metamour, a friend, or someone else in your anarcule, they may be well situated to offer you insight, support, validation, and fresh perspective in the relational challenges you're experiencing. But if the situation being navigated tasks their nervous system to the edges of their own capacity, their own relational landscape may feel depleted. Some people find it helpful to identify people who can be part of a support pod so that no one person feels the weight of being the only person offering support. Mapping out the Meta-Model dynamics helps us better understand our relationship dynamics, including identifying which relationship dynamics need attention when there is stress, conflict, or discord.

Ultimately, healthy triangulation is about using your understanding of these relationship dynamics to help bring more compassion and understanding to your connections, rather than creating distance or blame. Our relationships are inherently more stable when everyone in them is working within their capacity, when boundaries are honoured and needs are addressed. To work with this model invites us to work collaboratively, which is what we explore next.

17

CONSENT AND AGREEMENTS

What if it truly doesn't matter what you do, but how you do whatever you do?
—ORIAH MOUNTAIN DREAMER[1]

Relationship agreements are founded on consent—but what exactly is consent? While consent can absolutely involve giving permission and agreement to participate in someone else's desires, a more somatic, and perhaps anarchist, perspective is to see consent as collaboration. The permission-seeking model of consent might work adequately in a dyadic relationship, but as more people get involved, the scope of consent increases, and ambiguity can arise. Perhaps you've heard someone say, "I never gave permission for my partner to sleep with them," or found yourself wondering, *Do I need my partner's permission for this if they aren't involved in the experience I'm having with someone else?*

This uncertainty about who we need to include in the consent conversation can lead us to doubt ourselves and feel less somatically safe as a result. When we don't feel safe, we might slip into familiar adaptive behaviours, as we covered in chapter 4, aimed at making us feel safer: fight (pushing people away), flight (removing ourselves), freeze (saying nothing), or fawn (saying yes as a strategy for safety).

Self-protection can impact our experience of consent. We might grant or deny permission based on a primal instinct to protect ourselves as a strategy to avoid upset or distress. The expression "poly under duress," for example, describes a partner agreeing to be non-monogamous not because they want polyamory for themselves but because they fear that to refuse non-monogamy might end the relationship.

Real embodied consent lives in the nervous system. Our nervous system constantly assesses, *Am I safe?* When we can ascertain safety, we can more authentically consent or not. The most authentic way to arrive at embodied consent is through collaborative processes.

Collaboration Equals Equity

In chapter 2, where we explored non-monogamy, I offered an inquiry into what consent means in the context of polyamory as "non-monogamy with the consent of all involved." When it comes to Radical Relating, I propose that a consensual post-monogamous dynamic is where there is space for all who may be involved in or impacted by a relationship to be as collaboratively involved as they wish to be. This would mean that full disclosure and discussion of every detail of your relationships wouldn't necessarily be needed—only to the extent to which your partners benefit from and want disclosure and discussion, and, of course, within the bounds of what you are willing to include in that disclosure and discussion.

This can't be left ambiguous, and honesty with one another about what kind of disclosure and discussion each person desires, and has the capacity to give and receive, is important. For example, I let new partners know that it's my preference to share broad strokes about my relationship landscape, and they'll get details only to the extent that they are comfortable knowing. I'm also open about the fact that I do date openly. So if we're publicly dating, then others may understand that they are in a relationship with someone who is polyamorous. New partners can then let me know to what degree they want to hear about my other relationships—all the juicy details, or just the summaries and STI updates?—and consider for themselves to what degree they are comfortable with the social visibility of their relationship with me. I also like to know my partners' preferences. Can I expect to hear details about their other relationships? Will they tell me about who is important to them?

To explore this more, let's return to our hypothetical anarcule of Ali, Bea, and CJ and explore how they might approach collaborative consent. Bea and CJ are discussing going away for a weekend, which might impact Ali even though it doesn't directly involve them. Ali has a choice as to whether they want to be involved in the planning conversation: When will this weekend trip happen? But they may let Bea know there are weekends they were hoping to spend as just the two of them, and entrust Bea to make their plans with CJ with this in mind. But what if the issue at hand were different? Imagine that instead of a holiday, Bea and CJ were discussing having a child together, with Bea as the gestational parent. This might have a significant impact on Bea's relationship with Ali, so some three-way collaborative conversations about how Ali might be involved or not with the pregnancy and child care may be prudent.

The higher the stakes for any individual, the more likely they are to experience stimulation in their nervous system, which could impact how they respond in collaborative conversations.

Who Is It For, Why Is It Happening, and What Does It Mean?

As we explored in chapter 15, desires can be strategies for deeper needs. The simple question "Can I hug you?" could be a strategy for physical connection, nervous system coregulation, a response to thinking that the other person needs a hug as a precursor to more physical intimacy, or to create an opportunity for nonconsensual touching beyond the scope of a hug.

If I consent to a hug, to what extent am I aware of the need that I'm consenting to? Do I agree to the request because I would like some nervous system coregulation for myself? What happens if the hug, for me, is about comfort, but for the other person it's a precursor to more physical intimacy? Maybe this doesn't matter in the moment, but if we never get clear about what the hug meant, and it turns out that we had different understandings of its meaning, this could create conflict later.

Many of us have had experiences of saying yes to something, even when we weren't enthused about it, perhaps even when some part of us was screaming a no. Repeatedly saying yes when our nervous system is disrupted, either because we are intoxicated, fearful, or in any other way not ourselves, is not embodied consent. When we're exploring consent with a partner, whether they are someone new to us or someone we have known for many years, it can be helpful to pause and consider: when someone says yes to something, why is that so? Are they saying yes from an authentic place of feeling safe, open, grounded, and relaxed in their nervous system? Or does the yes come from anxiety, worry, or fear of saying no?

On a day-to-day basis in smaller incidental interactions, the difference here might not matter so much. But, in a higher-stakes conversation, such as agreements about what we communicate about others and when, if we aren't clear on our motivations and the motivations of our partners, our understanding of the agreement may differ. In other words, while the word of the law may seem straightforward, the spirit of the law may feel fuzzy, which could lead to future conflict and rupture.

Consent as Collaboration

Collaborative Consent can also help us navigate out of our necessary fantasy and slow down our journey through the layers of relating: awareness, safety, intimacy, and Relationship. Assumed consent brought on by the necessary fantasy might offer great scaffolding for the relationship, but ideally, that scaffolding isn't mistaken for the finished structure. If early on in a relationship I ask a partner, "Do you want to be my girlfriend?" and they say yes, I might assume that we're now in the deepest layer of relating and skip all the crucial collaborative work that allows us to build real safety and intimacy together. But if instead we open up a conversation about what the label "girlfriend" means to each of us, we may be able to arrive at an agreement that's not just about the labels we give our relationships but also what those labels mean for us. Collaborative consent can look like:

- recognizing when something you want with another person might impact a partner—be it practically, emotionally, erotically, or socially— and desiring to include them in a decision process

- identifying when you or a partner need more information from other people in your relational network before you can be fully engaged in a collaborative process

- cultivating intimate spaces between you and your partners where disagreement and distress can be talked about openly without fear of being shut down or dismissed

- ongoing communication about what's agreed to and what that means, rather than functioning on assumptions

If any of these feel challenging, know that that's okay. Many of us haven't grown up with collaborative communication models, nor have we learned how to create spaces where it's safe to have conflict. It takes time, patience, and a lot of practice to develop these skills. We'll be taking a deeper look at conflict in the next chapter.

Personally, I have never been a fan of "seeking and granting permission" relationship agreements. Before I had developed a well-honed sense of my own self-relationship, and before I knew how to recognize when my nervous system wasn't fully present, I would often agree to something a partner wanted simply because I didn't want to risk the relationship. I tried to push myself through discomfort, and in the process I said yes to lots of things I didn't actually want, including sex, marriage, moving countries for a partner, and more. As my own self-partnership journey deepened, I came to realize that abandoning myself for the sake of relationship agreements did not, in fact, make for healthy relationships.

Collaborative consent helps us arrive at explicit agreements rather than relying on implicit agreements. Remember, the expectation of mind-reading or telepathy is a hangover from monogamous mythology.

Types of Agreements

Let's break down the different types of agreements we can have.

Structure Versus Process

A structure-based agreement could cover the logistics of your anarcule, the frequency of dates with a partner, what relationship labels or terms of endearment you use for one another, and so forth. A process-based agreement focuses instead on how you engage with each other, for example, how you navigate conflict or how you agree to communicate about new relationships.

Structure agreements often involve conversations that address the design and form of your relationship landscape, starting from a place of your own self-relationship. You and your loved ones might sit down and map out the structure using Venn diagrams or tools like the Relationship Anarchy Smörgåsbord to help you explore where your desires and capacity in each quadrant overlap.[2] We look at this visioning process in chapter 20.

Process agreements may require more self-reflection, a deeper understanding of our values, why we relate the ways that we do, and even a recognition of our personal cosmology and how we relate to the world. These may be influenced by the cultures we grew up with, our spirituality or religious beliefs, our education, and even our politics. When I'm working with people who are navigating relationship conflicts, I find there is often conflict about the process by which they communicate or engage in conflict, and we have to navigate this first before we can go into any kind of restorative work together. Let's consider what this might look like for Ali and Bea as a dyad:

Structure agreement: Bea and Ali have one guaranteed date night each week, with both of them free to have dates with others on other nights.

Process agreements: Bea agrees to communicate to Ali a week in advance who they have dates with and when. Ali can ask for details about what Bea does on their dates, but Bea doesn't share those details without the permission of the people they date. If Ali feels uncomfortable about any of Bea's other relationships, they agree to get support from their coach to help sort through their feelings before bringing them to Bea. Bea agrees to hold space for any discomfort Ali experiences and work collaboratively to address any issues that arise.

Opening up from an existing relationship, relationship agreements about both process and structure offer needed scaffolding. Yet the fears and anxieties that arise when opening up can sometimes lead to agreements turning into rules and rules becoming tools by which to attempt to control one another—and potentially the others who may be involved in relationships with our loved ones. When this happens, what we have are not agreements grounded in collaborative embodied consent but rather coerced agreements arrived at through begrudging permission-seeking or under duress.

An agreement within an open relationship that says "We won't sleep with someone on the first date" might feel limiting or even controlling. In contrast, an acknowledgment of the root need gives more freedom. For example, "We both agree to ensure that the people we engage with are a good match for us because we value our relationship and don't want to destabilize it adversely, and will give due consideration to the impact new sexual connections might have on one another before engaging in sexual intimacy with any new partners."

Implicit Versus Explicit Agreements

Implicit agreements are based on our assumptions of what's happening, whereas explicit agreements are clearly and directly articulated.

Implicit agreements are based on shared cultural and subcultural understandings, such as shaking the hand of someone you meet, saying "Thank you" when someone holds the door for you, or calling the person you've been dating your girlfriend, boyfriend, or datefriend. According to Edward Hall's cultural iceberg metaphor, our daily interactions only capture the most superficial aspects of our culture, beneath which are the deeper beliefs, values, and ways of seeing the world that determine how we engage with it.[3] We might not think much about these culturally ingrained agreements until someone from another culture behaves differently than we expect.

Even when people follow the same outward behaviours, their implicit understandings of what those mean can differ. A great example of this is the physical motion of shaking one's head, which in much of the world is seen to mean "no," but in some parts of the Balkans in southeastern Europe has traditionally been a gesture for expressing "yes." Compare this to the many forms of head-movement gestures that exist in South Asia, which, depending on the context, speed, and conversation, could mean agreement, disagreement, gratitude, or even confusion. For folks who are neuro-diverse, the implicit agreements in their own culture may not make sense to them, and they may find that they always need to have explicit conversations about them. In contrast, some with neurodivergence may have learned one set of cultural rules so rigidly that it feels very challenging, and possibly scary, to adapt to different ones.

These implicit cultural agreements can impact our relational joy. As someone who grew up with two parents of very different cultures, I witnessed many times when conflict arose between them from misunderstandings about both the structure and process of their relationship. I saw the challenges they had around understanding the meaning-making they each did, based on their different cultural backgrounds and assumptions about what a good partnership was.

Explicit agreements help us avoid the ambiguity and confusion that can come with implicit agreements. By examining what they mean to us at a deeper personal level, we can find conscious explicit agreements with personal meaning that offer greater support for everyone's experience of somatic relational safety. Explicit agreements can include an understanding of who benefits from them: How, why, and to whom does an agreement matter? They are clear in how they honour everyone's needs and capacities. Where capacity may feel limited, agreements might explore how to enhance capacity, perhaps through working on resilience, both individual and relational. Explicit agreements can help:

- clarify expectations and capacity between all parties
- give guidelines for navigation of conflicts
- empower individuals seeking equity in multiple-person dynamics
- inform all parties about how they can support one another in support of attachment relationships, both dyadic and group-sourced
- create a framework of continuity during any kind of change in dynamics, for example opening up, escalating, or de-escalating
- sustain long term relationships by maintaining integrity and inviting accountability

Types of Explicit Agreements

Depending on which layers of relating you are exploring, you may want to consider different types of agreements to co-create:

APPETIZER AGREEMENTS: SUPPORT AWARENESS AND SAFETY

These often happen during the first months of a relationship. They establish the foundation of trust and safety, set the tone for how you connect, and may address the absolute minimums, for example, sexual health and safety, communication about other relationships, and open channels of communication between partners. Sometimes these agreements might look more like a mutual understanding of a clearly communicated pattern or boundary, for example, "I date openly," "I get my STI tests done every three to six months."

ENTRÉE AGREEMENTS: SUPPORT SAFETY AND INTIMACY

These develop over time, often involving some navigation of conflict, or they arise as part of the resolution around conflict and can be designed to help restore and rebuild trust. They can also be created pre-emptively to support conflict intimacy or to support a partner who may be struggling with trauma activation. They are focused on maintaining a good connection where everyone can experience safety and open towards more intimacy. This might include the frequency of dates, boundaries around navigating shared space with other partners, and giving some shape or definition to the relationship, such as making future plans.

SEASONING AGREEMENTS: SUPPORT INTIMACY AND RELATIONSHIP

Seasoning agreements can be made at any time and are about how you engage with power dynamics and differentials within your relationships, for example, couple's privilege, financial privilege, racial privilege, gender, and so on. These agreements aren't just situational; they reflect the values by which you commit to show up with one another. These agreements benefit from ongoing revisiting and reflection. In addition to this, we can explore agreements through the four quadrants—emotional, social, practical, and erotic—based on the types of boundaries or needs that they address. These might include financial process agreements to address an economic inequity in the relationship. For example, in our fictional anarcule of Ali, Bea, and CJ, when Ali and Bea go for dinner, as the higher wage earner, Ali covers the bill, but when Bea goes on dates with CJ, they split the bill between them. Financial structure agreements might look like arrangements for covering joint expenses or splitting the cost of shared travel to a festival.

DESSERT AGREEMENTS: SUPPORTING TRANSITION AND CHANGE

These are agreements about how to navigate a shift in the landscape, including a transition in the nature of the relationship or a break-up. These express how you will commit to treating each other with kindness and compassion, even if you find your relationship is no longer compatible. While we rarely want to consider that a relationship we're enjoying could end, many people find it valuable to have a conversation about this and make some agreements early on, often around the six-month mark into a connection. This can also prove helpful if you make decisions to dramatically shift the dynamic of your relationship, as when moving the relationship's focus from one quadrant to another. This could include process agreements about how to take space from one another, and structure agreements about the separation of belongings, custody of children, pets, and so forth.

AGREEMENTS IN THE FOUR QUADRANTS

You might also find it helpful to look at agreements through the lens of the four quadrants:

Practical agreements: protecting our physical and practical well-being, such as finances, home and nesting, scheduling, and time management.

Social agreements: supporting our mental health with information and disclosure about other relationships, and sensitivity to each person's capacity for holding and processing new info.

Emotional agreements: protecting our emotional well-being, titrating the process of forming new relationships, sensitivity to past hurts, and how we agree to navigate conflict or reconnect after any distance.

Sexual agreements: Supporting our sexual health with safety, STI disclosure, testing practices and frequency, and barrier and birth control use.

When you're exploring agreements in your relationships, whatever kind of agreements you are forming, I encourage you to think about the difference between limiting and expansive language. Limiting language, such as "We can't kiss a new partner without permission from our existing partner," tends to only address surface-level wants and may restrict individuals, never seeking to understand the core needs or boundaries at play. On the other hand, expansive language can acknowledge the core needs driving our desires and the bounds of capacity, allowing more freedom while honouring each individual. For example, "We recognize that new relationships can be scary for one another and our relationship, so we pace how we move into new connections, only moving into more physical intimacy, like kissing, when we are sure that there is the capacity to hold any discomfort it brings up." If a relationship agreement ever leaves you feeling small or restricted, it's probably time to refine it.

Checking Our Agreements

If you have a tendency towards people-pleasing or a strong fawn response, you may feel pulled towards agreeing to something your partner wants even when it isn't something you want or that you have capacity for. Similarly, if you tend towards fight, you may be so strong in your self-assertion that you don't notice your partner feeling imposed upon.

If agreements aren't rooted in your why and with a clear vision of where you hope the agreements will take you, they aren't agreements at all; they may hold smuggled desires. So when you are working on some explicit agreements in your relationships, it's worth taking a bit of time to check in and make sure that any agreements you arrive at support your individual needs and the vision you have for your relationship together. You might ask yourself:

- Am I agreeing to something because it is what the other person wants?
- Why does it matter to me to make and stick to this agreement?
- Am I willing to agree even though it's not something I would normally say yes to, and if so, why?
- Do I hold any resentment towards the other person about this agreement?
- Which relationships does this agreement support?

RELATIONAL TOOLKIT
Agreement Homework

To prepare for a conversation on agreements, consider the following:

- What core needs are needing support, and whose needs are those?
- How will supporting this need in turn support our relationship?
- What other possible strategies could we explore to meet these needs? For example, are the things to explore structure-based, process-based, different courses of agreements, or even different quadrants to make agreements in?
- What would be the consequences if this agreement isn't honoured, or the needs are unmet?
- What becomes possible when this need is met and this agreement honoured?

Write down your individual responses to all these considerations and ask your partner to do the same. As you discuss your responses, make sure to make a note of how you see things differently and where you are already in agreement.

Working with Agreements

Let's return to Bea and CJ to look at how we can work with agreements. In a past relationship, CJ's sexual health was put at risk when their previous partner was having an affair and not using STI protection with either CJ or the other person they were seeing. As a result, CJ has experienced a lot of hesitation about entering into a barrier-free sexual relationship, even though it's something they want to do with Bea.

While CJ has been affected by experiences that are in the past, Bea is in a position to support their journey of healing from that break of trust with partners. Bea and CJ might explore explicit agreements around their sexual health and how they navigate sexual health with other partners: Bea might choose to pause on engaging in new sexual relationships until new partners have been able to get a full STI panel done, or until CJ has been able to meet any new partners they have—an example of an entrée process agreement in the erotic quadrant. Bea might also agree to temporarily limit the kinds of sexual activities they do with others, or the frequency of seeing other sexual partners, for the first six months of Bea and CJ's sexual relationship. This would be an example of an appetizer process agreement.

A time-bound agreement, open to renegotiation, is a wonderful way to titrate and support any partner moving towards dynamics that have created stress or harm in the past. Bea and CJ might arrive at one agreement for the first six months, and at the end of that time they might make changes in the agreement, or they may find that a space of trust has developed that has overwritten the past relational experience of a break of trust, and entirely different agreements could be explored.

Charting Your Course:
Finding Your North Star

In any long-term committed relationship, developing a shared vision becomes important. I call this the North Star, a nod to historical traditions of navigating through charting the night sky and the importance of finding the star Polaris: a fixed point that would help travellers orient even in unfamiliar lands. The relational North Star becomes a compass by which you and your loved ones might navigate important decisions and choice points in your relational journeys. The North Star comprises four elements:

> What: What is it that you're doing together? This could include structure and labels but can also describe the landscape quadrants and layers of relating that form the sandbox of your relationship explorations.

Why: Why is it that this is what you're doing or not doing together? This acknowledges each person's needs and also their capacity and how it is that the what supports them.

How: What values and processes do you engage in together? What practices do you bring into your relationship?

Where: Where do you want to journey together? In five or even ten years, how do you hope you'll both feel in this relationship?

It's perfectly okay to answer any of these questions with uncertainty. Consciously acknowledging that something is unknown helps prevent us from filling in the blanks with our own assumptions or wishful thinking. And it's also okay for this to change over time.

RELATIONAL TOOLKIT
Your Personal North Star

In addition to having relational North Stars, we can also have a personal North Star. This might reflect your values, boundaries, desires, and capacity. What constitutes your personal North Star might also change over time. You may have noticed that this book is laid out in sections that correspond to these questions: Why do we do relationships, What kind of relationships do we want, How do we relate, and Where is it we want our relationships to go?

You may find it helpful to review your journaling reflections on the relationship landscape, the four quadrants, and the layers of relating, and consider your individual answers to these questions:

What: What kind of relationships do you desire to have?

Why: Why is it that you want these kinds of relationships? What needs would they meet for you?

How: What values do you lead with in your relationships?

Where: Where do you want your relationships to go? What vision do you have for your relationship landscape? What vision do you have for yourself and your life?

Remember that it's okay if some of these answers are vague to begin with. Sometimes just knowing that you don't know the answer can bring clarity.

In my journey as a solo polyamorist, I've created and ongoingly refined my own personal North Star as part of my self-partnership. Even though I have almost always been practising solo polyamory, the quadrants and layers I've been open to exploring in romantic partnerships have shifted over time. The vision for my relational future has become more refined as I've learned more about what works and doesn't work for me.

Relationship agreements can empower and support partnerships when they are consciously formed with a clear vision and understanding of everyone's needs and desires. Open communication helps us establish boundaries with honour and respect and supports us in treating all our loved ones with kindness and compassion.

Agreements help establish the boundaries and parameters of relationships. To sustain long-term relationships, romantic or otherwise, agreements can create a framework for continuity during changes in dynamics, clarify expectations and capacity, maintain integrity, provide guidelines for conflict resolution, support attachment relationships, and as if all that wasn't enough, empower each individual seeking equity in multi-partner relationship dynamics.

18

SHAME, SHADOW, AND CULTIVATING COMPERSION

Compersion is:

- a broad range of positive emotions experienced in relation to one's intimate partner's extra-dyadic intimate relations
- the broad range of positive attitudes, thoughts, and actions manifested in relation to one's intimate partner's extra-dyadic intimate relations
- the broad range of positive emotions, attitudes, thoughts, and actions manifested in relation to another person's gratifying experience in any context[1]

In this chapter we explore the inner experiences that can hinder or support the experience of compersion. To help us, we'll also explore shame and what Carl Jung called our shadow emotions. Coming back to the pillars of trauma-informed relating that we explored in the first part of this book, we'll explore some practical somatic activities that you can do to work with your shadow emotions and move towards embodying greater joy and ease.

The Kerista Commune coined the term *compersion* to describe the sympathetic and vicarious joy they experienced through multi-partner relating. The term is now used extensively in the non-monogamous world to describe vicarious joy even outside relational contexts. While this chapter looks at it in the context of non-monogamous relationships, remember that compersion can be experienced in friendships, and even felt for total strangers.

Compersion is sometimes described as the opposite of jealousy, although research on compersion has shown that the two can exist concurrently. Feeling compersion is often seen as a marker of success in non-monogamy—maybe, we might assume, it's a sign that we've overcome our monogamy hangovers! However, compersion isn't inherent to the experience of polyamory, and struggling to feel it doesn't necessarily mean open relating is not for you.

Those of us exploring alternative relationships, be we polyamorous, relationship anarchists, swingers, or something else, often long to experience a freedom within connection that we didn't find in exclusive relationships. We desire liberation from oppressive relational experiences, and compersion can represent the epitome of the expansive joy we seek.

Compersion isn't reserved for non-monogamists. The concept of empathetic and sympathetic joy can be found in non-Western and pre-colonial traditions. In Sanskrit, for example, *mudita* refers to joy for others, such as the elation a parent feels when they see their child delighting in a new experience, an empathetic response as the parent has their own emotion and joins their child in the experience, or the happiness when a dear friend shares good news, a sympathetic response where a person feels happiness for the other person but isn't in the experience with their friend.

In *What Is Compersion?*, Dr. Marie Thouin emphasizes the importance of developing a "non-mono-normative relationship to jealousy" and that jealousy is not something to be ashamed or avoidant of. She explores how personal values, self-love, relational security, positive relationships with metamours, and even a sense of community belonging can all contribute to experiences of compersion. You might notice that we have touched on most of these topics in this book.

Thouin also explains compersion can be hindered by individual, relational, and social elements. Individual factors include internalized mono-normativity, feeling under duress to be polyamorous, and unmet needs, among others. Relational elements include betrayal, feelings of exclusion, and distrust or dislike of metamours. Social factors centre on mono-normativity, the stigmatisation of non-normative relationships, and the lack of racial and cultural diversity in non-monogamous spaces.[2] What all of these experiences have in common is that they pull at the resources of your nervous system and potentially reduce your capacity for empathy, compassion, and sympathetic joy.

To explore how to cultivate compersion, let's look at the internal obstacles: distress in the nervous system (which limits our capacity for empathy) and the resulting shadow emotions that can arise. Carl Jung proposed the idea of a psychological shadow, defining shadow emotions as ones we try to repress, reject, deny, or ignore. He was strongly influenced by Eastern spirituality, but whereas in Buddhism the things that poison us are said to be greed, hatred, and delusion, Jung focussed on a shadow formed from jealousy, shame, anger, fear, and disgust, although any emotion can have its shadow side. We might understand these shadow emotions as clues from our nervous system about distress, be it a loss of connection or a lack of safety. Repressing them is a common cultural practice, and if you've been raised in Westernized and colonized spaces, you might never have learned how to sit with these emotions. Sometimes boys and men find that they've been encouraged to express and feel their anger but deny their fear, while girls and women may have been told, conversely, to suppress their anger and to express their fears.

My experience of compersion is that it contrasts all these shadow emotions. It is an expansive, warm sensation that acts as a balm for all my shadow emotions, not just jealousy. Anger, disgust, fear, and shame soften through the tenderness of empathy, whether that's me experiencing compersion for a partner or them experiencing it for me. I've found that compersion is a somatic experience: It arises more readily when the nervous system is resilient and supported. The more resilient our nervous systems, the more present we can be to our own experiences as they happen, and compersion can flow in abundance.

To cultivate compersion we grow both inner and relational resilience to distress. Deeply understanding the many things that can cause us relational distress can take years of work, and it may even need to touch on deep-rooted unaddressed traumas. Consider this the briefest overview to help you orient to, identify, and begin this work.

Somatic Compersion

In the sensation language of somatics, compersion might be described as openness, warmth, compassion, empathy, expansion. It brings a sense of abundance, gratitude, and deep affection. But the compersive experience isn't one-dimensional. Dr. Thouin explores attitudinal compersion and embodied compersion in her work, and blogger Zadena Love expands embodied compersion into emotional and erotic compersion in her article "3 Dimensions of Compersion."[3] I invite you to consider compersion in this way:

Intellectual compersion: A mostly mental experience. We intellectually understand that a partner is with another and hypothetically are okay with this. We feel relief in knowing that we do not need to provide for or be present with our partner for everything all the time. This experience can be considered sympathetic: We are not in the same emotional experience as our partner, but we can imagine how it might be enjoyable for them.

Emotional compersion: An experience of joy, happiness, and warmth. There may be excitement for a partner who has a date, or deep contentment when they return and tell us about it. This sensation could be described as empathetic joy: We have a personal emotional experience in response to the emotional experience of our partners. This might even feel like we are soaking up the extra joy they exude, or that we become an emotional mirror for them.

Erotic compersion: In some instances, knowing about a partner being with someone else brings arousal. This might feel like a rush of energy, and it might be confusing if intellectual and emotional compersion are absent. It can feel a lot like nervous system activation. For many, this is an embodied response and can sometimes be interpreted as erotic attraction to a partner's partner.

When you experience all these together, you might enjoy a full-bodied, integrated, somatic experience, which is as amazing as it sounds. However, for most, compersion arrives in one or two of these forms, and feeling all three simultaneously is not a daily event. All these aspects are equally valid experiences of compersion and may impact us and our relationships in different ways. Again, it is hard to connect to this experience when our nervous system is dysregulated. Many factors can contribute to that distress.

Distress and the Shadow

Distress can arise from any stimulation in the nervous system, even positive ones, that triggers self-protective responses. This natural somatic reaction occurs when we feel our safety, stability, or security is threatened, regardless of whether the threat is real. It could be triggered by something as simple as feeling disconnected from a partner or anxiety about relating in new ways, such as opening up a previously exclusive relationship.

A partner going on a date with someone might trigger a fear of abandonment, just as moving in with a dear friend might stir fears of losing privacy or even losing the friendship if it doesn't work out. New relationship energy can hold the distress of uncertainty, as we explored in chapter 9, and the necessary fantasy can offer temporary scaffolding through which to feel safe enough, but as reality replaces fantasy we may feel distressed. Looping thoughts around existing insecurities as we desperately seek solutions along with emotional dysregulation, or emotional avoidance, are common indicators of distress.

We looked at the self-protective responses of fight, flight, freeze, and fawn in chapter 5, but let's take another look to see how they might show up for you in your shadow emotions as you navigate distress.

Anger and the Impulse to Control: Fight Response

Somatically speaking, the desire to control is a sign of distress. The desire to have power over something or someone else can indicate that our nervous system perceives that thing or person as unpredictable, unsafe, or simply unknowable, and the urge to take over is a strategy for safety. Taking power over another is a self-preservation strategy and a form of fight response. This can be gentle: self-assertion and standing up for oneself in the face of bullying, erasure, and other forms of oppression. Bigger fight responses can sometimes take the form of emotional, mental, physical, or sexual violence. Veto power—forbidding your partner to be with someone—can be a strategy for maintaining control, sometimes to manage and avoid jealousy.

In fight, digestion slows down as the cardiovascular system prepares to defend or attack. Your pupils dilate, and you might even experience arousal. It may be time to slow down, check in with your partners, and ask for support with anything that feels overwhelming.

Fear and the Impulse to Avoid: Flight Response

Avoidance and withholding are impulses to steer away from potential harm or side-step anything that could risk rupture. It doesn't actually matter whether the danger is real or not; the internal response is the same. If we've experienced any kind of relational bullying, abuse, or cancellation, we may have learned to avoid by making ourselves small as a strategy for survival.

Somatically speaking, this impulse is a primal response to a perceived threat, wherein our nervous system prepares the body and mind to flee. In flight, the body prepares to mobilize: The legs, hip flexors, and lower back tense up. The hands might feel fidgety and restless. Thoughts might race fast. There may even be a sensation of feeling trapped.

If this primal impulse to flee is never able to resolve because we are not able to leave a situation that feels unsafe or harmful, or we are unable to come back into an experience of relational safety, the tension within the body that is preparing us to mobilize can stick around, leading to experiences of chronic pain and tension in our lower back and pelvis, or even heightening experiences of anxiety or insomnia.

We don't necessarily physically flee when the flight response is active. If the perceived danger is emotional or verbal, for example, we fear a partner berating us, or worry that we will be abandoned if we speak up for our boundaries, then instead of physically moving away, we might emotionally distance ourselves. This can look like not sharing how we are feeling, or even holding back on disclosing information that we worry might upset a partner.

Shame: Fawn and Freeze Response

Shame is often used as a tool for control and coercive conformity, with the threat of ostracization and loss of connection if we refuse to conform. In white supremacy culture, this shows up as the belief in one true way of doing things, perfectionism, and fear of conflict. Shame can leave us feeling frozen, distant, disconnected, and possibly unsure about connecting with ourselves. To survive in a world that seeks to control us through shame, many of us internalize it, sometimes to the point of feeling so familiar with it that we don't even realize it's there. Internalized shame can cause us to shrink away from connection, and we might:

- bend or break agreements
- withhold, lie, or otherwise betray the trust a partner has placed in us
- minimize, dismiss, or even gaslight our partners
- take unsafe risks in our erotic explorations
- avoid apologizing or acknowledging harm we have caused, refuse to do repair work, and reverse the focus of feedback onto the person giving it to us
- end a relationship

It is important to note that shame is a very different experience from remorse, which arises from loving self-awareness and pulls us back to our core values. Remorse is reflective recognition that our actions or inactions have had consequences for others that we wish were different or that could be changed. Acknowledging and expressing remorse can be an opening into reconnection. Shame, on the other hand, is a sensation that dwells in separation and tells us that we have no value. It carries with it the threat of ostracization from community, the loss of confidence in one's self, and feelings of smallness.

REFLECTIVE JOURNALING
Releasing Shame

Think about a time someone told you that you were wrong or made a mistake. What do you remember about how you felt at that moment? What emotions, thoughts, or impulses came up for you? As you remember that moment now, how does your body feel? Are there any words or phrases you find yourself saying, or can you remember someone else saying to you, that carry shame?

1. Write down on a piece of paper (not your journal!) any words you would use to describe the experience of knowing that you are imperfect at something when you have tried to be perfect at it.

You can repeat this exercise for as many situations as you like.

When you have a list of words that feel complete, take a moment to read through them, and remember that these words represent a narrative of your shame story. You might have words like *stupid, unworthy, waste of time, tightness, afraid, small, ignorant, cold,* and so forth.

Know that anytime these words or the sensations they describe arise, either from within you or directed at you by others, there's a chance that your shame story is being provoked.

2. Take these words associated with your shame and write their empowering opposites in your journal, for example, *smart, worthy, enriching to spend time with, openness, courage, big, wise, warm,* and so on.

Compare your shame stories to your empowering qualities and stories.

3. Optional: Rip up the list of shame stories as a way of symbolically saying goodbye to them.

4. Consider what activities, connections, or affirmations help you connect with your chosen empowering qualities. How could you incorporate these activities, connections, and affirmations into your life more regularly?

5. Who do you know who celebrates these qualities in you?

Disgust and Recoil:
Opposing the Fawn Response

Disgust can result from an impulse to recoil from something overwhelming. We may experience disgust about something that we don't understand, such as someone's sexual fetishes, or we might be disgusted by something that we recognize either isn't safe for us to participate in or that goes against our personal values. Think of the sensation you have when you walk into a space that has not been cleaned in a long time, or how it feels to hear someone sharing a political ideology that expresses violence to you or people you love. The impulse behind disgust is to take us away from a relationship that feels either unsafe or overwhelming.

Disgust can also be self-directed. If we have experienced self-abandonment and excessive people-pleasing (the fawn response), then disgust can show up as a mechanism for self-preservation. Disgust at the lack of care we have given ourselves might cause us to push back against our internal fawning tendencies. We may go from doting on a partner to recoiling away from them as our nervous system begins to regroup and move away from self-sacrificing for the sake of connection.

Jealousy and Global High Activation

Global High-Intensity Activation, or GHIA, is a Somatic Experiencing term for a nervous system state in which one is simultaneously scared and angry, wants to run away, puffs up and gets loud, rolls over and surrenders to something uncomfortable or unwanted, and feels frozen about what to do. In other words, every self-protective response feels activated at once or in very close succession. This can happen when unfamiliar circumstances threaten a core aspect of our relational safety and security. When you're in it, you may find yourself spinning in attempts to bargain with partners or metamours, wanting to end a partnership or cut off a connection, interfering or intervening in your partners' relationships with others, dissociating, or saying things are fine when they really aren't.

Some of us may have experienced GHIA repeatedly in our lives, particularly through any lived experiences of marginalization and oppression, or if our caregivers were absent or not consistently available during childhood. I think that the experience we describe as "jealousy" might more accurately be called GHIA-lousy. In non-monogamous relationships you may have felt this happening at the beginning of opening up, or when faced with disclosure of information about a partner and metamour's relationship, or even when the dynamics of your non-monogamy are feeling challenging and things are moving too fast, or perhaps while navigating the grief that comes alongside the process of exploring new ways of relating. It's a state that can be very confusing both for those experiencing it and for those trying to relate to folks experiencing it.

It's common to emerge from GHIA with either no memory or a fuzzy memory of what happened. It may be easier to remember the moments leading up to it and immediately afterwards.

Resolving Distress

Working with any kind of distress in the nervous system is twofold:

1. Internal resolution to the impulses for self-protection

2. External resolution through communication with our partners

We might forget important things that partners communicated to us, or find it challenging to identify what was so threatening to our nervous system. This is where the work on collaborative consent and relationship agreements that we explored in chapter 17 can be incredibly supportive. We also look at some communication tools to support this in chapter 19.

To support the internal resolution of self-protective impulses, you can explore, or even visualize, physical movements. As internal distress comes to have less of a hold, it may be easier to address the root causes of the distress with your partners and work on collaborative solutions that everyone can be on board with.

RELATIONAL TOOLKIT
Resolving Self-Protection Part 2

These suggestions build on the examples from chapter 6. More nervous-system capacity can come online when an impulse is allowed to complete. If you aren't sure what impulse you have, explore all of these. Doing these movements in slow-motion allows our nervous system to experience them more fully. If any movements are not available to you, you can imagine or visualize yourself doing them.

FIGHT
In fight, our shoulders and arms tense up to protect and defend—think of holding a sword and shield. Hold your arms up before you as if pushing someone away, and slowly push the air. You can imagine resistance to your push, or you can push against any solid surface. Alternatively, you can slowly sweep your arms before you, imagining you are clearing your way through a thicket of tall grass.

FLIGHT
In flight, our hip flexors tense up, ready to mobilize our body to leap or run. Explore peddling your feet back and forth very slowly. You can also lie down and practice moving your legs as if you were walking. Bend your knees so your feet are flat on the ground, keep them about hip distance apart, and let your

knees alternate slowly flopping into the centre and then coming back up, in a windshield-wiper motion.

FREEZE

In freeze, there is an impulse to move towards rest. You might wrap yourself in a blanket or build a blanket fort to help reduce sensory stimulation. Give yourself ten or twenty minutes in this state of rest, and as you come out of your rest, move slowly, gently waking each of your joints: wiggling your toes, rotating your ankles, gently bending your knees, slowly rocking from one hip to the other, rolling your shoulders and your wrists, wiggling your fingers, and gently rolling your neck from side to side.

FAWN

Fawn is an impulse to stay connected, and we can do that by gently resourcing the nervous system. Instead of staying connected with a stressful situation, practice staying connected with yourself by doing an activity you love for about twenty minutes. This might include journaling, making a warm beverage, spending time outside, playing with a beloved animal, or listening to a favourite piece of music.

Even if you cannot move, closing your eyes and imagining yourself performing a movement can help you resolve nervous system distress. As you learn to pendulate your nervous system and let go of patterns of people-pleasing and self-abandonment, you may be confronted by sensations of disgust, an impulse to recoil from connection with others, and shame. Sometimes the sensations of fight and flight feel stronger. Remember to stay kind and tender with yourself.

Dissociation as Safety

When we are pulled into our shadow self, whether through distress, overwhelm, or a lack of adequate support, we might also experience dissociation, a survival mechanism when we are overwhelmed. Temporary dissociation allows us to slow down the receipt of information and give ourselves time and space to process. We compartmentalize until we can have support to heal and integrate. In some instances of complex trauma, dissociation is not so temporary and can develop into dissociative conditions such as dissociative identity disorder. To be clear, this is not what we are discussing here. However, the advocacy work of therapists, clinicians, and those with forms of dissociative identity has helped enhance our understanding of how and why dissociation happens.

Dissociation allows us to take a break while minimally engaging in low-stress activity. You might gently dissociate by playing video games, scrolling on your phone, or going for a walk. Most of the time, all we need is a rest—think of how much easier it can be to tackle a harder task after a nap or a relaxing break. However, when facing more complex distress, we might need something more.

We might attempt a reset through altered states: the highs of drugs, the highs of new relationship energy, or through other means. While in an altered state, we might feel a little more integrated but still be internally catching up with our own experience.

Understanding the parts of ourselves that show up when scared, challenged, or angry can help us build a positive relationship with our shadows. I like to think about this through the framework of the four quadrants: the heart relates to our emotional quadrant, the mind to the social quadrant, the body to our practical quadrant, and the spirit to our erotic quadrant. When it feels unsafe to be in any of these spaces, we will naturally retreat to feel safe. We may even develop a preference about which quadrant we retreat into.

Retreat into the heart: Feeling things feels safe. We become emotionally volatile and reactive. It can be hard for people to reach us with reason and logic, and we may be overcome with strong emotions.

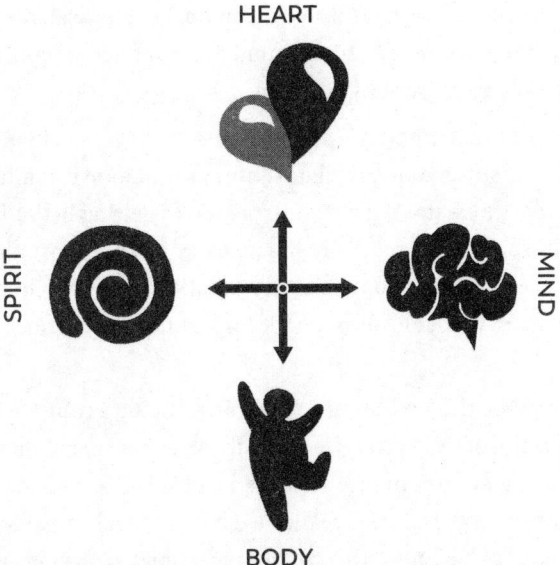

Figure 18.1. Dissociation (icons by Joan Trinh Pham)

Disconnect from the heart: Feeling things feels unsafe. We become dispassionate. We may be empathetically unresponsive; we might seem cold or harsh. We might even retreat into our rational mind and look for logic and reason to help us make sense of the experience.

Retreat into the mind: Thinking about things feels safe. We seek to intellectualize our experiences as part of processing them. We may rely on language, labels, and patterns to understand the situation and seek meaning. Sometimes our brains don't stop spinning, and we may be drawn to have an even more analytical approach to something than is typical for us.

Disconnect from the mind: Thinking hard feels unsafe. Our rational brain disconnects and we may struggle with comprehension, experience memory issues, or have brain fog. It might be hard for people to reach us with reason. We may lean into our emotional quadrant or seek comfort in our erotic quadrant.

Retreat into the body: Being in our bodies feels safe. We fixate on physical activities such as working out. This can also show up as a fixation on personal space, a strong desire to clean things, or obsessing about taking care of the home. You might also feel more enjoyment in physical touch and other sensory stimuli.

Disconnect from the body: Being in our bodies feels unsafe. We may lose awareness of hunger, pain, or other physical sensations. This could lead to things like disordered eating or freezing up during physical intimacy. We may struggle to recognize our physical boundaries and needs, and we might find others encroaching on our physical space.

Retreat into the erotic and the spirit: Being erotic or spiritual feels safe. We can be prone to spiritual bypassing; sentiments like "everything happens for the best" might come up. We may find ourselves getting hedonistic or getting immersed in spiritual or religious practices as a way of avoiding reconnecting to our whole. Some people may find that they use psychedelics more to alter their state of consciousness, and it may be hard to connect to the present moment.

Disconnect from the erotic and the spirit: Being erotic or spiritual feels unsafe. Our sense of reality may become distorted; we may experience depression. We might feel stuck or just frustrated and jaded. We might find ourselves fixating on physical pleasures. We may even find ourselves exhibiting compulsive or addictive behaviours. This could be as simple as playing video games for hours, marathoning through television shows, or disordered eating.

REFLECTIVE JOURNALING
Your Dissociative Patterns

What patterns do you have when it comes to dissociation?

Which places do you tend to feel safer hanging out, and which ones feel less safe when you are distressed?

How do you support yourself when resting in one of these quadrants, and what helps you reconnect with your whole self?

My own dissociation patterns have changed through the years. As a teen I felt safe in the theatre and playing at being someone else (spirit). After sexual trauma in adulthood, I began dissociating into my thoughts, retreating into intellect (mind). Following two miscarriages during my marriage, I turned to using the gym and the release of exercise as a way to avoid my grief and shame (retreating into my body). Later, I sought solace in dance, music festivals, and psychedelics (spirit and body). Today, I endeavour to notice how all these parts respond and honour the impulses I have to escape in non-destructive ways that support my nervous system to rest and come back into integration.

RELATIONAL TOOLKIT
Supporting Re-Integration

It takes twenty to thirty minutes for our nervous system to reset. These are examples of some practices that you can do that can help you reconnect to the place that you are feeling disconnected from.

Reconnecting with your heart: Spend time with a trusted friend or a favourite show or movie from childhood. Use soft textures and weighted blankets to bring you extra comfort.

Reconnecting with your mind: Journal privately or talk about your experience with a friend or trusted confidant. You might find it helpful to do things that engage your mind, like math, word puzzles, or reading a good book.

Reconnecting to your physical body: Intentional movement practice. This could be as simple as walking, taking a yoga stretching class, or dancing. Remember to hydrate and nourish yourself.

Returning into your spirit: Art, music, dance, writing, and other forms of creative self-expression are incredibly useful, as is spending time in nature. Spiritual practices and rituals, either solo or with community, are also fantastic.

Remember, the intention here isn't to force yourself to be chill about distressing things, or to like everyone in your extended network of relations. You don't have to feel compersion for someone you dislike, don't feel safe around, or who behaves in harmful or abusive ways to others. Even when you're working on your shadow emotions, completing your self-protection responses, and have ample opportunities for nervous system rest and integration, you might still dislike someone in your anarcule. That's okay. Take care not to gaslight yourself into a forced mimicry of compersion. Instead, turn back towards your self-relationship and the agreements you have made with yourself, and resource yourself in whatever way you need to courageously assert boundaries if and when you need to. We will look at this in more detail in the following chapter.

The goal is to resource your nervous system so that you can move towards experiences of empathy and compassion. Cultivating compersion is a process that thrives with trust, kindness, and care.

Tabitha's Story
The Gift of Compersion

Tabitha never thought she would feel compersion. In high school, she'd been in an intense relationship where she lost herself, leading her to avoid exclusive partnerships for years to protect her autonomy. But when she met Hank, she was determined to build a conscious relationship focused on open communication and working through challenges together. When they exchanged marriage vows, she couldn't promise "forever."

They enjoyed many incredible years together raising their daughter before Hank had an affair. The rupture of the affair rocked them both. Tabitha had desires for other people and didn't pursue them, believing she was honoring the agreement they made. She felt both envious that Hank had been able to pursue his desires and down on herself for not doing the same.

The conversation about having an open relationship was consistently in the background, but it took a decade before they were ready to explore it. Tabitha's interest in non-monogamy wasn't solely about sex; she longed to explore the kind of close, affectionate friendships she'd enjoyed before meeting Hank, and to be desired and courted. Hank was excited about the possibility of new experiences. He assured Tabitha that no one could replace her. Still, whenever he mentioned going on dates, Tabitha would feel as though she was reliving the distress of the affair, imagining the intimate moments he might be sharing with others.

They decided to see what it would be like to explore non-monogamous spaces together rather than separately. The hope was that they could provide each other with reassurance and connection rather than endure the stress of solo experiences. They attended a workshop for open-minded couples, going in nervously but holding hands and an agreement to stay close. The evening was a low-key "bottoms-on" event with ground rules that helped Tabitha feel safe. They met a couple on a similar journey and connected well with the wife of this couple, Abigail. Tabitha and Hank spent some time making out with Abigail before another woman approached Hank with an interest in connecting. As Tabitha and Abigail continued connecting, Hank continued to have occasional eye contact with Tabitha and touch her leg while he and this other woman were connecting. Tabitha found herself wanting to watch Hank with the other woman. Abigail checked in with her to see how she was doing, and Tabitha realized, much to her surprise, that she was feeling joy!

Seeing her husband enjoying himself, and another woman enjoying her time with Hank, something shifted in her. A warmth expanded through her heart and solar plexus: She was experiencing compersion. Something was arousing about the experience, but there was also a huge relief. She could exhale, with an embodied sense that nothing Hank was doing with anyone else was taking away from what she and Hank had together.

The openness, transparency, and boundaries of the experience helped her feel that Hank continued to honour their relationship—a stark contrast to her experience during the affair, when she felt their relationship had been disregarded. In the affair, she hadn't had a choice; she hadn't been considered or included. Coming to a place where they could embrace transparency, honesty, and have clear agreements about how she is included and how their relationship is continuing to be honoured has reinforced their connection.

That evening marked a turning point for Tabitha. She began to understand compersion as more than just an idea. Witnessing Hank's pleasure didn't diminish her; it brought her a sense of peace and even her own pleasure. Compersion, she realized, was less about eliminating jealousy and more about finding a way to embrace the complexities of love. She describes it as a feeling of wholeness, and it has given her a solid footing in the ongoing conversations about opening up, which can still at times be challenging. She says compersion feels like receiving something rather than something being taken away. It reminded her of who she remembered being before the rupture. And it also opened up a lot of new areas of pleasure and desire she is excited to explore.

As we move into deeper layers of relating, we may find that we also unlock more integrated experiences of compersion that nurture and nourish in profound ways. I've found that each drop of compersion has the potential to expand

and transform everything else in my relational landscape. Once you've tasted it, compersion will shift how you experience your relationship ecology. You might re-assess the relationship experiences through the lens of this new feeling and find subtle shifts in how you engage and connect with others. It might feel easier to let go of connections that bring too much destabilizing stress into your life, or you might feel inspired with a desire to do the deeper work with partners and loved ones to address the sources of relational stress and find a resolution.

19

COURAGEOUS COMMUNICATION AND CONFLICT INTIMACY

In this chapter, we explore how to navigate conflict in compassionate and loving ways by developing conflict intimacy. We build on the understanding of working with distress in the nervous system that we learned about in the previous chapter on cultivating compersion, alongside the work of collaborative consent from chapter 17, and set the foundation for communication practices and processes you can bring into your relationships.

It isn't just having conflict that can challenge our relationships; it's also the process of being in conflict. Without ongoing practices to help us reorient to connection amid conflict, it may feel difficult to move through the threshold of intimacy and come into that deepest layer of Relationship. For the purposes of this chapter, I offer a very broad definition of conflict: *any difference between needs, desires, capacity, values, or beliefs.*

Conflict can arise internally when we find differences between what we desire and what we have the capacity for. We might encounter it as we confront the necessary fantasy—the potential we have seen in a relationship and invested in as a strategy for safety—and transition towards figuring out what a connection actually is, beyond that fantasy. Conflict might arise after a loss of trust or even abuse of positional power. A conflict in values and principles, for example, over a political stance or spiritual belief, can lead to confusion about who a partner is, and if we ever feel that we have to capitulate or compromise on one of our values for the sake of a relationship, it can feel like we aren't being truly honoured or seen. Sometimes conflict happens because of misunderstanding or missing a bid for connection. We might also experience conflict about how to engage or disengage from conflict.

Conflict stimulates the nervous system, creating tension, activation, and vigilance. The energy of conflict is compelling: we may experience impulses to flee and to fight, to make ourselves smaller to avoid it, or to make ourselves bigger to hold power over it. We may feel overwhelmed by it, or even invigorated. You might experience conflict as creating distance between you and another. It might feel like you shift from one layer of relating into a less connected layer, which can in turn feel a lot like being abandoned.

At the heart of conflict is a fear of loss, instability, and changes in our connections with others. Conflict is essentially a disconnect: "I want one thing, you want another." Or, "I know what I want, but I imagine you want something different." There's that monogamy hangover of expecting telepathy again! Or even, "I know I don't want the thing that you want, and I'm not sure how to tell you." When we experience these disconnects, it can feel like we have slipped away from being in a relationship. This can stir up feelings of abandonment, loneliness, and sometimes even depression.

It takes courage, strength, and willingness to sit in the unknown and to lean into conflict intimacy. We have to feel supported enough to sit with the distress of the unknown. To do this, we need to know that we are safe. We need to have our core needs recognized by ourselves and others and be able to feel those needs are being met sufficiently.

Wanting to avoid conflict is a natural strategy for self-protection, especially if we have experienced conflict as leading to violence, be it physical, emotional, mental, sexual, or even spiritual. Remember: The existence of conflict does not necessarily mean there will be violence, and experiencing conflict isn't inherently violent, even though anger and aggression can be present. If you grew up around conflicts, being in conflict with loved ones might paradoxically feel like a familiar form of connection.

Conflict intimacy is the art of staying in connection while experiencing conflict. This kind of intimacy invites us to remain compassionate and present with our loved ones as we seek new understanding and return to trust. And when I say it is an art, I mean that it's not something we can ever perfect. It is an ongoing practice that will be slightly different every time we experience it. For me, the most beautiful thing about developing conflict intimacy with loved ones is that it allows me to remain connected to a sense of belonging without sacrificing any part of my autonomy. It means that conflict doesn't precipitate the end of a relationship.

I invite you to see conflict as a doorway, a moment of moving from one relationship experience into another. This door might well lead you out of the relationship, but it could also lead you into deeper intimacy and understanding in all your relationships.

REFLECTIVE JOURNALING
Your Relationship to Conflict

What's your relationship to conflict? Do you tend to feed conflict or avoid it? What was role-modelled for you growing up? How was conflict treated in your family of origin or your culture?

What sensations do you notice when you experience conflict? Do you grow tense in anticipation of conflict, or feel a temperature change? Does your mind race? Do you ever become emotionally guarded?

Conflict and Your Nervous System

To have healthy conflict, we first have to trust that we, both individually and relationally, mean enough to one another that no one will run away from the conflict or try to win at the others' expense. Being clear on your relational North Star, as we explored in chapter 17, can be helpful, but if you haven't worked on that yet, simply affirming your shared values can support more trust in a conflict process, and make a drastic difference in how we navigate it.

In other words, knowing the love, care, and significance that others place on you and your mutual relationship builds trust in the shared desire to maintain the relationship, and this resources the nervous system to feel safe enough to engage in conflict. Conversely, when we experience conflict with a stranger or acquaintance, or with a person we either don't have an emotionally invested relationship or a shared vision of a relationship with, the degree of mutual care will be unclear. In these circumstances, trying to engage in a process around conflict or repair following any harm or rupture can feel more distressing than avoiding the situation. Trying to engage in conflict intimacy where there's no trust in care and support might potentially be traumatic.

The stimulation of conflict can sometimes feel pleasing and energizing and even give the brain a hit of dopamine. In terms of what's happening in the nervous system, some mild stimulation can bring about rushes of energy, greater mental focus, and even sometimes sexual arousal. If that stimulation becomes too much and the nervous system becomes overwhelmed, this might lead us to shut down, minimize, or attempt to take control of a conflict. We might distract ourselves from conflict by seeking out new recreational relationships; investing our time, money, and resources away from the relationship; or even having an emotional affair. Some people find that their nervous system thrives on conflict, and that the cool numbness of an overstimulated nervous system experiencing shutdown after activation is a familiar form of comfort.

A desire to avoid conflict doesn't need to be pathologized. Looking at conflict from a somatic perspective, avoidance can be an indicator of overwhelm: stimulation overload, trauma memories, mental or physical health challenges, and other life stressors like work, money, and family problems all have the potential to take us beyond our capacity to engage with the emotional complexity that conflict brings with it. This can leave us with only one recourse: shutting down until the overwhelm disappears. But sometimes we keep shutting down, and end up numb to the issues that need addressing in our connections with others.

When one partner wants to run away, and the other wants to feed the conflict, we may even begin to experience conflict about the conflict, which is a challenging place to be in. Conversely, when one or more partners are impatient about addressing conflict, and the other partners don't yet have the capacity or trust to do so, this can feel like a boundary violation, leading to resentment and even further disconnection. And so, we have to find ways to support our nervous systems to overcome the urge to repress or react in harmful ways that might disrupt the relationship, such as the Relational Toolkit activity in chapter 18 on Resolving Self-Protection.

Dramatic Triangulation

In the storms of distress and uncertainty that conflict can bring, we may find ourselves experiencing triangulation—but not the healthy kind we explored in chapter 16. This dramatic triangulation arrives alongside three core fears: being abandoned by a loved one, hurting the people we love, and being treated as disposable or inhumanely.

If you've ever experienced being in the thick of what is sometimes called poly-drama, you'll know how much it can rock the proverbial boat of any multi-partner relationship ecosystem. As we looked at in chapter 16 when we explored the Meta-Model of Relating, triangulation can be a bid for stability, but in unhealthy triangulation, we enrol a third party, not as a mediator or healthy stabilizer, but to play a role in a system known as the drama triangle.

In the Karpman drama triangle, we cast ourselves in one of three roles—victim, rescuer, or persecutor—and then project others in our lives into the other roles to create a perpetual dynamic of intensity, confusion, chaos, and toxicity, otherwise known as drama.[1] This is the shadow side of triangulation. You may have been in situations where you've experienced playing these roles at different times in your relationships. When you're in relationship with someone playing one of these roles, you might have noticed how hard it is to resist playing one of the parts and joining them in the drama. The drama triangle exists somatically in the spaces of fight, flight, freeze, and fawn, and our primal survival instincts are activated by it. Being in drama together can feel like connection, although it's unsustainable. We might cycle through all these roles, caught in a sticky fly-paper-like vortex. This is the essence of so-called "toxic" relationship dynamics, and in this drama vortex, childhood wounds and any long-held relationship resentments can emerge.

I like to think of this cycle using archetypes rather than the commonly used labels of victim, rescuer, and persecutor. As a fan of Arthurian legends and Celtic lore, I've loved many a story of a brave knight rescuing a damsel in distress. These archetypes carry a lot of meaning for me, so I call them the damsel, the knight, and the dragon. I find this helps me think about their motivations and what each person might need, or what we might assume they want. I use all these terms as gender-neutral and applicable to anyone. If there are stories that you have grown up with that have similar archetypes, you might find it helpful to think of the characters in those stories to help you learn how to recognize these patterns of behaviour in the drama cycle.

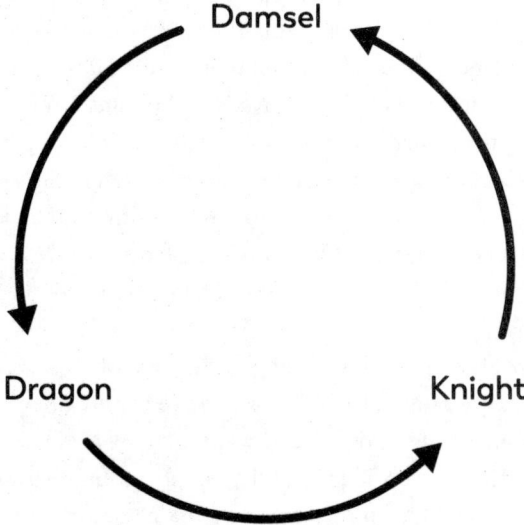

Figure 19.1. The drama vortex imagined as damsel, dragon, and knight

The damsel feels powerless, trapped by a dragon and seeking to be rescued by a knight. If their chosen knight fails to rescue them, they might conclude the knight is in cahoots with the dragon—maybe they are a dragon in disguise as a knight!—and seek out a new knight to rescue them. A damsel may struggle to assert their needs or ask for what they want. Instead, their words and thoughts may cycle continuously back to a misstep by a partner or some other wrong done to them. Their identity may reorient to be about this wrong. The damsel is often stuck in heightened nervous-system arousal, dancing between flight and freeze.

The knight finds purpose by saving damsels in distress. They may seek situations to triangulate themselves into, and often tend towards self-sacrificing in their quest. They might not even stop to check if their damsel wants their support, and may be keen to paint others as a dragon. Knights may hold deep wounds in themselves and seek to rescue others instead of working on their own healing journey. They have habitual fight and flight responses and try to stay connected with others through fawning and people-pleasing.

The dragon wants to hoard power and may struggle to recognize others' boundaries. Compassion is hard for them to access, and they might belittle or put down others to elevate their own sense of self-esteem. They may appear prone to angry outbursts and carry deep wounds. The dragon is often stuck in a highly aroused nervous system state, with strong fight responses moving towards freeze.

In a dynamic that has become drama-filled, we can cycle through all these roles. We may think ourselves to be one of them while fulfilling a different role to someone else. For example, I might see myself as the damsel, and my metamour as a dragon, but they might perceive themself as the knight saving our mutual partner from my fire-breathing ways. And our mutual partner may see themselves as the knight trying to rescue two damsels from one another simultaneously. Escaping this cycle can take persistent effort and dedicated focus. Even when you internally shift and are ready to leave it, others may still want to enrol you back into the drama with them.

Remember that when someone is angry, they are often scared. When someone is scared, they are often hurt. When someone is hurt, they are often feeling unloved. When someone is unloved, they want to be seen and heard for who they are and their experience. Consider what the people in the vortex need: A damsel in distress wants safety, a knight on a quest wants validation, and a dragon hoarding power wants security and stability. There are many ways to meet these needs that don't involve further feeding the drama and conflict.

Once you fully step out of the vortex, those still in it may triangulate new roles onto other relationships, or they might lose steam and eventually let go of the drama themselves. While we are in the cycle of drama, we negate responsibility and self-development, but the moment we escape the vortex, self-growth happens, and joyful relationships become possible again.

Other Experiences of Triangulation in Multi-Partner Relationships

Whether we are caught by the vortex of drama or not, conflict in our relationships can trigger three core fears: being abandoned, being treated as disposable, and hurting those we love. In multi-partner relationships, all three fears can show up simultaneously in the different people in the dynamic.

At the root of all these is a fear that relationships and connections will be lost, and the individual will be left alone and isolated. These fears can be treated as real and should not be ignored, dismissed, or minimized. Even if the real-life risk of these fears coming true seems low, our nervous systems don't necessarily know that. To support connection through conflict, we have to first establish safety, and to do so we must acknowledge that these fears come from a deep, instinctive drive towards belonging and companionship. The stakes are high: On a primal level, connection equals survival.

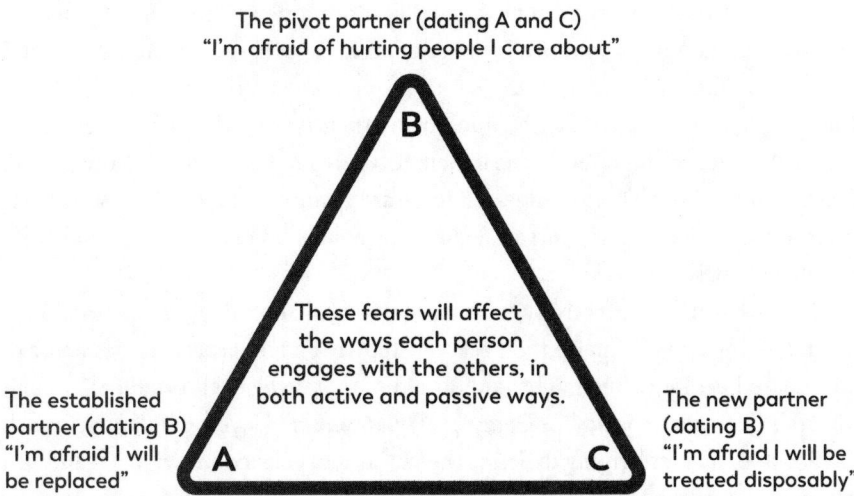

The pivot partner (dating A and C)
"I'm afraid of hurting people I care about"

B

These fears will affect the ways each person engages with the others, in both active and passive ways.

The established partner (dating B) "I'm afraid I will be replaced"

A

C

The new partner (dating B) "I'm afraid I will be treated disposably"

Figure 19.2. The polyamory fear triangle

Consider our theoretical anarcule again. Ali and Bea have an established relationship, and Bea has now started dating CJ. Ali may fear that Bea's new relationship with CJ will lead to an abandonment of their connection that has been deeply invested in with time, emotional energy, and effort. This fear might cause Ali to set ultimatums to control the relationship Bea has with CJ, or to seek more time with, or reassurance about, their relationship with Bea.

CJ as the new partner may fear that, given Ali and Bea's long-standing history together, they are at risk of being treated as little more than a recreational relationship and therefore will be disposable. CJ might feel anxious during the first few months of their relationship with Bea and may lean heavily into their necessary fantasy, or perhaps even avoid it altogether and instead anxiously seek out repeated clarity about Bea's capacity to be in a relationship with them. Bea, who loves Ali and is coming to care deeply for CJ, may fear making a mistake that could hurt either or both these people who are important in their life. Because of this, Bea might downplay or withhold any disclosures that could cause upset or pull them into a vortex of drama.

With each of these fears, there are both effective and ineffective approaches. Ineffective strategies could be passive (avoidance) or active (engaging). In our scenario with Ali, Bea, and CJ, Ali might respond by trying to impose rules on Bea and CJ's relationships, while also minimizing their fears or refusing to voice their concerns. CJ may become vocal in asserting themselves and not having their relationship with Bea be controlled by Ali, perhaps even making demands of Bea. Alternatively, they may start to push out Ali or other people in Bea's life, finding some consolation in an "out of sight, out of mind" approach. Bea may try to find peace by telling Ali and CJ each what they assume each partner wants to hear. They might also avoid conflict by minimizing their fears and concerns, and their inner perfectionist might even cause them to act as gatekeeper about how Ali and CJ are supposed to feel. To be clear, all these are examples of ineffective strategies, and they often leave each person feeling more isolated and disconnected from their loved ones.

To work with fear effectively, we have to work collaboratively. For Ali and Bea, that might mean working on their relationship vision and clarifying the shape of their shared ecology. Bea might find it helpful to get clear with both Ali and CJ what they have the capacity for, in terms of quadrants and layers of relating, in each relationship, further helping to define the sandbox of each connection. CJ and Bea might work together to determine what they hope their shared relational ecology holds, even if the relationship is still in early days. Ali and CJ might want to get to know one another better, or at least understand their respective relationships with

Bea. All of them will benefit from building more capacity in their nervous system so that the fears they hold cast less of a shadow over the relationships. We look at some specific examples of this below.

SOMATIC PAUSE
Successfully Navigating Conflict

Take a moment to stretch and take a few breaths.

We've been exploring hypothetical conflicts within a relationship, and maybe you're thinking about real-life conflicts you've experienced. Can you think of a time you've successfully navigated conflict in a relationship and returned to a positive feeling of connection?

What did it feel like to resolve the conflict?

What's the first moment you can remember when you felt reconnected to this person?

As you recall this memory, what sensations do you notice coming up for you?

If the sensations tied to thinking about successfully resolving conflict are comfortable for you, I invite you to stay with them for a few moments. Notice if other sensations start to come up: You might notice gratitude, some bittersweetness, or a sense of calm.

When you feel ready, gently shake your body in a way that feels good for you, and take a few breaths.

Transparency

Concealment and withholding are obstacles to healthy and thriving relationships. Sometimes conflict and drama start when someone could have voiced a need or boundary but didn't, or when someone might have been included in a conversation but wasn't. This isn't a suggestion that we abandon all personal privacy. A degree of privacy is essential to our psychological well-being. Instead, this is an invitation to explore more openness in how we openly relate as a step towards diffusing the power that shame, fear, and distress about conflict can have, thus mitigating their ability to disrupt our relationships.

Withholding our thoughts, feelings, curiosities, and impulses often buries them in our subconscious, where they may be acted out unconsciously through projections, and our minds may weave stories as we try to make sense of what isn't being said or addressed. We may sense intuitively that something is being hidden or not talked about, even if it isn't about us. Unconsciously our nervous system may respond to this as a possible threat, and our mind will create meaning out of it, possibly even filling in the blanks with a story that may or may not hold truth. Our shadow emotions may come into play.

Making time to make the unconscious conscious and visible, not just for yourself but whenever possible for everyone in your constellation, is key to addressing fears and conflicts and building long-lasting resilient relationships. The Open Window Check-In is a foundational practice for transparency. You can build it into your day-to-day interactions with loved ones. I use this tool myself, often weaving the questions into incidental conversations with my partners when we catch up and following it more formally when working through any challenges or repair.

RELATIONAL TOOLKIT
The Open Window Check-In

This exercise is about holding space to listen and tune in to where the other person is at. It is to help us build empathy and compassion and can be done with any number of people, although more than five might get overwhelming, depending on how much each person has to say.

It is best to do this with each person speaking uninterrupted. To support this, you could use an object to signify whose turn it is to speak, such as a hat, cup, crystal, or other item. As you listen to the person speaking, practice letting go of a need to respond or react to what they are saying. Remember that everyone is allowed to feel as they feel, and no one can be wrong about their feelings. When it is your turn to speak, practice speaking from a space of your feelings, and what feels true for you right now.

It can be helpful to relax your bodies and breathe together before starting. If you are physically present with one another, you could hold hands, and move together with your breath, raising your arms on the inhale and letting them down with the exhale.

You can take five to fifteen minutes each to share the answer to the following questions:

1. How is your relationship to yourself today?

2. How is your relationship to your world today?

3. How is your relationship to your partners (the people you're sharing this check-in with) today?

At the end of sharing, you can thank one another for being present, sharing, and listening. If there is something you want more clarity about, you can ask for clarification. If you feel inspired, you can offer a mirror of what you heard: a brief, compassionate summary of what you have seen through this open window into the other person's world.

Note: This isn't a time for problem-solving or exploring conflict. If you want to discuss something another speaker brought up, it is best to ask them if you can set aside time later to discuss it. Allowing time to pass before jumping into conflict and problem-solving gives everyone a chance to process and return to the subject from a more grounded space.

This exercise can be done daily, weekly, or at a frequency that makes sense for you. I recommend doing it in person if possible, but it still works over video or phone or through shared voice notes. It can be useful to do daily for several weeks when first practising it, or to do regularly over several months if you're working on repairing from rupture.

Repair Work and Accountability

Conflict, lack of trust, unaddressed self-protection, and nervous system distress can all lead to rupture, and for a relationship to continue, even after a conflict is resolved, we also have to work on repairing these ruptures. Relational rupture can feel a lot like loss or even death. Some might notice an overwhelming experience of grief and cycle through anger, sadness, denial, and bargaining before being able to come to a place of acceptance. We don't just mourn the harm and disconnection we have experienced; we also sometimes grieve for the relationship's future, especially if we feel deeply invested in it and struggle to see a way forward. These ruptures might land on top of wounds from past unhealed relational ruptures, including ones from childhood.

Repair cannot happen overnight, nor can it be approached disingenuously. Every party has to be on board with wanting to repair the trust in the relationship. We also have to be ready to do the repair work, which sometimes means doing a bit of work internally first, such as moving through any self-protection impulses we're holding on to. Relational repair requires us to work relationally rather than in carceral or punitive ways. Processes of restorative and transformative justice, such as the ones created by the Bay Area Transformative Justice Collective, offer pathways for large rupture repair processes, and we can apply principles from these to the smaller scale of our intimate relationships.[2] These practices, rooted in decolonized systems and inspired by pre-colonial Indigenous traditions, hold that no one is disposable within an ecology of relating, and our interconnectedness is vital for all of us to thrive.

Because repair can take time, we might need to navigate discomfort in our relationships during the repair process. Discomfort may not feel safe, and navigating repair can feel distressing to attempt alone. Reaching out to your wider relational ecosystem—your peers, elders, coaches, and guides—can help nourish and resource you.

Perhaps one of the most challenging things about this kind of repair work is that it requires each person to own their part, to take responsibility for their own foibles, shortcomings, mistakes, and harm. In relationship paradigms like patriarchal monogamy that expect perfection of a partner, to acknowledge anything less than perfection in oneself seems tantamount to shaming oneself. There is an internalized narrative for many that says, *If I take responsibility for doing wrong, I will be cast out; therefore I cannot take responsibility for doing wrong.*

When we are afraid to take responsibility for breaking trust, doing harm, or making mistakes, we might project blame onto another, triangulating ourselves as damsel and another as dragon. We might minimize or even gaslight a partner. Some may even dig their heels in and become more grandiose in extolling how perfect a partner they have been. Others may recoil internally, directed by shame to emotionally retreat or withdraw from their loved ones as a strategy to ensure no one can see their perceived failings.

Mary and Dan's Story
Rupture and Repair

Dan and Mary had been together for about a year and a half. At Mary's request, I'll be using he-him pronouns for him as he is a trans man and these events happened prior to him transitioning. Mary had introduced Dan to his community, where he also worked, and these friends welcomed Dan wholeheartedly. Dan was learning to identify and express his needs clearly and set boundaries. Unfortunately, one such attempt to set some boundaries was misunderstood by Mary as an ultimatum to precipitate the end of the relationship.

Mary had often experienced needing to remove himself from a community in the wake of break-ups; a stressful, but he felt necessary, move. The fear of losing the relationship with Dan also felt like it would mean a loss of the community he'd introduced Dan to in the first place. Scared about this possibility, he reached out to friends for support, which left Dan feeling betrayed.

Mary was distressed; the stakes felt high. His life was deeply embedded in this community, and leaving it might also mean leaving his job. Meanwhile, Dan felt frustrated. He thought he was simply expressing his needs, but Mary reaching out to their mutual friends poked at trauma from his past when people had believed untrue things about him, and he became defensive. This situation could have created major disruptions, not only in their own individual lives but also in their extended community. Neither of them was sure if a mediation process could help, but they were open to it.

I met with each of them separately to better understand what each was experiencing and to see if they were willing to meet together. Dan was willing to try mediation because he wanted to avoid burning bridges. For Mary, the idea of mediation was scary but also hopeful; he didn't think everything would be easy afterwards, but he felt it was at least worth trying.

Each of them invited three trusted friends as witnesses for the mediation to support them personally. The role of these friends was to observe the process without interacting with it, and to later help remind Mary and Dan of things that had been shared, even after the mediation concluded. The nine of us met in person, and the six witnesses, who all knew both Mary and Dan, formed a circle around us. We worked gently, slowly, checking in on what was understood when each person shared, and pausing to allow for feelings and emotions to be felt.

During the mediation, the initial misunderstanding became clear: Dan had stumbled in his expression of needs and desires and had hoped to find a way for the relationship to continue, and that the way he had done this had not landed well with Mary, and this set off a cycle of mutually triggering one another. As this all came to light, a space of softness and compassion was found.

Having friendly witnesses helped Dan feel calmer and better able to understand Mary's perspective. Coming out of it, Dan felt relieved that they had an agreed-upon path forward and that the community was holding them accountable to resolve things in a mature way. Without community support, Dan imagined that the situation could have easily spiralled, and he might have retreated out of fear and anxiety. The mediation process helped him stay present and have the necessary conversation.

For Mary, having witnesses during the mediation was intimidating. He was private about his struggles, but found that having people there made the process feel more supported, and eventually created deeper connections with those who were there to witness. The mediation left him with a different relationship to vulnerability and conflict. Even though the dating relationship did end, Dan and Mary were able to maintain a playful friendship that persists to this day. And even though they later shifted in their relationships to that community of friends, neither had to do so because of any rift.

This experience taught Dan how people could relate better and navigate conflict without resorting to fighting fire with fire. Dan felt it allowed him and Mary to find mutual understanding and compassion. For Mary, he came away with greater awareness of support in his life and the realization that he didn't have to face hard things alone. The mediation helped shift his perspective from "me versus him" to understanding that the relationship had just changed. For the first time, he got to experience a relationship transitioning in a healthy way, rather than ending completely.

Courageous Communication

I offer you the courageous communication guide to support you in navigating conflict. I've played with and developed this over the years, based on the difficult conversation formulas created by Marcia Baczynski and Reid Mihalko. This guide was developed in collaboration with Dr. Kimberly Dohms as part of our work in consent education in the Vancouver region, and I have refined this tool with influence from somatic practices.

You don't just have to use this when there are difficult things to talk about. It can be a model for all communications, including when supporting partners who are navigating rupture and repair. It can be a guide to help you prepare for a conversation and also to help you through as you have the conversation.

RELATIONAL TOOLKIT
Courageous Communication

PREPARATION PHASE
Can it be you? Can it be now? Is now the best moment for this conversation? Is there enough time to talk? Do you feel safe and resourced? Are either of you hungry, tired, or feeling raw and activated in this moment? Take the time to get resourced and come to the conversation from a supported and grounded space. It's important that everyone involved feels safe enough to be there.

CREATING CONTEXT
Fears and concerns: What potential obstacles are there to having this conversation? Do you have any fears about repercussions for yourself or others? Does it feel like there is space for empathy for your fears?

PREPARATION PHASE

Can It Be You?
Can It Be Now?

Yes, it can!

No, I'm too tired or scared to do this, or it's not a good time for me or my partner.

CREATING CONTEXT

Fears and Concerns
if you have them

Partner shares empathy, maybe shares their own fears and concerns.

Partner responds to fears with no empathy.

Hopes
why it matters, and why they matter!

Partner shares these hopes and affirms why it matters.

Partner doesn't agree or doesn't respond with empathy and understanding.

GET RESOURCED!

TALKING ABOUT THE THING

The Thing
need, desire, boundary, concern, inspiration

Partner is clear about what you've asked and responds supportively.

Partner dismisses or minimizes.

What Now?
What do you want them to do with what you've shared?

Partner makes a plan with you about next steps.

They can't do it

AFTERCARE: Care for your nervous system, make sure to follow up, and remember to play!

Resources can support you and your partner, and include:
• Asking for help from a friend, therapist, or mediator
• Hydrate, eat, move

• Completion of self-protection responses
• Somatic practices for nervous system support
Once you are resourced, go back to whichever stage you were at before needing to resource, and recap the conversation so far.

Figure 19.3. Courageous communication flow chart

Hopes: Why does it matter to you to talk about this situation? Why do you matter to one another? How do you hope this conversation will benefit you and others? Do you have a hope for how things might be after this conversation? Does your partner share your hopes and desires to have a conversation?

ACTUALLY TALKING ABOUT THE THING

The thing: Be as specific as possible! Depending on the situation, you may address what actions a partner did or didn't do and how that impacted you. Or you may have a boundary or limit to share. Or perhaps there is a need or desire that you have, or a concern that you want to raise, or maybe you've felt inspired and want to ask for something to change in your relationship.

What Now? Now that you've talked about the thing, what do you want them to do with what you have shared? Do you need a response right away, or would you rather they take some time before responding? Make a plan about what the next steps to address this topic are.

Aftercare: After any difficult conversation, make sure that you take time to care for your nervous systems, engage in activities that help release stress and resolve any forms of self-protection, and make sure to follow up.

Remember, you don't have to be perfect at this practice. It can take time to get used to resourcing your nervous system during conversations, or supporting your partner to do the same.

I encourage you to practise this with lower-stakes conversations at first to help you get used to the flow and pausing to resource when needed. This can help you prepare for any big conversations. Make notes together as you go through the conversation to help you track what is being talked about and shared as well as any decisions you make.

Nervous System Resourcing in Times of Conflict

As you work through any process of repair and grow conflict intimacy, it is important to remember to play. Play can resource us through discomfort and help us form new neural pathways of positive association between ourselves and the world we live in. Whether it's with the person you're in conflict with or someone else, play might well be the last thing on your mind when you are stressed or anxious. Play asks us to be a little vulnerable. When we play we open ourselves to the unknown, we invite interactions in novel ways, and sometimes we might sit at the edge of our comfort zones to explore beyond them. To put it simply: Play grants more capacity.

RELATIONAL TOOLKIT
Playful Activities to Support Healthy
Shadow Work in Relationships

These are examples of different play activities you can do with friends, loved ones, and partners to support mutual nervous-system regulation and positive connection. Choose the ones that you all enjoy.

- games: card games, board games, video games
- adventures and quests: going to a fairground, photo challenges, treasure hunts, playing hide-and-seek
- collaborative projects: art, cleaning, gardening
- play dress-up: cosplay, put together a costume, dress up fancy for a special occasion, wear a silly hat
- travel together: a day trip or weekend away
- participating in the arts: concerts, festivals, live theatre, comedy shows
- taking classes together or volunteering together

Balancing playfulness alongside attention to your needs and your partners' needs will help your relationships grow more authentic, joyful, and embodied. Over time, your nervous system will learn to be more comfortable with conflict. You'll develop resilience that allows you to feel connected with your loved ones, even amid challenging conversations. Conflict intimacy can strengthen and fortify your relationships from the roots to the branches and help you cultivate a vibrant and nourishing relational ecology.

PART 3 SUMMARY

In this section, we explored how to cultivate healthy, meaningful relationships through exploring new relational skills. Recognizing perfectionism as part of white supremacy culture and mono-normativity, we examined how post-monogamous relationships allow space for imperfection.

We've touched on how post-monogamous relationships can lead to the development of **anarcules** and relational networks through balancing a strong self-relationship with embodied, empowered connections to others, supported through **self-awareness, somatic practices, open communication, collaborative consent, relationship agreements,** and **courageous communication.** We also highlighted the importance of compassionately working with shadow emotions and nervous-system responses to stay connected through conflict, moving toward compersion.

You can revisit any of the activities in this section, especially the **Desire Dive, Open Window,** and **Courageous Communication** exercises, anytime. You may want to explore making a regular practice of the **Releasing Shame** and **Resolving Self-Protection** activities. Practicing these will help you grow healthier and more resilient and resourced post-monogamous relationships.

PART 4

Where Are You Going?

Throughout this book, we've explored alternatives to the nuclear family and other mono-normative relationship models, considering how to orient ourselves in a wide-open landscape rich with relational possibilities while learning to care for our nervous systems, and those of our loved ones, along the way. We've examined why these alternatives matter, what they might look and feel like, and how to cultivate them. Now, we'll look toward where they might lead.

We'll explore how to integrate your understanding of the **relationship landscape** and work within the **four quadrants** to form **resilient somatic attachment experiences,** and map your **relational ecology.** We'll also consider the possibility of including the nonhuman world in our relational ecosystems and discuss practices for navigating times of transition and change.

This section will conclude with an invitation to envision what **Radical Relating** and a **post-monogamous world** could mean for you—and for us all.

20

CHANGING LANDSCAPES

It's very strange to regard two people as community. Where is everybody else?
You know, with one person, it's hard to see very far. Two people, you can see a
bit more. But if you have a whole group of people around really caring about
you. . . it helps you fulfil your purpose.

—SOBONFU SOMÉ[1]

As individuals, we change over time; the world also changes, through seasons, economics, politics, emergent social movements, environmental forces, and more. When you're committed to authenticity in your relationships, you will undoubtedly experience changes over time. In mono-normativity, progression on the relationship escalator is the only endorsed form of change for a romantic connection. Any other kind of change is seen as negative or a precursor to break-up. But in a radical landscape, change is about honouring authenticity: finding the right pace, depth, and space for each relationship in a way that supports everyone's whole ecology. And this means that all things will change—and this can be good, nourishing, and even beneficial.

As you grow your own relational ecology and journey through a life of Radical Relating, how will you weather the storms of change and navigate the transitions and evolutions that naturally happen over time? How can you use these tools to help you orient to landscape changes, heal from the grief that change brings, and remain open-hearted and compassionate in all your relationships?

Networks of Attachment

In part 1, we touched on attachment theory and the precarity of romantic attachment in a monogamous paradigm. Let's examine how this shifts as we embrace a relational ecosystem.

To recap: Secure attachment is the experience of well-developed distress tolerance that helps us relate with a sense of safety, trust, and emotional security. By learning how to tolerate distress and understanding that our partners still exist in our landscape even when not visible or immediately available, we can develop somatic security that supports a positive attachment experience. As we get better at understanding and working with our nervous system responses effectively, it becomes easier to maintain connection and the feeling of belonging, even when there is relational stress.

However, when the nuclear family paradigms still dominate, and where supremacy cultures have sought to keep us divided, we suffer from the loss of community and the absence of extended family and village. Individualism in favour of small family units, along with the prioritization of romantic relationships over friendships, has impacted mental and social health. It is inherently precarious for our overall well-being when all our safety, security, and stability rests in a single set of relationships.

For many, consensual and honest non-monogamy offers a possibility of returning to extended family, kinship of choice, and poly-queer networks of attachment. Polyamory can provide support that mirrors the most committed of friendships. Much like in a friendship-affirming sitcom or movie, the people within a polycule—or anarcule—are there for you, even when it hasn't been, to quote a popular song from the 1990s, your day, your week, your month, or even your year.[2]

In the queer world, we see this through the practice of creating chosen family. Rooted in Black and Indigenous practices around kinship-making, intentional and chosen family offers a means to growing a network of attachment. We can also see similar practices within immigrant and refugee communities: Survival in a new land is more assured when you aren't alone, and people may form strong bonds based on their cultures of origin, sharing language, songs, and celebrations that contribute to resourcing their nervous systems. In turn, this helps each individual to cultivate the embodied experience of "I am not alone here."

Consider what your childhood might have been like with multiple adults you felt completely safe with and emotionally supported by. What might your experience of relationships be like today if you could feel safety, security, and deep belonging with multiple different people in long-term relationships and in myriad different ways?

I hold a diasporic identity: I'm a second-generation, third-culture kid who has faced alienation from their family of origin due to queerphobia and mental health stigma, and when I began exploring polyamory, there was absolutely a part of me looking for safe attachment experiences. Even as a solo polyamorist who did not desire life enmeshment or primary partnership, I still longed for consistency, reliability, and longevity. I would eventually grow my network of attachment by focusing on my friendships, nurturing greater depth and sharing with friends who sought the same and with whom I shared enough common values to feel truly safe as my fully expressed self.

I propose that creating attachment as a post-monogamous adult is about cultivating consistent experiences of belonging and safety within our whole relationship landscape. Instead of the secure, anxious, avoidant, disorganized categories offered by Western attachment theory, and heavily influenced by the nuclear family and white supremacist ideals of perfection, we can aim for a somatic experience of resilient attachment.

We cultivate resilient attachment through the network of our relationships: our peers, our friends, our neighbours, our pets, our communities. These all hold the potential to be part of a resilient network of attachment, and a constellation of loving and trusting relations can hold us through moments of distress and challenges much more effectively than we can alone or with just the support of a single partner.

Rose, Sophia, Blanche, and Dorothy
Chosen Family

When Rose's husband of thirteen years passed away suddenly in early 2020, her life was upended. Both she and her husband were queer and had been openly polyamorous for the entirety of their relationship. Still, they had never had any long-term partners who became part of their family. After his death, Rose faced difficult decisions about her living situation.

She had some experience living in communal houses and with roommates and knew that while in the depths of grief, she needed more than just a roommate—she needed a companion. After spending a few months living alone during the early stages of the COVID-19 pandemic, she reached out to her friend Sophia (they, them), who had recently moved back in with their parents during lockdown.

Rose and Sophia had known each other for a few years. Like Rose, Sophia was queer and familiar with non-monogamy. They also deeply understood grief, having provided emotional support to their parents after the death of their sister. When Rose invited Sophia to move in, they hugged and cried. Sophia arranged therapy for their parents and moved in with Rose the next day.

Rose and Sophia functioned amazingly well as nesting companions. A "two-person grief club," they were bonded by shared experiences of loss, even though the circumstances were different. However, three months into their living arrangement, the landlord informed Rose that they would be reclaiming the property. Sophia moved back in with their parents, and Rose began searching for an affordable room to rent.

After a period of uncertainty, Rose met Blanche. A single mother navigating the aftermath of separation and divorce, Blanche rented a four-bedroom house with a large garden and sublet two rooms. She made it clear that she wanted to live with people she enjoyed being around and who felt safe around her daughter, Dorothy. When Rose visited the house, she was open about her grief, and Blanche appreciated her honesty, offering her the room immediately. Upon discovering they had both been in polyamorous marriages, they felt an even deeper bond. For the first time, Blanche had someone to talk to about her experiences who wasn't part of her polycule. When the fourth room became available, Rose recommended Sophia. Blanche trusted Rose's judgment and didn't even need to meet them: Sophia joined the household.

This wasn't a hippie commune, nor were they just strangers sharing space. The three adults fostered a dynamic of independence and mutual support, grounded in shared values of openness, respect, and consideration. They rarely experienced conflict. When Blanche had a date coming over, she would send an emoji in their group chat. Household chores were shared without strict task lists or blame. If one person was struggling, the others would step up, focusing on community care rather than resentment; emotional support was freely given.

Blanche had always been open about being non-monogamous, so it was normal for seven-year-old Dorothy that her mother had different partners. This openness helped Dorothy understand that relationships take many forms, each valuable in its own way. Rose and Sophia became part of her family.

Rose and Sophia describe themselves as platonic life partners. Rose isn't ready to date yet, but Sophia had a partner for a few months who felt threatened by the deep bond between them. On the other hand, Blanche has a primary partner who lives an hour away and fully embraces the uniqueness of the household dynamic.

After living together for over a year, their landlord put the house on the market. Amid the disruption of real estate agent visits, Rose, Sophia, and Blanche discussed what this meant for their future, and decided they wanted to stay together as a household. For Blanche, living in community as a single parent provided the benefit of additional responsible adults to help with child care. For Rose, having a community of care has been invaluable as she navigates widowhood and disability. For Sophia, being surrounded by a supportive community during their social transition and hormone therapy has been a dream come true. While they didn't start as chosen family, they are now—and actively choose to be so every day.

A word of caution: The hunger for a network of secure attachment can sometimes cause us to overlook the shortcomings of community spaces. Landing in a ready-made community can feel like a huge relief, but the necessary fantasy can also be alive and well when we relate with groups, not just individuals.

I've seen many groups and communities get caught up in painful dynamics, struggling to hold space for relational rupture and repair. Some don't have the capacity or experience to navigate systemic traumas and may fear conflict. This is all to say, when you connect with pre-existing communities, treat your relationship with them like any other relationship: move with ease, honour your capacity, and stay discerning. Many find that having multiple groupings of friends and different kinds of communities can feel more resourcing. For example, your diverse ecology might include friends you do a hobby with, your non-monogamous partners, a spiritual community you participate in, and also some close and trusted confidants, all of whom form part of your attachment ecology.

Eco-Sexuality, Eco-Spiritualism, and Ecology Attachment

To grow a relational ecology that is resilient to change invites diversification. In Indigenous wisdom worldwide, one's family of origin wasn't just genetic relatives; it was the whole tribe, the village you were raised in, and even the land of your birth. Water, fire, sunlight, ocean, trees, soil, wind—all the elements of the local ecology might be considered persons to maintain a relationship with. In some animistic traditions, these elements might be personified as a deity or a character within a complex mythology that contains wisdom that helps grow a positive and affirming relationship with these elements.

In some cases, the relationship with these elements is the basis of rituals that have become part of cultural traditions. In the *Atmos* magazine article "Why the World Needs Spiritual Ecology," researcher Vijaya Nagarajan recalls,

> I was working on this incredible mandala tradition all over India—four hundred million Hindu women do this some time during the year, where they make designs on the household threshold with rice flour. Hundreds of women told me, "We do this every morning as our first ritual act of the day, before sunrise, to honor the earth goddess and to ask for forgiveness for all the actions that we are about to do that could harm her and all the actions that we have done in the past that have harmed her." . . . How do we create beauty that has ethics embedded within it? I call it embedded ecologies. We are swimming in

a sea of unravelled threads that have been undone by language, by actions, by rituals of modernity. We need to recall, through ritual action that we do daily, that we want to go towards the flourishing of life.[3]

What if we apply this to our relationship landscapes? Could we decolonize Western consciousness to relate to the elements of the ecosystem as living beings who are dynamic and with whom we could develop a more consciously connected relationship? I found that honing a relationship with my environment has deeply supported me through upheaval in the more human parts of my relationship landscape.

Even in Western traditions there are artists, writers, and poets who see the living world as a being we are in relationship to. Writing in the late 1700s, William Wordsworth's poem "Lines Written a Few Miles Above Tintern Abbey" is an ecstatic ode to the sacredness of nature, personifying the River Wye and exalting the power of an intimate relationship with nature to bring him into a more easeful relationship with himself:

> Therefore am I still
> A lover of the meadows and the woods,
> And mountains; and of all that we behold
> From this green earth; of all the mighty world
> Of eye and ear, both what they half-create,
> And what perceive; well pleased to recognize
> In nature and the language of the sense,
> The anchor of my purest thoughts, the nurse,
> The guide, the guardian of my heart, and soul
> Of all my moral being.[4]

Since the late twentieth century, the eco-sexuality movement has celebrated a sensual essence within nature and forming a more intimate, and perhaps sometimes erotic, relationship with the ecosystem one lives within.

Consider how you might honour nonhuman life. This could be as simple as keeping plants in your home or spending more time in nature. Some find it rewarding to be around animals by adopting pets or volunteering for animal rescue organizations. You might enjoy taking a few days each year to put away all your technology and spend time off-grid. Or you might join a local gardening group and learn more about growing food in keeping with your local environment and climate.

Building a Village, Growing an Ecosystem

Psychologist Robin Dunbar's research on friendships led to a proposal that humans have an upper limit to how many people we can cognitively build meaningful relationships with. He suggested this number was 150.[5] In the social media age we might feel connected to a larger number of parasocial relationships, but how many do we hold within our close ecosystem, and how many of these relationships are deeply meaningful, or form part of our attachment experience?

If you don't feel safe or seen in your current relationships, I recognize that this idea of a network of attachment might sound a little scary. I know from my own experiences that cultivating an attachment experience won't always make sense in every relationship, and for me, it's only once I have experienced enough consistent safety and intimacy with someone that I feel like we can even consider attachment dynamics. I've also experienced the pain of assuming I had found an ecosystem where I could experience village-like attachment, and then in trying to reverse-engineer my way to relational safety, had it come crashing down, fracture, and fall apart over value differences, unaddressed internalized white supremacy, and an inability to challenge systems of oppression.

My own experience of attachment is now fluid, within the context of a resilient and decentralized ecosystem. As a consequence, my non-monogamy is no longer just about dating and having erotic experiences with multiple people. It has come to be about growing meaningful bonds with the extended network of humans in my world. Some are lovers; some may have been lovers or the partners of lovers in the past. What matters the most for me is the quality of connection we co-create with one another, even when there is physical distance. When we connect, whether online or in person, we find our nervous systems settling in the presence of our deep knowledge and understanding of one another. For me this has been a healing balm for the pain of separation from my family of origin, the trauma of othering and dehumanisation experienced by my Greek and Roma matrilineal ancestors, and it has helped me to counter the impacts of isolating colonialism and individualism. And I'll own that metamour relationships—that is, the relationships I have with the partners of my partners—are ones that I still find challenging. I've come to terms with this and know it's okay for there to be people in my partner's ecosystems that I'm not enthusiastic about including in my own.

Within your relationship ecology, you may find anchoring connections that are evergreen, lasting through the seasons and years. There may also be perennial relationships that come and go. Some may blossom and wither, while others may need to be transplanted to thrive. As you work on undoing the hold of mono-normativity, you will begin to cultivate your own resilient network of attachment relationships. While any network will inevitably undergo shifts and morph through the seasons, a well-permacultured relational landscape will continue to sustain you through the seasonal changes. Growing a resilient network of somatic attachment might be the most profound work any of us do.

Non-Escalator Relationships and Measures of Relational Success

The relationship escalator has implicit marks of commitment and investment, and being off the escalator—without a predetermined trajectory—doesn't mean that we lack commitment or vision, or don't invest in repair. In post-monogamy, we can still form commitments, but it's a commitment to cultivating and caring for our relationship landscapes, not a relationship escalator. We commit to mutual growth, relational transformation, and the ability for everyone in relationship with us to be truthful and authentic to themselves.

In escalating relationships, we look for external markers of success, like moving in together, meeting one another's families, and getting married, but in a relational ecology, you might consider the experiences of transitioning through each layer and each quadrant and what personally holds meaning and significance. This idea of customizing what has meaning and significance for you has inspired relationship anarchists to have open conversations about customizing what their relationships include. Heather Orr and Lyrica Lawrence created the first draft of what would become known as the Relationship Anarchy Smörgåsbord: a graphic that outlines different features of relationships and invites users to pick and choose what they include and what they don't. In the spirit of anarchism and community-building, the Smörgåsbord has been added to, refined, and edited through the years, with input gathered from the Relationship Anarchy and Solo Polyamory Facebook groups, collated by artist Maxx Hill. You can find the current edition of the Smörgåsbord in a Google Drive account hosted by Hill.[6]

I love the Smörgåsbord and have deep respect for its creators. I have seen so many people benefit from it and have shared it with many of my clients. I also find that as it has become more complex, I've craved a way to consider it through the lens of the four quadrants. The Relational Ecology Map is my attempt to explore how the Relationship Anarchy Smörgåsbord might align in the four quadrants of the relationship landscape, and even perhaps within different layers of relating. Some elements could easily go in multiple quadrants, or they may land in different layers from the ones I've suggested. Where you would put some of these things might be different, and I think that's okay. I offer it here as another way you might envision your relationship landscape and as a tool that might support your conversations with loved ones.

Relational Ecology Mapping

EMOTIONAL — HEART	EROTIC — SPIRIT AND CREATIVITY
• emotional presence: recognizing and validating a partner's emotional state	• What erotic names have significance? E.g. sweetheart mistress, lover
• emotional availability: sharing a continuous emotional experience	• boundaries for sexual exploration: kissing? orgasms? genitals?
• knowing each other's love languages	• creative expressions and explorations; co-creating together
• emotional secure attachment?	• romantic dates, e.g. cooking together, dancing, sensual explorations
• regular check-ins about your feelings	• spiritual intimacy
• sharing emotionally vulnerable experiences	• sensuality and hedonism
• giving and receiving emotional support; confidante; empathy	**• erotic or sexual exclusivity**
• emotional availability: sharing a continuous emotional experience	• conscious exploration of sexual dynamics: sacred sexuality, kink, power play, fetishes, etc
• aware of past traumas	• physical intimacy: dancing, cuddles, massage, holding hands, co-sleeping
• What relationship labels have emotional meaning?	**• erotic commitment to one another's erotic being, honoring erotic wounds**
• emotional rapport: being kind, sensitive, doing repair work when trust is broken	

PRACTICAL — BODY AND PHYSICAL BEING	SOCIAL — MIND AND INTELLECT
• practical collaboration, e.g. sharing chores, sharing a garden.	• social displays of affection
• How often are dates, and how do you decide the schedule?	• sharing about ideas and values, exploring oneanother's belief systems
• practical exclusivity	• socially out and open about the relationship?
• physical activities: gym, biking, hiking, etc	• community event participation
• visa or financial sponsorship	• frequency and methods of communication
• physical caregiving, meal trains during crises, living will support, elder care	• Does this relationship interact with others? E.g. friends, other partners
• practical anchor?	**• What relationship labels have social significance?**
• shared medical insurance	**• social events together: concerts, festivals, conventions group dinners, excursions**
• joint financial planning: savings, retirement, business, vacations	**• Is this someone you explore your ideas and values with?**
• nesting, co-parenting, legal entwinement, next-of-kin, marriage or civil partnership?	**• part of your network of secure attachment?**

Figure 20.1. The Relational Ecology Map. A guide for discussion when identifying the aspects of relationship you experience or desire. The examples given are not exhaustive and may cross multiple quadrants for some. Inspired by the Relationship Anarchy Smörgåsbord created by Lyrica Lawrence and Heather Orr, refined and developed by Maxx Hill with support of Relationship Anarchy, Polyamory, and Solo Polyamory Facebook groups. Icons by Joan Trinh Pham. A more comprehensive version of this guide can be found at radicalrelating.ca.

You can also use this tool to aid you when you need help reconfiguring any aspects of a relationship. For example, if you've felt that the physical and sexual intimacy in a particular relationship hasn't been working for you, but you still love and value this person's presence as an anchoring partnership in your life, it might help you consider other ways to grow intimacy together.

Change, Differentiation, and De-Escalation

Break-ups, de-escalation, transitions—changes in the relationship landscape can challenge us, especially when our ecologies have felt stable and supportive. But change is also inevitable. All relationships will one day end, be it by break-up or bereavement.

Break-ups in polyamory come with not just the grief of an intimate relationship ending but also the grief of losing a network of people. If non-monogamy has helped you to grow a community that has been a balm for any attachment wounds, the distress of loss can be amplified. Break-up and de-escalation of a relationship can bring grief and regret: how did we not see an incompatibility sooner? Is it some fault of ours that the potential we had envisioned for the relationship will never be met? How do we trust our own hearts as we move forward? And how do we stay in a space of kindness and compassion with one another through the medley of feelings?

Many non-monogamists might use the term *de-escalating,* which, as someone who doesn't seek out the relationship escalator in the first place, has always felt confusing for me. Rather than endings or de-escalations, I prefer thinking of transitions, using language like "shifting gears" or "transplanting" when I talk about changes in my relationships. The connection moves to the part of our shared landscape where it will have a better chance of thriving. Just as we might go from friends to lovers, we might transition from partners to friends. We might also de-nest but maintain emotional intimacy. For me, it's about honouring my own capacity and a desire to never try to force a dynamic to be something that it isn't.

Whether you think of it as de-escalating or transitioning, there is very often a sense at the outset, from at least one partner, of what level of enmeshment they are or are not comfortable with. The de-escalation for a partner who already knows their reduced capacity and is ready for the change may stall as the other partner works through their grief at the loss of enmeshment. In these instances, the process of de-escalating is one partner shifting and essentially waiting for the other to reconcile to the shift. It's helpful when the process can be collaborative, but this won't always be possible. If having a collaborative process about changes in your relationship landscape proves challenging, I encourage you to consider approaching it with kindness, compassion, and patience for yourself and one another. It may be helpful in these moments to seek out support from outside of your relationships through peers, elders, or even with a therapist or experienced non-monogamy coach.

Finding new ways to assess the success of a relationship, and letting go of the "forever" metrics, allows for more present, honest, and authentic relationships to flourish. While no person or relationship should ever be treated as disposable, honouring when a relationship has run its course, or when the needs and capacity of the people in the relationship have shifted, liberates each person to move towards their pleasure rather than sitting in a state of tension, anxiety, and endurance.

Rituals for Grief

Grief has come up repeatedly in this work. I think that growing our capacity for resilience and with grief is a specific kind of relational work that doesn't get talked about enough in polyamorous and polyamorous-adjacent circles. In mono-normative paradigms, grieving a lost connection often happens in isolation or perhaps with the support of a few trusted friends. In the complex landscapes of non-monogamy, sitting with the grief of change, transition, and loss, and spending time isolating from connections, such as taking a break from dating, may not always make sense.

Rituals are a powerful way to work with grief, creating grounding for the nervous system. A one-off ritual could be a longer, epic exploration of all the facets of grief, giving them space for expression and possible catharsis. But an epic ritual can be overwhelming for the nervous system and require a lot of integration time afterwards. You may find it easier to explore smaller, more regular rituals for yourself as you navigate your way through grief.

I've helped a few couples facilitate un-weddings: a symbolic release of marriage vows or relationship agreements where they affirm new commitments, often to their self-relationships, and celebrate one another's truth and how they will relate going forward. These have been incredibly moving events; I've created a few myself with former partners. Sometimes there is a small fire to burn things from the relationship, or water to bathe their hands or bodies in to represent renewal. Some dance or play music, while others have done this in silence. Some have invited loved ones to witness them, but most prefer to keep it small. And sometimes the grief ritual is a solo journey.

REFLECTIVE JOURNALING
Creating Your Own Solo Grief Rituals

How can you invite in elements of nature: plants, water, scent? Do you want to burn something, or have a candle lit?

Do you want to bathe your body or some part of it? Water has a potent soothing power for the nervous system and can symbolize washing away what you are letting go of.

What emotions need to have expression, and what might support you with that?

Anger: Consider a large pillow to hit or scream into if there is anger to release. Is there something you can responsibly destroy? Consider breaking pottery or burning a copy of relationship agreements to mark the end of a relationship.

Longing: writing poetry, making art, or engaging in self-pleasure. You may want some paper, colouring pencils, or canvases and paint nearby. Explore what it's like to paint using your hands, and let your emotions flow into the canvas this way.

Sadness: What helps you feel safe enough to let your sadness out?

You might want to consider whether you'd like to do this solo or if you'd like a friend or someone else to witness your ceremony.

If you work with plant medicine, do you want to include it in your ritual, and if so, how?

Aftercare: How will you integrate this experience afterwards? What might comfort your nervous system? Are there foods or drinks that make sense to include as aftercare? Calorie- and mineral-dense foods such as chocolate or bananas can help the body to soothe and relax without altering the brain's chemistry as something like alcohol might do.

Aftercare helps to integrate the experience of a ritual in our nervous system. Giving yourself lots of time is important to integrate the grief and any expressions you accessed through ritual. Things that help our nervous system integrate include movement and immersing our bodies in water, for example, taking a shower, having a bath, going for a swim, a sensory deprivation float, or something similar.

Practise relating with your grief. You might name the feelings that arise: *I feel sad right now,* or give voice to your state of being, *I don't know what happens next.* You may find it helpful to give your grief a relevant name: *That pandemic break-up grief is really present right now.* As it becomes more familiar to name and sit with your grief, you may find it helpful to have boundaries to hold you with care and kindness as you grieve. You may hold off on beginning new relationships or making big changes in others. This could be a time boundary, like six weeks or six months; feel into what would work for you. It could also be criteria-based, for example, once you have gone several weeks without dreaming about them. During the process of grieving, your nervous system is working to adapt to sudden and often unexpected changes in your landscape's attachment network, and more change, even if it's a pleasant change, can sometimes feel overwhelming. Make sure to take time for your self-relationship. Go on self-dates and do things that bring you joy. You may want to learn a new skill or revisit an old one, such as music, gardening, working out, sword fighting, or something else that inspires you.

Practising Compassion for Sustainable Anarcules

Anarchism, queerness, polyamory, and somatics all support and encourage wider scopes of relationship building, but systems exist that oppose these. White supremacy culture, which affects us all, thrives on individualism and separation. We have been told to hoard resources rather than share them, to treat anything or anyone that says otherwise as a threat, to judge one another, and to push away what we either don't understand or don't have the capacity for.

As we explored in chapter 19, compersion is often touted as the pinnacle of the polyamorous experience, but there's little compersion without compassion, the capacity to remain sensitive and responsive to how adverse experiences impact us and others. Compassion offers a balm for all the shame, judgment, separation, and individualism that is part of white supremacy culture. Fostering compassion through learning to see all our harmful actions and inactions as consequences of individual, systemic, and intergenerational traumas, and a quest for safety, is transformative. Compassion creates a space where we no longer have to bind ourselves to an identity dictated by our grief experience. Compassion also helps us to be gentle with ourselves and others during the exhaustion that grief can bring.

Cultivating compassion is a trauma-informed strategy for kinder relationships. Compassion becomes the fertile soil in which we can plant new seeds of hope and empowered relating that can grow out of the decomposing shadow of grief. Compassion creates spaces of softness when things get hard, helping us lead with kindness so we can get through the tough times without losing connection. Compassion opens the door to even greater compersion and a deep experience of respect for the ineffable essence we all share.

21

RADICAL RELATING

What is liberation if not the work of love, every day, including love for ourselves because we are not separate from the world? What is love if not liberation for each and every one of us?

—ALEX IANTAFFI[1]

As I write these concluding thoughts, I cannot help but wonder what the future holds for our world. I put these words to paper as unprecedented floods, droughts, fires, and other climate disasters wreak havoc on the livelihoods of so many worldwide. Large corporations holding monopolies on industries further the damage through destructive and exploitative policies. Wars are being fought over resources, land, and more. Many people face economic instability, housing insecurity, and other challenges to their survival. By some estimates, 1.2 billion people will have been displaced by climate events alone by 2050.[2] This number does not factor in the many who are facing displacement due to colonial occupation, genocides, and wars.

I share that my not-so-secret polyamorous agenda is to build a world where we can all be more loving, kind, and compassionate with one another while staying true to ourselves. My goal has never been to teach people my way of doing relationships; rather, I hope to share wisdom, insights, and tools that can help everyone feel empowered with the skills to navigate whatever style or path of relating feels authentic for them. And in so doing, maybe we can all move a bit closer to a post-monogamous world that can indeed be more loving and kind. In this chapter, I'd like to share what I hope that will look like.

Why: Divesting from Systems That Divide and Separate Us

- healing from oppression
- collectively surviving and thriving

Recognizing that the structures of colonialism, late-stage capitalism, patriarchy, white supremacy culture, and the nuclear family have fragmented connections and constrained our abilities to live and love, we are motivated to build relationships that are rooted in healing from the systems and experiences of oppression. Our relationships can offer us pathways for reclaiming not just individual agency against these systems but also our collective power. We survive and thrive together through mutual support, prioritizing mutual aid, care, compassion, and shared resilience. Our networks of solidarity empower us to flourish amid systems that seek to divide us.

What: Diverse, Interdependent, Relational Ecosystems

- celebration of self
- networks of secure attachment
- trauma-informed and integrated
- interdependence

Radical relationships are spaces where you can be fully yourself without hiding any part of who you are. They create networks of secure attachment, nourishing the roots of your relational ecosystem with safety, love, and support. In these relationships, everyone is trauma-informed, sensitive to how past experiences affect our bodies and emotions, fostering interactions that are compassionate and empathetic. Radical relationships embrace interdependence, where individuals maintain autonomy while co-creating supportive and nurturing bonds. Relationships thrive through mutual care, allowing for growth and connection within shared landscapes.

How: Becoming Somatically Aware

- queering and anarchising
- somatic awareness
- conflict intimacy

Growing somatic awareness means we can attune to the sensations, emotions, and responses our bodies hold, offering more profound insights into how internalized narratives of competition and scarcity shape our feelings and how we relate. As our awareness of these embodied patterns grows, our minds, bodies, hearts, and spirits can be liberated from the oppression-based stories that have fed into isolation and conflict. With increasing resilience and capacity to navigate the tensions of conflict, we become more resourced to be in disagreement and still hold empathy and compassion. The barriers that separate us tumble down, and we come together to thrive.

Where Is It Going: A Post-Monogamous World

- kinship and chosen family
- resource sharing, not hoarding

In a post-monogamous, post–nuclear family world, the future of relationships shifts towards more fluid, expansive networks of kinship and chosen family. These relationships negate the rigidity of colonial and patriarchal monogamy, making space for diverse, intentional forms of relating that centre connection and can include sexually and romantically fidelitous relationships. Rather than prioritizing individual ownership and resource hoarding, communal resource sharing and collaborative processes can offer healthier relationships to both local and global ecosystems. With a broader network of support across emotional, social, practical, and erotic landscapes, a culture of abundance where love, care, and resources are distributed collectively can lead us towards more sustainable living and loving.

Your Map Towards Radical Relating

We've explored the pillars of trauma-informed relating: orientation, resilience, resolution, and embodiment. We've outlined the four quadrants of the relationship landscape: emotional, social, practical, and erotic. We've dug through the soil of the layers of relating: awareness, safety, intimacy, and Relationship. We've learned how to move through all these spaces as we relate to ourselves and others while growing loving relationships with our own shadows and the self-protective responses of our loved ones.

Radical relationships are grounded in the recognition of shared humanity and belonging. They invite deep connection, where we see reflections of ourselves in others and foster the experiences of safety, security, and belonging we all so dearly seek. Our bodies and nervous systems find ease: Emotional safety allows us to nurture, care for, and support one another in ways that promote growth, self-actualization, and community resilience. Radical relationships offer a dynamic space for authentic communication and the freedom to express changing desires, boundaries, and needs without fear.

At the heart of radical relationships is a commitment to honour change and diversity, with compassion for mistakes, messiness, and support for healing and repair. Intimacy isn't limited to the erotic, and it isn't limited to a single partner. Radical relationships flourish in these rich ecosystems where diverse connections—perennial or seasonal—are cultivated with care and nurturance. Together, we foster resilience and make space for conflict and healing, all while weaving wider webs of care, compassion, and understanding that go far beyond what traditional mono-normative frameworks have been able to offer.

SOMATIC PAUSE
The Possibilities of Radical Relating

I invite you to take a moment to pause and let yourself enjoy stillness in any way that feels good and accessible for you. In this moment of stillness, perhaps you notice your breath. You may notice a pleasing sound or the textures of your clothing. Or maybe your gaze falls on a cherished memento in your space.

Consider what you have learned through your journey with this book. Notice the thoughts, feelings, ideas, and sensations that arise in you.

Think about the shape of your relationship landscape: where it is now, and what you now imagine it could grow to be. As you think about this possible future, notice again the sensations, thoughts, feelings, and ideas that arise within you.

If you step into this possible future, what then becomes possible?

Notice what you feel. Notice what you sense. Notice any ideas, images, or thoughts that come up.

If you like, you can take a moment to write these down.

Thriving Together

The world we live in today has been shaped by acts of anger, fear, jealousy, and future hoarding. It has also been shaped by love, passion, empathy, connection, and friendships. Even in the darkest times, the resilience of the human spirit burns bright still, seen in the acts of compassion we are all capable of.

I would love to exist in a world where relationships function on a basis of abundance and sharing, where our lives are collaborative, where we together overcome the limitations and binds of oppression and separation and where we thrive, together, because of one another and not in spite of one another.

I dream of a world where we are motivated by passion and care for the land and the creatures in it, where we recognize our roles as stewards of the earth and act accordingly. A world where the power systems of rampant destructive capitalism have given way to organic interdependence and communitarianism, and where we work together to heal from our collective centuries and millennia of trauma. It's a world where we honour our shadows and are liberated from the binds of shame. It's a future where every person's individual autonomy and sovereignty are held sacrosanct while we co-create communities of nurturance, compassion, and love.

Whether your journey towards this future includes romantic relationships that are polyamorous, monogamous, or anything in between, my deepest hope is that this book inspires and empowers you to radicalize the way you relate.

It might be many years before anyone will know just how this invitation to relate may impact the world. I invite you to stay open to possibilities, honour yourself, and celebrate one another. Try things out, use what works, and leave what doesn't—and let's see where this takes us.

A Prayer for the Radicals

May we grow and sustain loving, kind, and compassionate relationships.

May we orient to safety and connection through growing relational ecologies.

May our ways of loving be embodied and liberatory.

May we know resilience as softness and the nourishing of somatic capacity.

May we come back to ourselves as we resolve and heal relational wounds.

May our desires to expand intimacy dissolve the differences that impede our ability to resist oppression.

May we survive, and thrive, together.

And may our search for liberated love include liberation for all.

GLOSSARY

anarcule A play on the word molecule. A network of connections formed on an anarchist basis; a relational structure that defies the nuclear family. Anarcules form through mutuality and alignment of values and interests. Could include non-monogamous partners, close friends, family or family of choice, emergency contacts, creative collaborators, and more.

asexual A sexual orientation where a person experiences no sexual desire or attraction to anyone.

attachment theory A psychological theory concerning relationships between humans, originating from studies on infant behaviour when separated and then reunited with their primary caregiver. Often applied to understanding the romantic dynamics of adult relationships.

bonogamy Coined by Victor Warring. An umbrella term for the diverse spectrum of multi-partner relating that decenters monogamy as the default relationship style. Also includes decolonization, rewilding, and rematriation values and practices. A portmanteau of bonobo, a species of great apes known for their matriarchy, non-violence, and diverse sexual practices, and the suffix gamy, meaning to mate, partner, or marry.

cancel culture A cultural condition in which an individual believed to have behaved in unacceptable ways is socially ostracized without any possibility of repair and re-inclusion.

cis-heteronormativity A social construct that considers cis and heterosexual people to be the norm.

codependency A state of enmeshment in relationships where one or more partners rely on one another for their experience of emotional, mental, social, or spiritual well-being. People in codependent dynamics or with codependent tendencies may struggle to desire connections beyond a single partner, or experience distress when a partner's attention is not on them.

colonialism The control and exploitation of land and living beings by a foreign group. Typically refers to European colonial powers and their policies of expansion across the world.

comet An occasional partner, often long-distance and with whom connecting happens infrequently but is still significant in a person's relationship landscape.

compersion Experiencing joy when witnessing or hearing about another person's joy. Sometimes defined as the opposite of jealousy, but can exist alongside jealousy.

conflict intimacy A concept and practice where conflict is seen as an opportunity to develop deeper intimacy.

consensual non-monogamy (CNM) The clinical umbrella term for non-monogamy that happens with the full knowledge and consent of all parties. Because of the honesty involved, it differs from cheating.

consent Legally defined as a "meeting of minds," can be defined as (1) permission, for example, when a person consents to medical care from a doctor; (2) an embodied state, for example, the full-body sensation of enthusiasm about an experience or an invitation that has been given by another person; (3) collaboration, for example, two or more people working together to find a common consensus and build an experience that everyone can enjoy.

cosmology A personal way of seeing one's relationship to the universe and all the beings and phenomena within it. Can be influenced by religion, spirituality, personal experiences, and more.

couple's privilege The culturally entrenched measure of value awarded to couples by society in public perception and legal status. Couples can't opt out at will. Not the same as hierarchy, though they often co-exist. Couple's privilege can harm the noncoupled partners connecting with the members of a couple.

date zero Coined by Xianny Ng. The first meeting one-on-one with a new person that an individual has romantic or sexual interest in. Not necessarily as high stakes as a date. Intended to be a shorter meetup in a casual setting to get a feel of chemistry and in-person compatibility.

demisexual A sexual orientation where a person only experiences sexual feelings and attraction after first developing an emotional relationship.

desire smuggling Coined by Marcia Baczynski. Hiding what one really wants from oneself or from a loved one, then finding covert strategies to get at least some of what is wanted.

dharma A Sanskrit term meaning "right action." Used in Buddhism and Hinduism. Often implies a healthy, ethical, kind way of living.

differentiation In relationships, a process of redefining one's self or reclaiming agency, often following a period of feeling enmeshed or subsumed by a relationship.

dissociation An experience of being disconnected from oneself or the world.

distress tolerance The ability to manage the inner experience of distress, whether the source of distress is imaginary, for example, the result of pre-emptive worry, or real, for example, a routine with a partner is disrupted.

don't ask, don't tell An extreme form of compartmentalization in polyamory where partners share an agreement to not proactively share information about their other relationships and only share if their partner asks. There are often implicit or explicit agreements within this to ensure sexual health and safety, for example, the use of barriers or regular STI testing.

eco-sexuality Coined by Annie Sprinkle and Beth Stephens. A sexual orientation, environmental activist strategy, and grass-roots movement that considers the earth and all elements of nature as conscious beings we can be in relationship with.

embodied An integrated experience of being aware of the present moment. Includes an ability to sense, feel, and respond to bodily sensations, emotions, and internal cues. Allows for an authentic, lived experience that enhances self-awareness, emotional regulation, and responsiveness by grounding awareness in the physical and sensory aspects of one's being.

emotional affair A non-sexual relationship where a close emotional bond is formed, often in contradiction to monogamous expectations of monogamous fidelity.

emotional labor The process of managing the feelings and expressions of others. Can include supporting a person through an emotionally difficult time, helping a person de-escalate from anger, or helping a person better understand their own feelings and those of others.

enmeshment A state of relating between two or more people where the boundaries between them are unclear.

established relationship energy The comfortable and secure feeling associated with a well-established relationship.

ethical non-monogamy (ENM) An outdated and subjective term for open relating. Implies a set of ethics for doing non-monogamy; ethics can be culturally subjective, and much of the written material discussing ENM focuses on Western-colonial-centered ethics.

feminism A set of values and practices that recognizes women and other non-men as equals to men and challenges the patriarchal default that men must hold power in all relationships.

friendtimate A friend that a person shares intimacy with. Denotes warmth, care, and that the friendship is prioritized.

gender essentialism A theory that seeks to define gender as a binary of being either male or female and leaves no space for gender non-binary or nonconforming. Also implies that there are specific characteristics that can only be held by men and others that are innate to women. Upholds outdated patriarchal values about relationships.

GHIA-lousy A portmanteau of jealousy and GHIA, global high-intensity activation, a term from Somatic Experiencing. GHIA describes massive stimulation and arousal of the entire nervous system, often resulting in overwhelm and a self-protective response that is either fully on or fully off. This in turn can lead to a pattern of dramatic energy storms or emotional responses even with very little stimulation.

ghosting Ending a personal relationship suddenly and without explanation. Usually means withdrawing from all communication once a relationship has been clearly established.

greysexual A sexual orientation where a person experiences low levels of sexual attraction.

hierarchy The prioritizing of one relationship over another. Prescriptive hierarchy is assumed based on the relationship type; a loss of hierarchy is perceived to mean something is missing or the end of the relationship. Descriptive hierarchy is an organic dynamic that emerges over time; fluid and mutable, the relationships maintain an openness to change.

hinge partner A person in a non-monogamous relationship who is dating two or more other people.

honest non-monogamy Non-monogamy done with honesty and transparency. Can include exclusive lifetime commitments with multiple partners (polygyny, polygamy, polyandry, polyfidelity); having a core secure attachment partner and additional date friends; being one's own primary partner as a solo polyamorist; casual sex.

incel Short for "involuntary celibate," this term has been adopted by men who blame feminism for hindering their ability to develop intimate relationships with women. Incels often behave violently towards women.

interdependence A state where each person exists as an autonomous and sovereign human being with an active awareness of their relationship and inescapable reliance on one another. Neither the loss of self in codependency nor the loss of community in individualism.

kitchen table polyamory All partners and metamours in a polycule share a close level of emotional and social familiarity and can comfortably share time together, such as a group meal, an outing, a board game, a movie, or similar.

late-stage capitalism The changes in capitalism since World War II. Characteristics include increasing commodification, such as the arts, into consumables; the rise of celebrity culture; multinational corporations and the international division of labour; and the emergence of large umbrella corporations that maintain an illusion of consumer choice while reducing actual choice.

love bombing Overwhelming a new partner with positive attention, affection, and gifts. Can sometimes be a precursor to abusive dynamics but can also be a strategy for establishing security when a person feels anxious in new relationships.

metamour The partner of a partner. Sometimes called a partner-in-law. Often abbreviated to "meta." Some polyamorists like to form close friendships with their metamours; others prefer to keep their distance from their metas. Either is a valid choice.

misogyny Ingrained prejudice against women.

monogamish A relationship that is mostly monogamous in appearance and function but where both partners are mutually free to engage in occasional extra-marital relationships, usually sex-based or short-term.

monogamy Typically defined as lifelong or long-term, mutually exclusive, sexual or social, and a dyadic pair bond exclusively between two people.

monogamy hangover The internalized and often unconscious stories originating from patriarchal monogamy, also sometimes called toxic monogamy, that hold us back from authentic joy in our intimate relationships, be they polyamorous, monogamous, or other styles of relating. Recovering from the hangover of monogamy doesn't happen overnight, and expectations based on monogamy can sneak up even in non-monogamous relationships.

mono-normativity Coined by Marianne Pieper and Robin Bauer. The social assumption that couple-shaped relationships are the principle of social relations, an essential foundation of human existence, and the elementary, almost natural pattern of living together.

mudita A Sanskrit term meaning "empathetic joy." Considered in Buddhism to be one of the four qualities of the heart, the others being kindness, compassion, and equanimity.

multiamory An alternate term for multiple loving relationships. Popularized by a podcast of the same name.

multigamy Coined by Roy Graff. An umbrella term for all multiple-relationship dynamics. Unlike non-monogamy, has no negative implications. Ethics and consent are a given, and as in monogamy, individuals behaving unethically do not represent the entire community. Multigamy doesn't mean those involved are polyamorous; they may be, for example, monoamorous and multisexual.

the necessary fantasy A strategy for nervous-system safety that helps a person feel safe enough to stay engaged and invested in a new relationship when there is much to learn about a new partner and the potential of the relationship.

nesting partner A partner one lives with. May or not be a primary partner.

new relationship energy (NRE) The oxytocin and dopamine buzz of novelty and infatuation that occurs when a new relationship is inspiring and exciting.

non-monogamy Literally, anything that is not monogamy. Honest forms could include sexually open relationships, such as swinging, and emotionally open relationships, such as polyamory. Non-monogamy can also be dishonest, such as in cheating.

nuclear family A family system of two parents, typically a mother and a father, and their offspring.

open relationship Any kind of relationship allowing for additional partners, whether they are emotional, erotic, aromantic, transactional, or otherwise. Can mean forms of polyamory but also includes open marriage agreements, where one partner might have additional partners for specific needs, for example, kink play, or a lover who is known but whose presence doesn't affect the partners in a marriage together.

parallel polyamory A compartmentalized style of polyamory where metamours interact either minimally or not at all. They may know one another or have met in passing but do not share social, emotional, or intimate space.

patriarchal monogamy Traditional monogamy that centres the power of men over women and children. Men are considered the head of the household, and women are considered the property of their fathers until they became the property of their husbands. In modern times many elements of patriarchal monogamy remain in how monogamy is practised: expectations between partners of ownership, control, gender-defined roles such as one partner being the breadwinner and the other raising children, and so forth.

patriarchy A system based on dominance that centres men as holding power over women, other genders, animals, nature, and more. Among men, patriarchy holds that only certain men can hold power and prescribes restrictive parameters; men who are unable to meet these parameters are also considered subservient.

pendulation A natural process of moving between states of contraction and expansion in the body and the nervous system. It's a basic rhythm of life, similar to the ebb and flow of the tides or the opening and closing of a bird's wings.

polyamory Coined by Morning Glory Zell-Ravenheart. A type of non-monogamy where people have multiple romantic or sexual relationships at the same time.

polycule The expanded network of a person's non-monogamous connections.

polyfidelity A relationship style where multiple partners agree to maintain long-term exclusivity with one another. This could look like polygyny (more than one wife), polyandry (more than one husband), or egalitarian forms of exclusivity within a closed group on a relationship escalator together.

polynormativity The "two-plus" model of polyamory often popularized in the media. An existing couple maintains a primary relationship with one another and date additional individuals as secondary partners, often prioritizing the needs, status, visibility, and social value of the primary partnership over the secondary.

primary partner A hierarchical term denoting that one partner takes priority: a spouse, a nesting partner, or a partner with whom the person shares other legal agreements, such as co-parenting or next of kin.

purity culture A set of beliefs that emphasizes sexual abstinence before marriage. Can also include gendered structures of behavior and modesty.

queer A sexual, gender, or relational identity that does not correspond to established ideas of sexuality and gender, especially heterosexual norms.

relationship anarchy (RA) A guiding set of principles for relationships that values autonomy, non-hierarchical practices, and community interdependence. Can include polyamorous relationships but does not exclude sexual and emotional monogamy.

relationship ecology The interconnected relationships that people share through co-existing as humans together. What impacts one individual or group of individuals may have impacts and consequences for others as well; no person can be truly isolated from others.

relationship escalator Coined by Amy Gahran. The default set of societal expectations for intimate relationships; partners follow a progressive trajectory toward the goal of lifelong monogamy. The standard by which most people assess a relationship's significance and worth. For many, being on the escalator is a cherished goal; for others, stepping off the escalator can be an empowering experience.

relationship landscape Instead of a relationship escalator, a landscape: vast, open, filled with possibilities, waiting to be explored. People exist in relationship with this landscape, just as they do with the surrounding real-world ecology.

relationship libertarianism A callous cousin of relationship anarchy in which individuals view any kind of relationship agreement or accord as an infringement on their personal rights. An extreme form of individualism that is often practised with little to no consideration of or accountability for the impact of actions on others.

secondary partner A non-primary partner who is still considered to be long-term and consistent. The degree of commitment may vary.

self-relationship The practice of developing and maintaining a secure, healthy relationship with oneself, sometimes called self-secure attachment. A healthy self-relationship involves understanding and accepting one's individual needs, values, and emotions and learning to care for oneself in a nurturing and supportive way.

sex positivity An open, tolerant, progressive attitude toward sex and sexuality.

sneakyarchy Coined by Keiren Stephenson. Concealed hierarchy in relationships. A portmanteau of sneaky and hierarchy.

social capital The potential ability to obtain resources, favours, or information from one's personal connections. In Arabic called wasta.

solo polyamory Non-monogamy with no desire for, or expectation of, riding the relationship escalator. "SoPo" individuals may have short-term casual relationships but enjoy long-term committed partnerships that don't conform to mainstream expectations of relating, such as marriage or nesting together.

somatics An approach to therapy, healing, and self-care that focuses on the body's physical responses to thoughts, emotions, and nervous system responses. Somatic practices use body-based tools such as mindful movement, massage, breathwork, and meditation to help individuals connect with their bodies and gain insight into their inner experiences.

swinging Initially a form of organized partner-swapping, these are consensual relationships based on sexual intimacy. Partners who swing together might have an emotional relationship, but they do not form enmeshed connections, explore the relationship escalator together, or participate in one another's lives.

toxic monogamy An unhealthy form of monogamous relationship often characterized by possessive and controlling behaviour, lack of respect and communication, and a focus on power dynamics rather than mutual respect and understanding. Toxic monogamy can cause physical, mental, and emotional harm to those involved and can be damaging to both individuals and the relationship as a whole.

trad wife A married woman who embraces patriarchal gender roles, with a tight focus on having many children, doing all the housework, and supporting her husband to be the sole or primary breadwinner.

trauma The consequence of being overwhelmed by situations beyond a person's ability to cope with them. Can arise due to emotional, physical, mental, or spiritual factors. Can be brought about either from direct experience or vicariously, for example, through witnessing something overwhelming.

trauma-informed relating Building connections with attention for transparency, trust, mutuality, autonomy, choice, and spaciousness. Also, connecting with awareness of the impact of cultural, historical, gendered, and other experiences that contribute to trauma and impact relationships.

triangulation Introducing a third party into a relationship dynamic, for example, a therapist, friend, or new partner. Healthy triangulation means consensual involvement of an outsider who can bring balance and perspective, which often helps generate stability. Unhealthy triangulation creates a scapegoat outside a dyad who can be blamed instead of a partner taking responsibility; this often increases relational drama.

unicorn A person of any gender and orientation, but typically a bisexual female woman, who wants to be the third party in a threesome with an existing couple.

unicorn hunting A couple aggressively seeking a third. Generally considered nonconsensual objectification, but some individuals enjoy being a unicorn with a couple. See www.unicorns-r-us.com.

unicorning Seeking or being a third party to join an existing couple for a casual sex experience.

veto power The power to end, or impose limits on, a relationship with a partner's other partners.

white supremacy culture Coined by activist Tema Okun. The ways in which the ruling-class elite or the power elite in the colonies of what was to become the United States used the pseudo-scientific concept of race to create whiteness and a hierarchy of racialized value in order to disconnect and divide white people from Black, Indigenous, and people of colour; disconnect and divide Black, Indigenous, and people of colour from each other; disconnect and divide white people from other white people; disconnect and divide people from nature; disconnect and divide people from themselves and from source.

RESOURCES TO
SUPPORT YOUR JOURNEY

Mel curates resources to support your journey through their relationship coaching practice at www.radicalrelating.ca and shares regularly on social media with @radicalrelating. They also offer regular workshops and courses, including the Monogamy Detox Course (https://monogamydetox.com). You can find somatic meditations from Radical Relating on Insight Timer: https://insighttimer.com/radicalrelating.

Additional Learning Materials and Resources
Challenging Mono-Normativity

Meg-John Barker, *Rewriting the Rules: An Integrative Guide to Love, Sex and Relationships* (Routledge, 2012).

Mark A. Michaels and Patricia Johnson, *Designer Relationships: A Guide to Happy Monogamy, Positive Polyamory, and Optimistic Open Relationships* (Cleis, 2015).

Libby Sinback, *Making Polyamory Work,* podcast, www.makingpolyamorywork.com.

Tema Okun, "White Supremacy Culture," website and essay, https://whitesupremacyculture.info.

Amy Gahran, *Stepping Off the Relationship Escalator: Uncommon Love and Life* (Off the Escalator, 2017).

Somatics and Trauma-Informed Work

Kathy L. Kain and Stephen J. Terrell, *Nurturing Resilience: Helping Clients Move Forward from Developmental Trauma* (North Atlantic Books, 2018).

Anjuli Sherin, *Joyous Resilience: A Path to Individual Healing and Collective Thriving in an Inequitable World* (North Atlantic Books, 2021).

Peter A. Levine, *Healing Trauma: A Pioneering Program for Restoring the Wisdom of Your Body* (Sounds True, 2005).

Eleanor Criswell, *How Yoga Works: An Introduction to Somatic Yoga* (Freeperson Press, 1987).

Thomas Hanna, *Bodies in Revolt: A Primer in Somatic Thinking* (Holt, Rinehart and Winston, 1970).

Queerness and Anarchy

Juan-Carlos Pérez-Cortés, *Relationship Anarchy: Occupy Intimacy!* (published by the author, 2022).

Meg-John Barker and Alex Iantaffi, *How to Understand Your Gender: A Practical Guide for Exploring Who You Are* (Jessica Kingsley, 2017).

Meg-John Barker and Alex Iantaffi, *How to Understand Your Sexuality: A Practical Guide for Exploring Who You Are* (Jessica Kingsley, 2021).

Relationship Ecologies

Roger Kuhn, *Somacultural Liberation: An Indigenous, Two-Spirit Somatic Guide to Integrating Cultural Experiences Toward Freedom* (North Atlantic Books, 2024).

Sophie K. Rosa, *Radical Intimacy* (Pluto, 2022).

Alex Iantaffi and Meg-John Barker, *How to Understand Your Relationships: A Practical Guide* (Jessica Kingsley, 2025).

Victor Waring, somatic coach, Rewilding Eros, www.rewilderos.com.

The Emotional Quadrant

Rhaina Cohen, *The Other Significant Others: Reimagining Life with Friendship at the Center* (St. Martin's, 2024).

The Social Quadrant

Mia Birdsong, *How We Show Up: Reclaiming Family, Friendship, and Community* (Hachette, 2020).

The Practical Quadrant

Laura Boyle, *Monogamy? In This Economy? Finances, Childrearing, and Other Practical Concerns of Polyamory* (Jessica Kingsley, 2024).

The Erotic Quadrant

Miranda Shaw, *Passionate Enlightenment: Women in Tantric Buddhism* (Princeton University Press, 1994).

Sherronda J. Brown, *Refusing Compulsory Sexuality: A Black Asexual Lens on Our Sex-Obsessed Culture* (North Atlantic Books, 2022).

Institute of Authentic Tantra, www.authentictantra.com.

Self-Partnership

Marcia Baczynski, coach, Asking for What You Want, https://askingforwhatyouwant.com.

Bella DePaulo, *Single at Heart: The Power, Freedom and Joy of Single Life* (Apollo, 2023).

Dr. Sophia Graham, therapist, Love Uncommon, https://loveuncommon.com.

Brené Brown, *Braving the Wilderness: The Quest for True Belonging and the Courage to Stand Alone* (Random House, 2017).

Consent and Agreements

Marcia Baczynski and Erica Scott, *Creating Consent Culture: A Handbook for Educators* (Jessica Kingsley, 2022).

Helena De Felice, facilitator, Our Sacred Body, www.helenadefelice.com.

Shadow Work and Compersion

Marie Thouin, *What Is Compersion? Understanding Positive Empathy in Consensually Non-Monogamous Relationships* (Rowman & Littlefield, 2024).

Cara Page and Erica Woodland, *Healing Justice Lineages: Dreaming at the Crossroads of Liberation, Collective Care, and Safety* (North Atlantic Books, 2023).

Courageous Communication

Dedeker Winston, Jase Lindgren, and Emily Sotelo Matlack, *Multiamory: Essential Tools for Modern Relationships* (Cleis, 2023).

Community Building

Wahinkpe Topa and Darcia Narvaez, *Restoring the Kinship Worldview: Indigenous Voices Introduce 28 Precepts for Rebalancing Life on Planet Earth* (North Atlantic Books, 2022).

angel Kyodo williams, Lama Rod Owens, and Jasmine Syedullah, *Radical Dharma: Talking Race, Love, and Liberation* (North Atlantic Books, 2016).

Network for a New Culture, www.networkfornewculture.org.

NOTES

Chapter 1. Unravelling Monogamy

1 Esther Perel and Mary Alice Miller, "5 Myths We Tell Ourselves When We're Dating," Esther Perel's Blog, n.d. www.estherperel.com/blog/5-myths-we-tell-ourselves-when -were-dating.

2 Cat Bohannon, *Eve: How the Female Body Drove 200 Million Years of Human Evolution* (Random House, 2023); Christopher Ryan and Cacilda Jethá, *Sex at Dawn: How We Mate, Why We Stray, and What It Means for Modern Sexuality* (Harper, 2010).

3 bell hooks, *The Will to Change: Men, Masculinity, and Love* (Atria, 2003), 18.

4 Kim Tallbear, "Making Love and Relations Beyond Settler Identities," video, February 24, 2016, YouTube, www.youtube.com/watch?v=zfdo2ujRUv8.

5 Kim Tallbear, "Making Love and Relations Beyond Settler Identities."

6 David Brooks, "The Nuclear Family Was a Mistake," *The Atlantic,* February 11, 2022, www.theatlantic.com/magazine/archive/2020/03/the-nuclear-family-was-a-mistake /605536.

7 Tema Okun, White Supremacy Culture, 2021, www.whitesupremacyculture.info.

8 Ian F. Hancock, *We Are the Romani People* (University of Hertfordshire Press, 2002).

9 Divorce.com, "51+ Divorce Statistics in the U.S., Including Divorce Rate, Race, & Marriage Length," July 15, 2024, https://divorce.com/blog/divorce-statistics.

Chapter 2. Exploring Non-Monogamy

1 Sarah Carter, *The Importance of Being Monogamous: Marriage and Nation Building in Western Canada to 1915* (University of Alberta Press, 2008).

2 Jeff Willet, "Tibetan Fraternal Polyandry: A Review of Its Advantages and Breakdown," *Nebraska Anthropologist* 14 (1997), 96–107, https://digitalcommons.unl.edu /nebanthro/113.

3 Wikipedia, "Polygamy in Christianity," last modified November 19, 2024, https:// en.wikipedia.org/wiki/Polygamy_in_Christianity; My Jewish Learning, "Polygamy in Judaism," n.d., www.myjewishlearning.com/article/polygamy-in-judaism.

4 Wikipedia, "Polygyny in Islam," last modified September 7, 2024, https://en.wikipedia .org/wiki/Polygyny_in_Islam; Leila Ahmed, *Women and Gender in Islam: Historical Roots of a Modern Debate* (Yale University Press, 1992).

5 Emma Goldman, "Marriage and Love," in *Anarchism and Other Essays* (Mother Earth, 1914), 233–46.

6 Andie Nordgren, "The Short Instructional Manifesto for Relationship Anarchy," 2006, https://theanarchistlibrary.org/library/andie-nordgren-the-short-instructional -manifesto-for-relationship-anarchy.

7 Organization for Polyamory and Ethical Non-Monogamy, "Non-Monogamy Facts," n.d., www.open-love.org/fact-sheet.

8 Polyamory UK, "How Common Is Polyamory in the UK?" n.d., https://polyamoryuk .co.uk/how-common-is-polyamory-in-the-uk; Isambard Wilkinson, "Survey Shows Nearly Half of Spaniards Approve of Polyamory," *The Times,* April 13, 2023, www .thetimes.com/world/europe/article/survey-shows-nearly-half-of-spaniards-approve -of-polyamory-nnzp8fgd8.

9 Morning Glory Zell-Ravenheart, "A Bouquet of Lovers: Strategies for Responsible Open Relationships," *Green Egg* 23:89 (1990), 228–31, www.scribd.com/document /630883185.

10 Robyn Trask and Alan M., "What Is Polyamory?" Loving More, 2013, www .lovingmorenonprofit.org/home/new-what-is-polyamory.

11 Wikipedia, "Polyamory," last modified October 7, 2024, https://en.wikipedia.org /wiki/Polyamory.

12 Canadian Polyamory Advocacy Association, "What Is Polyamory," n.d., https:// polyadvocacy.ca/what-is-polyamory.

13 Coined by therapist Roy Graff, "Multigamy," December 10, 2022, https://openrelating .love/multigamy.

14 Coined by somatic liberationist Victor Warring, ReWild Eros, www.rewilderos.com.

Chapter 3. Post-Monogamy

1 Amy Gahran, *Stepping Off the Relationship Escalator: Uncommon Love and Life* (Off the Escalator, 2017).

Chapter 4. Becoming Trauma-Informed

1 Ofer Perl, Or Duek, Kaustubh R. Kulkarni, Charles Gordon, John H. Krystal, Ifat Levy, Ilan Harpaz-Rotem, et al., "Neural Patterns Differentiate Traumatic from Sad Autobiographical Memories in PTSD," *Nature Neuroscience* 26:12 (2023), 2226–36, https://doi.org/10.1038/s41593-023-01483-5.

Chapter 5. Why Somatics?

1 Thomas Hanna, *Bodies in Revolt: A Primer in Somatic Thinking* (Holt, Rinehart and Winston, 1970), 16–17.

2 Eleanor Criswell, *How Yoga Works: An Introduction to Somatic Yoga* (Freeperson Press, 1987).

3 ICPIT, "Historic Page," n.d., https://icpit.org/historic-page.

4 Peter A. Levine and Ann Frederick, *Waking the Tiger: Healing Trauma* (North Atlantic Books, 1997), 2.

Chapter 6. The Pillars of Trauma-Informed Relating

1 Gabor Maté and Daniel Maté, *The Myth of Normal: Trauma, Illness and Healing in a Toxic Culture* (Avery, 2022).

Chapter 7. Queerness and Anarchy

1 Juan-Carlos Pérez-Cortés, *Relationship Anarchy: Occupy Intimacy!* (pub. by author, 2022).
2 Juan-Carlos Pérez-Cortés, *Relationship Anarchy.*
3 Juan-Carlos Pérez-Cortés, *Relationship Anarchy.*

Chapter 8. The Relationship Landscape

1 Roger Kuhn, *Somacultural Liberation: An Indigenous, Two-Spirit Somatic Guide to Integrating Cultural Experiences Toward Freedom* (North Atlantic Books, 2024), 111–12.
2 Stephen R. Covey, "Voices of Leadership: Stephen R. Covey," *Washington Post,* July 17, 2008, www.washingtonpost.com/wp-dyn/content/discussion/2008/07/16/DI2008071602427.html.
3 Mark A. Michaels and Patricia Johnson, *Designer Relationships: A Guide to Happy Monogamy, Positive Polyamory, and Optimistic Open Relationships* (Cleis, 2015), 10, 14.

Chapter 9. The Layers of Relating

1 Being Held Community, www.beingheld.ca.

Chapter 10. The Emotional Quadrant

1 Thich Nhat Hanh, *How to Love* (Parallax Press, 2015), 39.

Chapter 11. The Social Quadrant

1 Prentis Hemphill, *What It Takes to Heal: How Transforming Ourselves Can Change the World* (Random House, 2024), 120.
2 Brené Brown, *Braving the Wilderness: The Quest for True Belonging and the Courage to Stand Alone* (Random House, 2017), 157.
3 Martin Keogh, "101 Ways to Say No to Contact Improvisation: Boundaries and Trust," in *Dancing Deeper Still: The Practice of Contact Improvisation* (Intimately Rooted Books, 2018), 22, https://martinkeogh.com/?page_id=108.
4 angel Kyodo williams, Lama Rod Owens, and Jasmine Syedullah, *Radical Dharma: Talking Race, Love, and Liberation* (North Atlantic Books, 2016), xi.

Chapter 12. The Practical Quadrant

1 Laura Boyle, *Monogamy? In This Economy? Finances, Childrearing, and Other Practical Concerns of Polyamory* (Jessica Kingsley, 2024), 63.

2 Geranda Notten, "Getting a Fuller Picture of Poverty in Canada: Why the Government's Official Poverty Measure Is Insufficient," *The Conversation,* March 22, 2023, https://theconversation.com/getting-a-fuller-picture-of-poverty-in-canada-why-the-governments-official-poverty-measure-is-insufficient-201629.

3 Anjuli Sherin, *Joyous Resilience: A Path to Individual Healing and Collective Thriving in an Inequitable World* (North Atlantic Books, 2021), 348.

4 Laura Boyle, *Monogamy? In This Economy?,* 73.

5 Kerista Commune, "History of the Kerista Commune," 1979, www.kerista.com/herstory.html; Leonard Dau Freitag, "History of the Communal Utopian Spiritual Movement," 1984, www.kerista.com/dauhistory5.html.

6 ZEGG Gemeinschaft und Bildungszentrum, "Zegg Forum," video, November 9, 2018, https://youtu.be/_ghG38ufiQQ?si=6l612kyVpU-PniyF; ZEGG Forum, www.zegg-forum.org/en.

Chapter 13. The Erotic Quadrant

1 Alan M., "Deborah Taj Anapol, 1951–2015," *Polyamory in the News,* blog, August 19, 2015, https://polyinthemedia.blogspot.com/2015/08/deborah-taj-anapol-1951-2015.html.

2 Tom Hickman, *God's Doodle: The Life and Times of the Penis* (Counterpoint, 2012), 65.

3 Audre Lorde, "Uses of the Erotic: The Erotic as Power," Fourth Berkshire Conference on the History of Women, Mount Holyoke College, Hadley, MA, August 25, 1978, printed in Audre Lorde, *Sister Outsider: Letters and Speeches* (Crossing Press, 1984).

Chapter 14. Embrace the Mess

1 Tema Okun, "One Right Way," White Supremacy Culture, 2021, www.whitesupremacyculture.info/one-right-way.html.

Chapter 15. Self-Relationship

1 Audre Lorde, *A Burst of Light: Essays* (Firebrand, 1988), 97.

2 Marshall B. Rosenberg, *Nonviolent Communication: A Language of Compassion* (PuddleDancer, 2000).

Chapter 16. The Meta-Model of Relating

1 Emmi Bevensee, "Widening the Bridges: Beyond Consent and Autonomy," Center for a Stateless Society, March 17, 2018, https://c4ss.org/content/50557.

Chapter 17. Consent and Agreements

1 Oriah Mountain Dreamer, *The Dance: Moving to the Deep Rhythms of Your Life* (HarperOne, 2001).

2 Lyrica Lawrence, Heather Orr, and Maxx Hill, "Relationship Anarchy Smörgås-bord: A Tool for Discussion," 2022, https://drive.google.com/drive/folders /17Hc3UFkDX3qA4IGYmjxEQhMW9BUOdPxt.

3 Edward T. Hall, *Beyond Culture* (Anchor, 1976).

Chapter 18. Shame, Shadow, and Cultivating Compersion

1 Adapted from Marie I. Thouin and Sharon M. Flicker, "Compersion," in *Springer Nature Encyclopedia of Sexual Psychology and Behavior,* ed. Todd K. Shackelford (Springer, 2022), https://doi.org/10.1007/978-3-031-08956-5_2472-1.

2 Marie Thouin, *What Is Compersion? Understanding Positive Empathy in Consensually Non-Monogamous Relationships* (Rowman & Littlefield, 2024).

3 Zadena Love, "3 Dimensions of Compersion," blog, May 4, 2016, https:// zadenalove.wordpress.com/2016/05/04/3-dimensions-of-compersion.

Chapter 19. Courageous Communication and Conflict Intimacy

1 Stephen B. Karpman, "Fairy Tales and Script Drama Analysis," *Transactional Analysis Bulletin* 7:26 (1968), 39–43, https://karpmandramatriangle.com/pdf/DramaTriangle.pdf.

2 Mia Mingus, "Pods and Pod Mapping Worksheet," blog, Bay Area Transformative Justice Collective, June 2016, https://batjc.wordpress.com/resources/pods-and-pod -mapping-worksheet.

Chapter 20. Changing Landscapes

1 Sobonfu Somé, *The Spirit of Intimacy: Ancient African Teachings in the Ways of Rela-tionships* (William Morrow, 1999).

2 "I'll Be There for You" by The Rembrandts, better known as the theme song for popular 1990s TV sitcom *Friends*.

3 Mary Evelyn Tucker, "Why the World Needs Spiritual Ecology," *Atmos*, August 21, 2024, https://atmos.earth/why-the-world-needs-spiritual-ecology.

4 William Wordsworth, "Lines Written A Few Miles Above Tintern Abbey," in *Lyrical Ballads, with a Few Other Poems* (J. & A. Arch, 1798), www.gutenberg.org/files /9622/9622-h/9622-h.htm#poem23.

5 Robin Dunbar, *Grooming, Gossip, and the Evolution of Language* (Harvard University Press, 1998).

6 Lyrica Lawrence et al., "Relationship Anarchy Smörgåsbord," https://drive.google .com/drive/folders/17Hc3UFkDX3qA4IGYmjxEQhMW9BUOdPxt.

Chapter 21. Radical Relating

1 Alex Iantaffi, Instagram post, August 22, 2024, www.instagram.com/p/C -_HWb0Jwu-/?img_index=9.

2 Saverio Bellizzi, Christian Popescu, Catello M. Panu Napodano, Maura Fiamma, and Luca Cegolon, "Global Health, Climate Change and Migration: The Need for Recognition of 'Climate Refugees,'" *Journal of Global Health* 13:03011 (March 24, 2023), https://doi.org/10.7189/jogh.13.03011.

BIBLIOGRAPHY

Ahmed, Leila. *Women and Gender in Islam: Historical Roots of a Modern Debate.* Yale University Press, 1992.

Anapol, Deborah M. *Polyamory: The New Love Without Limits.* IntiNet Resource Center, 1997.

Baczynski, Marcia, and Erica Scott, *Creating Consent Culture: A Handbook for Educators.* Jessica Kingsley, 2022.

Barker, Meg-John. *Rewriting the Rules: An Integrative Guide to Love, Sex and Relationships.* Routledge, 2012.

Barker, Meg-John, and Alex Iantaffi. *How to Understand Your Gender: A Practical Guide for Exploring Who You Are.* Jessica Kingsley, 2017.

Barker, Meg-John, and Alex Iantaffi. *How to Understand Your Sexuality: A Practical Guide for Exploring Who You Are.* Jessica Kingsley, 2021.

Bellizzi, Saverio, Christian Popescu, Catello M. Panu Napodano, Maura Fiamma, and Luca Cegolon. "Global Health, Climate Change and Migration: The Need for Recognition of 'Climate Refugees.'" *Journal of Global Health* 13:03011 (March 24, 2023). https://doi.org/10.7189/jogh.13.03011.

Bevensee, Emmi. "Widening the Bridges: Beyond Consent and Autonomy." Center for a Stateless Society. March 17, 2018. https://c4ss.org/content/50557.

Birdsong, Mia. *How We Show Up: Reclaiming Family, Friendship, and Community.* Hachette, 2020.

Bohannon, Cat. *Eve: How the Female Body Drove 200 Million Years of Human Evolution.* Random House, 2023.

Boyle, Laura. *Monogamy? In This Economy? Finances, Childrearing, and Other Practical Concerns of Polyamory.* Jessica Kingsley, 2024.

Brooks, David. "The Nuclear Family Was a Mistake." *The Atlantic.* February 11, 2022. www.theatlantic.com/magazine/archive/2020/03/the-nuclear-family-was-a-mistake/605536.

Brown, Brené. *Braving the Wilderness: The Quest for True Belonging and the Courage to Stand Alone.* Random House, 2017.

Brown, Sherronda J. *Refusing Compulsory Sexuality: A Black Asexual Lens on Our Sex-Obsessed Culture.* North Atlantic Books, 2022.

Cameron, Julia. *The Artists Way: A Spiritual Path to Higher Creativity.* Jeremy P. Tarcher, 1992.

Canadian Polyamory Advocacy Association. "What Is Polyamory." n.d. https://polyadvocacy.ca/what-is-polyamory.

Carter, Sarah. *The Importance of Being Monogamous: Marriage and Nation Building in Western Canada to 1915.* University of Alberta Press, 2008.

Cohen, Rhaina. *The Other Significant Others: Reimagining Life with Friendship at the Center.* St. Martin's, 2024.

Crenshaw, Kimberlé. "Demarginalizing the Intersection of Race and Sex: A Black Feminist Critique of Antidiscrimination Doctrine, Feminist Theory and Antiracist Politics." *University of Chicago Legal Forum* 1989:1 (1989), 139–67. https://chicagounbound .uchicago.edu/cgi/viewcontent.cgi?article=1052.

Criswell, Eleanor. *How Yoga Works: An Introduction to Somatic Yoga.* Freeperson Press, 1987.

DePaulo, Bella. *Single at Heart: The Power, Freedom and Joy of Single Life.* Apollo, 2023.

Divorce.com. "51+ Divorce Statistics in the U.S., Including Divorce Rate, Race, & Marriage Length." July 15, 2024. https://divorce.com/blog/divorce-statistics.

Dunbar, Robin. *Grooming, Gossip, and the Evolution of Language.* Harvard University Press, 1998.

Easton, Dossie, and Janet Hardy. *The Ethical Slut: A Guide to Infinite Sexual Possibilities.* Greenery Press, 1997.

Freitag, Leonard Dau. "History of the Communal Utopian Spiritual Movement." 1984. www.kerista.com/dauhistory5.html.

Gahran, Amy. *Stepping Off the Relationship Escalator: Uncommon Love and Life.* Off the Escalator, 2017.

Goldman, Emma. "Marriage and Love." In *Anarchism and Other Essays.* Mother Earth, 1914.

Graff, Roy. "Multigamy." December 10, 2022. https://openrelating.love/multigamy.

Hall, Edward T. *Beyond Culture.* Anchor, 1976.

Hancock, Ian F. *We Are the Romani People.* University of Hertfordshire Press, 2002.

Hanh, Thich Nhat. *How to Love.* Parallax Press, 2015.

Hanna, Thomas. *Bodies in Revolt: A Primer in Somatic Thinking.* Holt, Rinehart and Winston, 1970.

Hemphill, Prentis. *What It Takes to Heal: How Transforming Ourselves Can Change the World.* Random House, 2024.

Hickman, Tom. *God's Doodle: The Life and Times of the Penis.* Counterpoint, 2012.

hooks, bell. *The Will to Change: Men, Masculinity, and Love.* Atria, 2003.

Iantaffi, Alex, and Meg-John Barker. *How to Understand Your Relationships: A Practical Guide.* Philadelphia: Jessica Kingsley, 2025.

ICPIT. "Historic Page." n.d. https://icpit.org/historic-page.

Jesse, Caffyn, Cassie Moore, and Mehdi Darvish Yahya. *Healers on the Edge: Somatic Sex Education.* Published by the authors, 2017.

Kain, Kathy L., and Stephen J. Terrell. *Nurturing Resilience: Helping Clients Move Forward from Developmental Trauma.* North Atlantic Books, 2018.

Karpman, Stephen B. "Fairy Tales and Script Drama Analysis." *Transactional Analysis Bulletin* 7:26 (1968), 39–43. https://karpmandramatriangle.com/pdf/DramaTriangle.pdf.

Keogh, Martin. *Dancing Deeper Still: The Practice of Contact Improvisation.* Intimately Rooted Books, 2018.

Kerista Commune. "History of the Kerista Commune." 1979. www.kerista.com /herstory.html.

Kuhn, Roger. *Somacultural Liberation: An Indigenous, Two-Spirit Somatic Guide to Integrating Cultural Experiences Toward Freedom.* North Atlantic Books, 2024.

Lawrence, Lyrica, Heather Orr, and Maxx Hill. "Relationship Anarchy Smörgåsbord: A Tool for Discussion." 2022. https://drive.google.com/drive/folders /17Hc3UFkDX3qA4IGYmjxEQhMW9BUOdPxt.

Levine, Peter A. *Healing Trauma: A Pioneering Program for Restoring the Wisdom of Your Body.* Sounds True, 2005.

Levine, Peter A., and Ann Frederick. *Waking the Tiger: Healing Trauma.* North Atlantic Books, 1997.

Lorde, Audre. *A Burst of Light: Essays.* Firebrand, 1988.

Lorde, Audre. *Sister Outsider: Letters and Speeches,* Crossing Press, 1984.

Love, Zadena. "3 Dimensions of Compersion." Blog. May 4, 2016. https://zadenalove .wordpress.com/2016/05/04/3-dimensions-of-compersion.

Maté, Gabor, and Daniel Maté. *The Myth of Normal: Trauma, Illness and Healing in a Toxic Culture.* Avery, 2022.

Michaels, Mark A., and Patricia Johnson. *Designer Relationships: A Guide to Happy Monogamy, Positive Polyamory, and Optimistic Open Relationships.* Cleis, 2015.

Mingus, Mia. "Pods and Pod Mapping Worksheet." Blog. Bay Area Transformative Justice Collective. June 2016. https://batjc.wordpress.com/resources/pods-and-pod -mapping-worksheet.

Mountain Dreamer, Oriah. *The Dance: Moving to the Deep Rhythms of Your Life.* Harper-One, 2001.

My Jewish Learning. "Polygamy in Judaism." n.d. www.myjewishlearning.com/article /polygamy-in-judaism.

Nordgren, Andie. "The Short Instructional Manifesto for Relationship Anarchy." 2006. https://theanarchistlibrary.org/library/andie-nordgren-the-short-instructional -manifesto-for-relationship-anarchy.

Notten, Geranda. "Getting a Fuller Picture of Poverty in Canada: Why the Government's Official Poverty Measure Is Insufficient." *The Conversation,* March 22, 2023. https:// theconversation.com/getting-a-fuller-picture-of-poverty-in-canada-why-the -governments-official-poverty-measure-is-insufficient-201629.

Organization for Polyamory and Ethical Non-monogamy. "Non-Monogamy Facts." n.d. www.open-love.org/fact-sheet.

Page, Cara, and Erica Woodland, *Healing Justice Lineages: Dreaming at the Crossroads of Liberation, Collective Care, and Safety.* North Atlantic Books, 2023.

Perel, Esther, and Mary Alice Miller. "5 Myths We Tell Ourselves When We're Dating." Esther Perel's Blog. n.d. www.estherperel.com/blog/5-myths-we-tell-ourselves -when-were-dating.

Pérez-Cortés, Juan-Carlos. *Relationship Anarchy: Occupy Intimacy!* Published by the author, 2022.

Perl, Ofer, Or Duek, Kaustubh R. Kulkarni, Charles Gordon, John H. Krystal, Ifat Levy, Ilan Harpaz-Rotem, and Daniela Schiller. "Neural Patterns Differentiate Traumatic from Sad Autobiographical Memories in PTSD." *Nature Neuroscience* 26:12 (2023), 2226–36. https://doi.org/10.1038/s41593-023-01483-5.

Pieper, Marianne, and Robin Bauer. "Polyamory and Mono-Normativity: Results of an Empirical Study of Non-Monogamous Patterns of Intimacy." Unpublished manuscript. Hamburg: Research Center for Feminist, Gender, and Queer Studies, University of Hamburg, Germany. 2005.

Polyamory UK. "How Common Is Polyamory in the UK?" n.d., https://polyamoryuk.co.uk/how-common-is-polyamory-in-the-uk.

Rosa, Sophie K. *Radical Intimacy.* Pluto, 2022.

Rosenberg, Marshall B. *Nonviolent Communication: A Language of Compassion.* PuddleDancer, 2000.

Ryan, Christopher, and Cacilda Jethá. *Sex at Dawn: How We Mate, Why We Stray, and What It Means for Modern Sexuality.* Harper, 2010.

Shaw, Miranda. *Passionate Enlightenment: Women in Tantric Buddhism.* Princeton University Press, 1994.

Sherin, Anjuli. *Joyous Resilience: A Path to Individual Healing and Collective Thriving in an Inequitable World.* North Atlantic Books, 2021.

Somé, Sobonfu. *The Spirit of Intimacy: Ancient African Teachings in the Ways of Relationships.* William Morrow, 1999.

Tallbear, Kim. "Making Love and Relations Beyond Settler Identities." Video. February 24, 2016. YouTube. www.youtube.com/watch?v=zfdo2ujRUv8.

Thouin, Marie. *What Is Compersion? Understanding Positive Empathy in Consensually Non-Monogamous Relationships.* Rowman & Littlefield, 2024.

Thouin, Marie I., and Sharon M. Flicker. "Compersion." In *Springer Nature Encyclopedia of Sexual Psychology and Behavior,* edited by Todd K. Shackelford. Springer, 2022. https://doi.org/10.1007/978-3-031-08956-5_2472-1.

Topa, Wahinkpe, and Darcia Narvaez. *Restoring the Kinship Worldview: Indigenous Voices Introduce 28 Precepts for Rebalancing Life on Planet Earth.* North Atlantic Books, 2022.

Trask, Robyn, and Alan M. "What Is Polyamory?" Loving More. 2013. www.lovingmorenonprofit.org/home/new-what-is-polyamory.

Tucker, Mary Evelyn. "Why the World Needs Spiritual Ecology." *Atmos,* August 21, 2024. https://atmos.earth/why-the-world-needs-spiritual-ecology.

Wilkinson, Isambard. "Survey Shows Nearly Half of Spaniards Approve of Polyamory." *The Times,* April 13, 2023. www.thetimes.com/world/europe/article/survey-shows-nearly-half-of-spaniards-approve-of-polyamory-nnzp8fgd8.

Willet, Jeff. "Tibetan Fraternal Polyandry: A Review of Its Advantages and Breakdown." *Nebraska Anthropologist* 14 (1997), 96–107. https://digitalcommons.unl.edu/nebanthro/113.

williams, angel Kyodo, Lama Rod Owens, and Jasmine Syedullah. *Radical Dharma: Talking Race, Love, and Liberation.* North Atlantic Books, 2016.

Winston, Dedeker, Jase Lindgren, and Emily Sotelo Matlack. *Multiamory: Essential Tools for Modern Relationships.* Cleis, 2023.

Wordsworth, William. "Lines Written A Few Miles Above Tintern Abbey." In *Lyrical Ballads, with a Few Other Poems.* J. & A. Arch, 1798. www.gutenberg.org/files/9622/9622-h /9622-h.htm#poem23.

ZEGG Gemeinschaft und Bildungszentrum. "Zegg Forum." Video. November 9, 2018. https://youtu.be/_ghG38ufiQQ?si=6l612kyVpU-PniyF.

Zell-Ravenheart, Morning Glory. "A Bouquet of Lovers: Strategies for Responsible Open Relationships." *Green Egg* 23:89 (1990), 228–31. www.scribd.com/document/630883185.

INDEX

ABOUT THE AUTHOR

Mel Cassidy is a somatic relationship coach committed to the path of liberatory love and rewilding intimacy. They specialize in working with queer and questioning humans (and those who love them), exploring post-monogamous relationships with a focus on polyamory, solo polyamory, and relationship anarchy.

They are of Irish, Greek, and Khorakhane Romani descent and have lived in three countries across three continents. They currently live in British Columbia, Canada, and work with clients and students around the world.

ABOUT
NORTH ATLANTIC BOOKS

North Atlantic Books (NAB) is an independent, nonprofit publisher committed to a bold exploration of the relationships between mind, body, spirit, and nature. Founded in 1974, NAB aims to nurture a holistic view of the arts, sciences, humanities, and healing. To make a donation or to learn more about our books, authors, events, and newsletter, please visit www.northatlanticbooks.com.

01 14

J